TROUBLESOME WOMEN

Troublesome Women

Gender, Crime, and Punishment in
Antebellum Pennsylvania

ERICA RHODES HAYDEN

The Pennsylvania State University Press
University Park, Pennsylvania

Frontispiece: County map of Pennsylvania. © 2006 Derek Ramsey (Ram-Man) (from U.S. Census Bureau).

Library of Congress Cataloging-in-Publication Data

Names: Hayden, Erica Rhodes, author.
Title: Troublesome women : gender, crime, and punishment in
    antebellum Pennsylvania / Erica Rhodes Hayden.
Description: University Park, Pennsylvania : The Pennsylvania
    State University Press, [2019] | Includes bibliographical references and
    index.
Summary: "Examines the lived experiences of women criminals in
    Pennsylvania from 1820 to 1860, mainly as they navigated the
    nineteenth-century legal and prison systems"—Provided by publisher.
Identifiers: LCCN 2018035752 | ISBN 9780271082264 (cloth : alk. paper)
Subjects: LCSH: Female offenders—Pennsylvania—History—19th
    century. | Women prisoners—Pennsylvania—History—19th century.
Classification: LCC HV6046.H39 2019 | DDC 364.3/740974809034—dc23
LC record available at https://lccn.loc.gov/2018035752

Published by The Pennsylvania State University Press,
University Park, PA 16802–1003

The Pennsylvania State University Press is a member of the Association of
University Presses.

It is the policy of The Pennsylvania State University Press to use acid-free
paper. Publications on uncoated stock satisfy the minimum requirements
of American National Standard for Information Sciences—Permanence of
Paper for Printed Library Material, ANSI z39.48–1992.

For J. C. and Jamie, with love always

CONTENTS

Researching and writing a book is not completed in a vacuum. It takes numerous people to accomplish this task. This book would not have been possible without the financial support from Vanderbilt University, which facilitated research for this manuscript. I also wish to thank the American Philosophical Society for their support as a Nancy Halverson Schless Fellow in 2010, and I particularly want to thank Earle Spamer and Roy Goodman for their interest and guidance in my project while in residence at the Society library. Furthermore, the librarians and archivists at county archives, historical societies, and courthouses across Pennsylvania have been invaluable sources of information and help.

I am grateful to all those who provided feedback on portions of this project. I especially thank professor Richard Blackett, who has offered patient, unending guidance and motivation throughout the years and has taught be how to be a good historian. He does so with a great sense of humor, sage advice, and a keen eye for writing.

Friends make projects like these bearable. The support of Caree Banton, Frances Kolb Turnbell, Nicolette Kostiw, Angela Sutton, and Nick Villanueva has been invaluable, as they provided endless laughter, helpful ideas and suggestions, and group "therapy" sessions over the years.

My current and former students also have inspired me along the way. They listened intently as I lectured on prisons and crime, asking probing questions that not only made class enjoyable but also challenged me as a scholar while I worked on this project. I especially thank my history students at Trevecca Nazarene University who have read portions of this work and provided many useful comments and recommendations. Kirsti Arthur, in particular, gave her time to help scroll through microfilmed prison records and painstakingly transferred her findings into spreadsheets for statistical analysis. She is a dedicated historian in the making. This book has given me the opportunity to demonstrate to my students one aspect of what it means to be a historian and engage them with the process.

Trevecca Nazarene University has been a nurturing place to continue this project. Supportive colleagues in the Department of Social and

Behavioral Sciences and a campus-wide appreciation for faculty research at a teaching-intensive university have enabled me to pursue my research and writing. Parts of this manuscript have been presented at the Faculty Research Symposium in 2015 and 2016.

Excerpts from this work have been previously published, and it is with gratitude that I have been given permission to reprint them here. Excerpts from my chapter "Letters from Inside: Prison Writings from Eastern State Penitentiary in the Nineteenth Century," part of the edited collection *Incarcerated Women: A History of Struggles, Oppression, and Resistance in American Prisons*, published in 2017, can be found in chapter 4 and is reprinted with permission from Lexington Books. Portions of chapters 4, 5, and 6 originally appeared in my article "'She keeps the place in Continual Excitement': Female Inmates' Reactions to Incarceration in Antebellum Pennsylvania's Prisons" in the journal *Pennsylvania History: A Journal of Mid-Atlantic Studies* in 2013 and are reproduced here with the permission of the Pennsylvania Historical Association.

It has been a pleasure to work with Kathryn Yahner and the editorial and production staff at Penn State University Press. Thank you all for your guidance in this process!

The History Department at Juniata College is deserving of my gratitude as well. The dedication to their fields and students of the history faculty in particular, and the institution as a whole, is astounding. The seeds of this project were planted as I researched and wrote my senior thesis in 2006–7 on capital punishment in small-town Pennsylvania. As part of a summer internship at the Huntingdon County Historical Society, I stumbled across the noose from the last hanging in the county as I organized excess collection materials for the Society. That find set me on a path to research the social ramification of capital punishment in the nineteenth century and, later, the experiences of women criminals. The History Department at Juniata have kept tabs on my work as I completed graduate school, inviting me back to campus to lecture on my research and continuing to provide support and advice, for which I am appreciative.

A very special thank-you is given to my family, who have been supportive of my pursuit to become a historian. My parents and grandparents instilled the importance of the past in my life through an appreciation of family and local history, and their understanding of and dedication to higher education gave me the encouragement needed to fulfill that dream.

My parents and brothers humored me with trips to historic sites and listened to me graciously as I told them about my research findings. They have been an unfaltering support system and sounding board over the years. My son, Jamie, has provided countless smiles, giggles, and chatter throughout the revision process, reminding me that there is much more to life than work. Most importantly, I wish to thank my loving husband and best friend, J. C., as he has encouraged and inspired me throughout this process. I cannot thank him enough for putting up with me during this endeavor—his patience is admirable.

Introduction

In April 1839, the *Philadelphia Public Ledger* reported on a crime, as the newspaper did daily. Mary Stealingoods, who, the newspaper reporter quipped, had "an appropriate name!" stole three handkerchiefs and was sentenced to a year in the county prison. In a later article, readers learned that Mary's true surname was Woodward.[1] While inside the prison, Mary Stealingoods was punished for talking out of the ventilator.[2] A year later, a Mary Woodward was sentenced to two years in the state penitentiary by the Court of General Sessions. Woodward, a black woman, was "charged with stealing a shad, a loaf of bread, a pound of butter, and a bowl ... altogether of the value of $1.25." The newspaper reported that Woodward had "an extraordinary appetite, and accounts for it by being afflicted with a tapeworm." The reporter humorously pondered if "the prisonkeepers received instructions to gratify Mary's appetite with shad." Prison records indicate that Woodward entered Eastern State Penitentiary at the age of thirty-two and was a servant. She served her full sentence and was released on May 14, 1842.[3]

Mary Woodward represents an archetype of antebellum female criminals and their experiences. Many committed petty, nonviolent offenses, with larceny being among the most common crimes. She also exemplifies the commonly shared theme of repeat offenses, resulting in longer prison sentences or moves from the county jail system to the state penitentiary. Underlying her story is the ongoing problem of the difficulty in reforming prisoners. Furthermore, the way in which the public is exposed to Mary's crime and experience in court, through dramatically portrayed newspaper articles, has much power to shape how society viewed Mary and other women for their crimes. In Mary Woodward's case, the portrayals likely provided entertainment for the readers, undermining the seriousness of her seemingly difficult life. Although Mary's voice is absent from the records available today, one can still piece together the experience of Mary Woodward. The crimes suggest a level of want for the items stolen, signaling that Mary lacked sufficient funds to meet her needs. We know she is black, and her race may have shaped how the reporter viewed her and chose to portray her situation, perhaps showing her less sympathy. And we know that Mary Woodward spent two years in Eastern State Penitentiary in Philadelphia (and possibly other stints in the county prison), an institution renowned for total isolation and silence—a daunting experience, indeed. What happens when she leaves the historical record is unknown, which, unfortunately, is another common theme in the experiences of female criminals and prison inmates. They fade from the record, yet their experiences illustrate the varied struggles they encountered in their time within the legal and prison systems of the antebellum era.

This book examines the lived experiences of women criminals in Pennsylvania from 1820 to 1860, mostly, as they interacted with the nineteenth-century criminal justice system. While women constituted a small percentage of those who faced courtrooms or prison sentences, their experiences remain an important aspect of understanding the struggles faced by all those involved: defendants, inmates, employees, reformers, and the viewing public. Their individual struggles illuminate larger issues that troubled society at the time, including race, class, criminal punishment, reform, and gender roles.

This book traces the full experience of these criminal women, from the committing of the crimes through efforts to reform convicted women in prison, placing the women themselves, as much as possible, at the center of the story. I argue that instead of simply letting the legal process happen to them and allowing authorities to use preconceived notions of nineteenth-century womanhood and female criminals to dictate their circumstances, these women actively shaped and influenced their situation—in the commission of crimes, in court, and in prison. In this capacity, women demonstrated that they were aware of their place in society, understanding nuances of society's values and mores, particularly in the way antebellum America viewed women. This societal view was often defined around the middle-class white woman, so many of these female criminals who did not fall into that category had to negotiate a societal standard that was, realistically, not achievable for them. Issues of class, race, and ethnicity added layers and complications to the ways these female criminals interacted with legal systems within their communities. And yet, this cognizance of place in society did not limit these women from taking control of their circumstances, rather it empowered the women caught in the legal system. Many of them either used these societal expectations of women in their favor, or rejected these norms and challenged the role of women in antebellum society by their actions. The women in this study exhibited a strong ability to manipulate society's beliefs about how a middle-class white woman should act—the standard at the time—to their advantage.[4] These women garnered sympathy from juries for acquittals or lighter sentences, maintained a manner of respectability as a cover to commit crimes, or challenged the legal limitations placed on married women to extricate themselves from marriages through criminal acts like murder. Some women even challenged the fact that antebellum society believed they should be politically voiceless by participating in riots, allowing their actions to become the voice for their views and desire to create social change. Women convicted of crimes and sent to prison continued to demonstrate their awareness of their rights, both as inmates and as women, to challenge the expectation that female inmates were beyond redemption through interactions with employees and reformers. Although most of the women in this study were not members of the white middle or upper classes, the demographic categories often used in defining the proper role of women in the antebellum era, these women showed an awareness of those characterizations and co-opted or challenged them in ways that benefited their individual situations as they navigated the antebellum legal and prison systems.

Women caught in the legal and prison systems faced continuous opposition in their pursuit to maintain or redeem their reputations. Definitions of female respectability played a critical role at every stage of the female offender's "career," and this idea of respectability was employed by criminal women in numerous ways. Some women, such as female swindlers or shoplifters, used the trappings of respectability to commit crimes. Others had to combat societal definitions of respectability while on trial for crimes, attempting to convince jurors through appearance and demeanor that they had not become fallen or broken women. Almost all these women had to struggle against stereotypes, in some way, due to their poverty, race, or immigrant status, making this task of demonstrating respectability even tougher. After conviction, some female inmates sought to regain some level of respectability by taking advantage of reform programs established by philanthropic female prison reformers, who used their status as upstanding ladies to influence the character reformation of convicted women, while others eschewed reformation efforts and continued to rebel against prison officials' and reformers' expectations. This study emphasizes the actions and experiences of the women criminals and prisoners themselves, as much as the sources allow, to recover the lived experiences of these women—a significant shift from past studies focusing on the structure and leadership of penal institutions and reform organizations.

Scholarship on female criminals and prisoners in the antebellum decades of the United States is relatively sparse. Most previous scholarship that examined prisons during this period centered its focus on the institutional level, not on the offenders themselves. Landmark works such as *The Discovery of the Asylum* by David Rothman and Michel Foucault's *Discipline and Punish* of the 1970s examine the trend of "institutionalization" and prevailing efforts to discipline and control society through institutions like penitentiaries. Foucault argued that the development of the penitentiary system, a form of punishment designed to reach the core of the soul of the offender, created "'docile' bodies" which were "subjected and practised" under a disciplinary routine that controlled every aspect of the inmates' existence. The goal of the prison, according to Foucault, was "not to punish less, but to punish better; to punish with an attenuated severity perhaps, but in order to punish with more universality and necessity."[5]

By the 1990s and 2000s, scholarship shifted course, with works on punishment reform moving away from the argument that penitentiaries managed social control and toward the idea that penitentiaries protected liberties and emphasized the need for virtuous citizens. This newer trend is more amenable to the idea that the need for humane treatment of inmates and benevolence influenced the rise of the penitentiaries. Michael Meranze, in *Laboratories of Virtue*, argues that discipline was a central element in the spread of liberal institutions: it restrained direct violence from the state in public punishments and instead adopted the hidden techniques of constant surveillance. Meranze contends that attempts to reform punishment led to more patriarchal and paternalistic systems that undermined, to an extent, reformers' original goals to foster virtue and self-discipline among inmates in the wake of the American Revolution. Mark Kann, in *Punishment, Prisons, and Patriarchy*, argues that first-generation penal reformers set the price of liberty for Americans at the perpetuation of patriarchal political power over those in marginal demographic groups; they denied liberty to some to protect liberty for the majority. Kann asserts that institutions like prisons were designed to warehouse undesirable portions of the population: immigrants, African Americans, and sometimes women.[6]

My emphasis on the experiences of female criminals challenges these important works in several ways. First, by looking at the crimes women committed themselves, one sees the agency and empowerment women had to shape their circumstances in a society that ideally wanted to limit their public presence. Once in prison, the female inmates in my study demonstrated that they were not the "docile bodies" that Foucault had predicted would develop in the penitentiary. The women posed problems for prison officials, both at the state and county level, sometimes solely by the simple fact that they committed crimes and were present in these institutions. Employees were not sure how to deal with the small but persistent population of female prisoners, and their presence undermined the penal institutions' authority. Women in Pennsylvania prisons found ways to challenge the penal discipline, ranging from subtle to overt forms of resistance. Because women tested prison authority, and often succeeded, the nineteenth-century penitentiary failed to coalesce into the total institution that several early scholars posited. Exploring the experiences of women criminals and prisoners helps to provide a more comprehensive, richer portrait of the lived experiences of these individuals in the nineteenth century.

This is not to say that there is no scholarship on women criminals and prisoners. Works by Estelle Freedman and Nicole Hahn Rafter pioneered this path of scholarship, examining the hardships faced by women committed to prison, particularly those institutions designed for men. More recent works in the vein of recovering women criminals' experiences include Kali Gross's *Colored Amazons* and Susan Branson's *Dangerous to Know*. Furthermore, there has been an increasing trend to recover the voices of inmates in the nineteenth century with collections such as *Buried Lives: Incarcerated in Early America* edited by Michelle Lise Tarter and Richard Bell. Jen Manion's *Liberty's Prisoners* uncovers for the period of the Early Republic the experiences of women prisoners, noting that the shift in criminal punishment "was defined in relation to and on the backs of a diverse and motley crew" of immigrants, the working poor, and African Americans, arguing that the new form of punishment served to control these groups in the new nation.[7] This study builds on this growing body of scholarship of putting the criminals and inmates themselves at the center of the work and focuses its attention on a wider scope of Pennsylvania as a whole rather than centering only on Philadelphia. This work centers its attention mainly on the antebellum decades, a period in which the scholarship on female criminals and inmates is relatively thin. Similar to Manion's research on the Early Republic, this book looks at the societal norms and expectations of the antebellum decades and seeks to understand how they had an impact on the way that women of various races, ethnicities, and class standings dealt with the legal and prison systems of Pennsylvania.

At the heart of this book is an examination of antebellum female criminality and punishment in Pennsylvania in order to reconstruct the lived experiences female criminals by analyzing their offenses, court experiences, and subsequent treatment as prisoners. Pennsylvania provides an ideal location to study female criminality and punishment as it was home to the internationally renowned Eastern State Penitentiary, as well as the Western State Penitentiary, and acted as a seat of critical debates over criminal punishment reform during the nineteenth century.

The antebellum era stands as an essential period to explore female criminality for several reasons. In addition to Pennsylvania's strong ties to the establishment of the penitentiary systems described in more detail below, these decades also witnessed profoundly shifting expectations for women in society. Women's societal roles became more specifically defined, particularly centered on the separate spheres ideology and the cult of domesticity; yet such roles were being challenged by female reformers in the crusades for abolition, temperance, women's rights, and punishment reform. Female criminals also challenged these predefined roles in numerous ways—using expectations of proper behavior to mask their crimes or receive lenient sentences or to outright challenge their limited position in society by committing crimes to procure more social mobility and freedom. This book highlights the agency that women exhibited in their committing of crimes and resistance to punishment—powerful statements in an era when institutions such as the penitentiary, and society as a whole, attempted to control and limit the influence of women, particularly African American, immigrant, and poor women, a trend that preceded and continued after the antebellum period.[8] Furthermore, the antebellum years were a time of increasing political tension regarding race and ethnic relations, particularly in the 1840s and 1850s. The riots that wreaked havoc on Philadelphia and other locales in Pennsylvania provide a gateway to exploring crimes that embodied political overtones and the roles women played in these politically charged events. These occurrences help us to reconstruct how some women demonstrated political, ethnic, and religious views through their criminal activity in both rural and urban settings.

To understand the world women entered when they committed crimes in Pennsylvania in the antebellum period, it is important to examine the roots of criminal punishment and reform in Pennsylvania. The state in the Early Republic was focused on what to do with crime and how best to punish those who broke the laws:

> Let a large house, of a construction agreeable to its design, be erected in a remote part of the state. Let the avenue to this house be rendered difficult and gloomy by mountains or morasses. Let its doors be of iron; and let the grating, occasioned by opening and shutting them, be encreased [sic] by an echo from a neighboring mountain, that shall extend and continue a sound that shall deeply pierce the soul. Let a guard constantly attend at a gate that shall lead to this place of punishment, to prevent strangers from entering it. Let all the officers of the house be strictly forbidden ever to discover any signs of mirth, or even levity in the presence of the criminals. To encrease [sic] the horror of this abode of discipline and misery, let it be called by some name that shall import its design.[9]

In 1787, founding father and philanthropist Dr. Benjamin Rush detailed what he believed would be a superior system of punishment, one meant to both humiliate and punish criminals. He described in the words above what would later become the penitentiary system, an institution pioneered in Pennsylvania, one that would, theoretically, be the ideal, modern, and humanitarian way to punish offenders. Pennsylvania's first penitentiary, Walnut Street Jail in Philadelphia, opened three years later. Rush's *Enquiry into the Effects of Public Punishments,* and his 1792 publication *Considerations on the Injustice and Impolicy of Punishing Murder by Death,* spoke to his long-standing efforts to improve the criminal punishment system. In

1682, only murder was punished by death in Pennsylvania; other crimes resulted in penalties such as monetary restitution, whipping, and imprisonment, among other forms of punishment. At the time of Pennsylvania's formation, the colony had a very mild criminal code.[10] His work reflects some of Pennsylvania's earliest efforts in criminal punishment reform work, dating even back to the colonial period—an endeavor that continues to the present day with the Pennsylvania Prison Society.

But the idealism and emphasis on peace and conciliation advocated by the Quakers fell short of the mark in criminal proceedings. Between 1718 and 1794, the number of crimes resulting in the death penalty fluctuated. The Act of 1718 codified much of the English criminal law, with many of the harsh punishments common to the English code. By 1794, however, only first-degree murder remained a capital crime. Women became caught up in these changes specifically when they were accused of infanticide.[11] During the eighteenth century, public punishments became the norm. These ritualistic spectacles of punishment were meant to educate the public on the consequences of committing crimes and to deter individuals from becoming criminals. In the post-Revolution years, reformers grew more concerned with the usefulness and morality of public criminal punishments, which according to Mark Kann "were suitable for monarchies but not republics."[12]

The idea of the penitentiary, as described by Benjamin Rush, was conceived in this post-Revolutionary era. The belief emerged that criminals could be reformed. Corporal punishments, which focused on physical pain and humiliation as means of control, no longer seemed to be the only solution to dealing with crime. By creating a new form of punishment, significantly longer in duration, reformers hoped to alter the behaviors of criminals through a rigorous rehabilitation program that would enable convicted criminals to return, rehabilitated, to society after their sentence. Thus the penitentiary system in Pennsylvania reigned over the state's criminal punishment system for over a century.

As reformers considered ways to improve the efficacy of criminal punishment, contemporary society's views on the causes of crime also changed as the nation moved into the nineteenth century. By the 1820s and 1830s, crime was no longer seen as a consequence of sin, but came to be viewed as the result of social problems, associated with the rapidly expanding nation. The anxiety over growing social disorder, poverty, and mental illness, largely

the result of growing urbanization, led to attempts to remove social miscreants who threatened social order. Institutions such as the penitentiary, the
poorhouse, and the insane asylum fit this need to protect and strengthen
civil society.[13]

In Pennsylvania, Quakers were often at the forefront of this new
approach of institutionalization, and they pushed to improve the prisons
that already existed in the state. Pennsylvania reformers became pioneers
in the quest to find a better way to punish criminals as well as to improve
inmate discipline. The prisons constructed in the eighteenth century simply
corralled prisoners into large and often overcrowded rooms. To them, these
jails were simply "breeding-places of crime" and they insisted that imprisonment *"should not be viewed as a punishment, but as a means to reform."*[14]

After seeing the plight of prisoners in their city during the Revolutionary War, a group of concerned Philadelphians began to work for change.
On May 8, 1787, the Philadelphia Society for Alleviating the Miseries of
Public Prisons (presently known as the Pennsylvania Prison Society) was
organized. Early on, the group moved to end cruel and humiliating public
punishments. Dr. Benjamin Rush was one of the Society's driving forces.
He strongly opposed public punishments, including capital punishment,
because, as he noted, "all public punishments tend to make bad men worse,
and to increase crimes, by their influence upon Society" and as they were
"always connected with infamy, [they] destroy in the criminal the sense
of shame which is one of the strongest outposts of virtue." Additionally,
public, physical punishments were so short in duration "as to produce
none of those changes in body and mind, which are absolutely necessary to reform obstinate habits of vice."[15] Rush's sentiments, influenced
by Enlightenment and utilitarian theories, exemplified a larger trend of
moving away from corporal, public punishments and toward humane character reformation.

On April 5, 1790, Rush and the Society's requests to end public punishments succeeded when the state adopted a regime of solitary confinement
with work. Walnut Street Jail in Philadelphia became the first penitentiary
in the state, even though it had been functioning as a jail since 1784.[16] The
isolation of the inmates and the policy of silence changed the way this jail
operated. Through their prison reform efforts, the Society made the state's
penal institutions a model for the modernization and restructuring of punishment systems which other states and nations would emulate.

The opening of Walnut Street Jail as the state's first penitentiary signified an important shift in the system of punishment. In the past, criminals were crowded together without classification according to crime and with no hope of rehabilitation. These old, crowded jails allowed inmates to interact with one another, so reformers called for the separation of inmates as a way to create more healthful living conditions and to allow for rehabilitation. Separation encouraged repentance and rehabilitation. The penitentiary system, beginning with Walnut Street, and continuing with Eastern and Western State Penitentiaries, which opened in the 1820s, promoted a style of punishment that combined isolation, silence, and rehabilitation. This disciplinary plan was seen as an innovative and more humane way to penalize offenders.

It is in these early prisons—Walnut Street, other county jails, and Eastern and Western State Penitentiaries—that women were incarcerated in small numbers, alongside men. Prior to incarceration in these institutions, the women navigated the antebellum legal system in tandem with an acute cognizance of their place in society as women and the impact that being female might have on them in their commission of crimes, in court, and, ultimately for many, in prison. Using their awareness of their position in antebellum Pennsylvania, these women empowered themselves as best they could to influence the court outcome or improve their experiences in prison.

———————

Unlike past scholarly work on crime and punishment in Pennsylvania, which has focused almost exclusively on Philadelphia, this book widens the orbit to look at women's crime and punishment across the state. It is important to consider the ways in which communities beyond the eastern urban center dealt with female criminals. Comparing the rural and urban attitudes toward female criminality and how women's criminal punishment differed depending on location offers a more comprehensive picture of antebellum female crime and punishment patterns. I examine female crime and punishment in sixteen counties in the state, providing 6,035 cases for my sample: three counties with large urban centers, Philadelphia (Philadelphia County), Harrisburg (Dauphin County), and Pittsburgh (Allegheny County). The other counties were chosen based on their proximity to these centers as well as the quality of their available source material.[17]

Most of these rural counties are located in the southern half of the state. Historical population patterns suggest that as Pennsylvania (near the state's

TABLE 1. Breakdown of types of crime for entire sample

	Violent	Property	Moral/petty	Total
Number of offenses	1,986	1,714	2,335	6,035
% of crimes	32.91	28.40	38.69	100

Note: Percentages were drawn from county quarter sessions dockets for the sixteen counties making up the research sample. Dockets for all years between 1820 and 1860 were examined, where they existed. Some counties, such as Allegheny, only have a small portion of their dockets surviving. Due to the large numbers of cases in Philadelphia, I took a sample of docket books (1820, 1825, 1830, etc.).

southern border) was populated during the seventeenth, eighteenth, and nineteenth centuries, most settlers moved west from Philadelphia. As a result, historically, the state's southern half is more densely populated than the northern half.[18] Chester, Berks, Cumberland, Adams, York, Lancaster, Westmoreland, and Washington counties were selected as outlying zones to the three main settlement areas. Because there is a wide geographic gap between Harrisburg and Pittsburgh, I have also included the counties of Mifflin, Huntingdon, and Bedford, to provide a more specifically rural perspective. Two northern counties, Erie and Luzerne, were added to provide a perspective from the less densely populated northern tier of the state.

These counties offer the basis for analysis of this study, which is split into two parts. Part 1, consisting of chapter 1 through 3, examine women's entrance into the legal system through the commission of crimes. These chapters look at the ways women interacted with the police and court system, focusing on the methods women used to either mitigate their circumstances in court or outright challenge their legal limitations through their criminal actions. Chapter 1 concentrates on women who used traditionally expected female behaviors to commit crimes and to garner sympathy in the court. These women demonstrated awareness of the prevailing expectations of women to be demure, sympathetic, passive, and respectable, and used these characteristics to commit crimes or to portray themselves in this light while in court to perhaps earn an acquittal, or, at the very least, a lighter sentence. Chapter 2 looks at women who committed crimes as a result of the legal limitations women faced in this era, with a heavy focus on women who committed murder to get out of marriages. These women knew the obstacles they faced in getting out of unwanted relationships and turned to crime as a means to achieve their goals when a

legal path remained unavailable. Their actions demonstrated a direct challenge to the antebellum period's expectations of women's status in society.
Chapter 3 goes a step further when looking at the ways women challenged
their place in society. Women across Pennsylvania became involved in riots
over nativism, fugitive slaves, and labor issues. Their participation in these
criminal acts demonstrated an acute political awareness of their circumstances, and they used rioting as a way to have a political voice.

Part 2 turns to the experiences of female criminals once convicted
and in prison and examines how they continued to actively shape their
experiences even in settings where their personal control and freedom was
severely limited. Chapters 4 and 5 look at the struggles women faced in the
state penitentiaries and county prisons, respectively. Officials were often at
a loss about what to do with these women who were sent to their prisons,
and thus treated them differently than the male convicts, ultimately creating disorder, security concerns, and neglecting their needs. The women
inmates were not passive victims in the prison. Rather, they showed their
worth as women and individuals and resisted the oppressive nature of the
penitentiary system. As a result of these problems that female inmates
faced, institutional reform and inmate rehabilitation were paramount
in the eyes of benevolent individuals who advocated for prison reform,
which is the focus of chapter 6. The final chapter, while shifting focus to
look more closely at the reformers' work with the inmates, examines the
theories behind prisoner rehabilitation and how, initially, this played out in
the penitentiaries with chaplains and moral instructors. Female reformers,
however, remained unconvinced that these programs were the solution to
aid in the reformation of female convicts, so this chapter also analyzes the
efforts of these activists in their quest to aid incarcerated women. Such
reformers sought to help the inmates and released prisoners in their quest
for personal empowerment and set forth the groundwork for life outside
of prison. The philanthropists advocated for the imprisoned women and
helped to channel their individual agency that they exhibited in prison into
means that would facilitate transition to the free world.

PART I

The Crimes

CHAPTER 1

"With a World of Tears"

Women Criminals and the Use of Mercy and Femininity

In April 1836, Mary Moffat was arrested and taken to court in Philadelphia. Upon Moffat entering the courtroom, the *Philadelphia Public Ledger* crime reporter noted that in her "stood the victim of intemperance." Moffat's physical appearance revealed "the deep and damning consequences" of habitual drinking. Her face showed "the faded graces of feature and form—lovely even in their ruin," and her mannerisms in the courtroom told of "evident emotions of sorrow." The court looked sympathetically on Mary Moffat and did not convict her for her public drunkenness.[1]

Mary Moffat was fortunate that the court took pity on her situation. Her alleged beauty, although marred by drinking, perhaps allowed her to avoid a criminal sentence. Many other women in Philadelphia, Pittsburgh, and other locations across Pennsylvania were not so lucky. Women across the state committed a whole host of criminal offenses. Petty crime, including moral offenses such as public drunkenness, disorderly conduct, vagrancy, adultery, fornication, and myriad property crimes, made up a significant number of the infractions, although women also committed more violent crimes like assault and battery, infanticide, and murder. Newspaper accounts of these offenses remain the most significant way to glimpse into this world of crime committed by women in the nineteenth century, particularly in urban settings. Most newspaper entries were brief, simply stating the crime, the name of the offender, and the sentence. Other cases warranted more space in the columns, allowing one to understand how these women who became caught up in the web of crime, courts, and prisons navigated this terrain. The fact that so many women entered the court records offers an opportunity to examine female criminal behavior. Furthermore, these articles allow a glimpse into the ways in which the courts dealt with and the public viewed these misbehaving women. These reports also enable scholars to begin to understand the experiences of these women in their decisions to commit crime and the ways they navigated the legal system in antebellum Pennsylvania. The increase of newspapers in the 1830s and 1840s allowed crime reporting to become a mainstay in the columns and situated crime within changing social structures.[2] This can be seen in the *Philadelphia Public Ledger* and other urban newspapers' coverage of female offenders. In rural communities where crime was seemingly less prevalent, newspapers reserved their reporting for more heinous, violent offenses, which still illustrate communities' viewpoints and reactions to women's crimes.

This chapter uses these and other sources to explore the ways in which some of these women marshaled their feminine characteristics and played on the mercy of the court and community to earn an acquittal or perhaps a lighter sentence, if convicted. In this way, these women demonstrated their awareness of what mainstream society expected of women of the time, using these values as a means to influence the court system and public opinion, a tactic also used by women embroiled in the legal system during the Early Republic.[3] These women showed cleverness at utilizing their individual power to protect themselves and to demonstrate their worth and capability in antebellum society. At the same time, these cases, and women's involvement in them, illuminate broader societal concerns and attitudes regarding crime, urbanization, race and ethnicity, and female morality. Women who committed crimes represent a tension in antebellum society. Many in these communities were loath to think that women were capable of such behavior, yet at times, as is the focus of this chapter, women who committed crimes used this powerful knowledge to improve their situation in the court system and in their community's public opinion.

WOMANHOOD IN ANTEBELLUM AMERICA

Before delving into how women criminals used feminine characteristics, played on the court's mercy toward them, or, as is the subject of the next chapter, directly challenged the court system and society's oppression of women, it is necessary to look at the prevailing attitudes of antebellum society concerning women. To clarify, the baseline against which the female criminals of this study worked centers on the social expectations set forth for white middle-to-upper-class women. Some of these characteristics, particularly those noted by Barbara Welter, include purity, piety, submission, and domesticity, while other historians include compassion, charity, and a tendency toward nurturing and morality as important traits. Barbara Cutter suggests that women's inherent qualities of morality and virtue constituted the "ideology of redemptive womanhood" giving women a special responsibility to protect the nation's virtue.[4] These characteristics, influenced by the notion of Republican Motherhood, also shaped the idea of the "separate spheres" ideology of men and women in the nineteenth century, where women were not necessarily unequal but had distinct roles to fulfill in the domestic arena.[5]

These characteristics of antebellum womanhood only provide one perspective on the experiences of women—the white middle-to-upper-class women experience—and there is an extensive historiography that discusses the ways in which many women did not fit this mold, often due to class, race, or ethnic background.[6] Women moved in the public sphere as well, helping to shape nineteenth-century American character and demonstrating that not all women were content to stay focused on or constrained by domestic life.[7] Criminal women played a role in shaping this identity, too—albeit in a very different setting. Many of the women who entered the courts of antebellum America for committing crimes were not of the same social class or race of the "ideal woman" described above. Recent studies by Clare Lyons, Susan Klepp, and Jen Manion have all shown that women were eschewing social expectations long before the more prescribed norms of the antebellum period.[8] Yet, some of the criminal women employed these characteristics of respectability or ideal womanhood to alleviate their situation. This showed awareness of not only their place in society, but how others around them expected antebellum women to behave. By using feminine demeanor, playing on the court's sympathies, or acting and dressing respectably, female criminals wielded power to manipulate societal norms in their favor, even if in other circumstances these same women would be viewed beyond the scope of traditional femininity. Although they likely would never break into the ranks of middle- or upper-class white society due to their race, ethnicity, or class, their use of values held dear in other sections of society enabled some criminal women to improve their outcome in court and preserve a better place in public opinion. These criminal women were well aware of the power of perception and the need to be seen in a respectable light during this period.

GARNERING SYMPATHY

Many women crossed the threshold of the Mayor's Office in Philadelphia and entered the crime record as vagrants. The *Ledger* reported on August 8, 1836, that eighty-year-old Catharine Shiber "was found sleeping in a privy." The paper continued: "Her emaciated and aged form elicited much sympathy." She was sent to the almshouse because, not able to afford her rent, she lived on the streets. Cases such as Shiber's litter the paper. Catharine Clark, "a poor destitute Irish woman, whose reason appeared to be partly unsettled by intemperate habits," took shelter in an alley until arrested by an officer and escorted to the watch house. In front of the judge the next morning, she "begged to be sent to the almshouse" instead.[9] The judge acquiesced.

The discussion of the almshouse in these two cases necessitates understanding the function of the institution in nineteenth-century Philadelphia. Although the almshouse was not necessarily a prison (the watch house functioned more like a prison), official reports referred to the inhabitants as inmates. The conflation of the almshouse and prison, in the idea that there needed to be work to achieve reform, illustrates the nineteenth-century social desire to improve society and discipline individuals. Later almshouses incorporated a house of employment for inmates to continue working to pay off debts. In addition, the inhabitants of the almshouses might learn a useful skill to help improve their employment chances. We see the emphasis on work also play a significant role in the early penitentiaries for the same reasons. For some, the almshouse was a place of relief, somewhere to get shelter, food, and medical attention in order to get back on one's feet. For others, the almshouse was like a prison and meant to be a place of behavioral correction.[10]

Communities have long been plagued by how to explain the existence of crime in their midst. By the early nineteenth century, reasons for why people committed crimes shifted away from the colonial emphasis on sin to the idea that changes and problems in society influenced people to break the law. American society experienced an unraveling of tight-knit communities and networks to which they were accustomed; and growing populations provided a blanket of anonymity that often made crime easier to get away with, particularly in urban settings. Contemporaries grew increasingly concerned over the rise in crime, fearing that the growing cities and their populations would devolve into its of lawlessness.

The antebellum fear over the increase in crime necessitated a change in dealing with social deviants. This anxiety over a growing social disorder with criminals, the poor, and the mentally ill led to the trend of institutionalization.[11] Institutions such as the penitentiary, the poorhouse, and the insane asylum opened in cities and removed from the streets these social miscreants who threatened the community's stability. Removing the troublemakers from public spaces provided protection for the law-abiding citizens and fulfilled the purpose of strengthening civil society.[12]

The first two cases of vagrancy illustrate a level of sympathy toward the plight of these women. Shiber's age and health evoked a sense of compassion for her situation, thus allowing the judge and observers to view her crime perhaps as an unfortunate situation as opposed to a disorderly act. Sending her to the almshouse was not a punishment but rather a remedy for her poverty and a chance to preserve her frail health. Shiber did not have to do much to elicit a lighter sentence from the court—her gaunt appearance and advanced age were enough.

Clark's case demonstrates a limited level of sympathy. While authorities granted her request to be lodged at the almshouse, the classification of Clark as "a poor destitute Irish woman" with "intemperate habits" might have curtailed the amount of sympathy she actually received from the reading audience. While we see this disdain for the poor in these examples from the antebellum decades, this sentiment is not new. This class of men and women faced criminalization for their idleness and vagrancy reaching back to the post-Revolutionary period as elites put mechanisms in place to control the immigrant population and limit their mobility.[13] The distinction of her ethnicity in the report also highlights a sense of dislike or distrust of the Irish population as a force that lowered the city's quality of life by their poverty and foreignness. While the report does not explicitly demonstrate hatred for her Irish ethnicity, the fact that the reporter mentions it at all illustrates the judicious determination to set this woman apart from other women. The prejudice is subtle but apparent. Vagrants became expenses to the city, thereby prompting frustration among the larger public (illustrated by the reporters' remarks). Cases like Shiber's are common in the newspapers.[14] Because many of the city's poor were immigrants, ethnic tensions were heightened during the nineteenth century. The correlation between the Irish, drinking, and vagrancy speaks to the stereotypical view of Irish immigrants that antebellum citizens held. Dale T. Knobel suggests that the ethnic stereotype and Irish distinctiveness was "environmental" during this period. The traits that many considered to be Irish—excessive drinking, ignorance, superstition, habitual poverty—were formed by environmental factors they experienced in Ireland, like poverty and governmental oppression. These conditions affected to various levels the character of the immigrants to the United States. Native-born Americans seemed to latch onto these character traits, thus forming a distinct, negative stereotype of the Irish, which is trotted out time and again in newspaper reports of criminal activity concerning immigrants. By the 1850s, the Irish stereotype was formed less by environmental factors, but took on a more racial bent. Irish immigrants were considered "low-browed" or "brutish" rather than "dirty" or "ragged," descriptors more commonly used in the 1820s and 1830s.[15] Even so, Clark employed begging in the courtroom to adjust her sentence. While the nature of the scene was not described, it must have been persuasive, emotional even, to sway the judge. Clark played an active role in the courtroom, choosing to behave in ways that she believed would help her. In her case, it succeeded.

Clark's case represents a broader issue regarding issues of race and ethnicity in relation to crime. Throughout the court records and newspaper reports, women of color or immigrants tend to be prevalent. These trends in arrests and reporting reflect the ways that authorities categorized and treated certain criminals. Newspaper reporters had power also to influence the ways these criminals were portrayed to the public, oftentimes reinforcing negative stereotypes about certain ethnic groups. This plays out time and again in cases of antebellum crime, in a period of heightened racial and ethnic tensions. One editorial in the *Ledger* discussed the role of ethnicity in crime, referring to German immigrants as "ignorant, besotted, destitute, they wander about our streets, begging, pilfering and . . . extending their depredations to offences of a bolder character."[16] Editorials like this one serve to mold public opinion against the growing immigrant populations in the antebellum decades in Pennsylvania's cities by reinforcing stereotypical views of certain groups and linking immigrant status with crime.

Contemporaries of the Early Republic and antebellum years, such as Alexis de Tocqueville and Gustave de Beaumont, contended that misbehavior by European immigrants and free blacks were causes of social unrest. They believed that upon finding liberty for themselves, these groups could not handle the freedom and thus failed to control their actions. Furthermore, the sense that urban centers attracted population groups located on the fringes of mainstream society caused a great sense of anxiety for the populace and may help to explain a higher percentage of convicted free blacks and immigrants in Philadelphia and other cities. Reformers managed these less desirous residents convicted of petty crimes by incarcerating them in high percentages to county jails and state prisons, following the historical precedent from the post-Revolutionary period of communities using prisons as a way to control certain portions of the population.[17] Prison records of the nineteenth century corroborate this suggestion, as population documents for Eastern State Penitentiary and Western State Penitentiary show that the institutions' female inmates often hailed from minority groups (see appendixes B and C).

The tenuousness of race and ethnic relations in the nineteenth century suggested by scholars and contemporaries demonstrates the prevalence of this anxiety and helps to explain why there might be a higher proportion of minority criminal offenders. According to an editorial comment in the *Ledger*, the "mass of our convicts may be divided into two classes—the free colored persons, and foreigners." The author continued: "The number of colored persons in our prisons is, when the extent of that population is compared with the other, fearfully great ... [but] their various social disadvantages are so great, that we need not marvel at their moral debasement."[18] White prejudice stood in the way of equality and manifested itself in Philadelphia's numerous race riots during the antebellum era. Characteristics that shaped the United States in the nineteenth century, such as urban development, the rise in industrial production, and immigration, led to the prevalence of racism in the city. While these racial attitudes were directed at men and women, criminal women, particularly those of minority status, faced rigid stereotypes about their character and were considered beyond redemption.[19] Race and ethnicity seemed to influence how courts handled criminal offenders, as is evident from the treatment of female criminals in this chapter and throughout the study. The sentencing patterns also reflect a wider social mind-set toward marginal populations that prevailed in the antebellum era.[20]

The cases of Shiber and Clark described above demonstrated that women were sometimes able to prompt sympathy from the court, even if they were of a minority group. Although appearance or a show of emotion might be enough in some cases, other women's appearances worked against them. The case of Isabella Smith in 1841 illustrates such an example. The newspaper reported that the woman referred to as Bell Smith "is such a belle as would not be likely to do much heart-breaking among the beaux." The reporter noted, "Would she call herself Bill Smith instead of Bell Smith, the question of her manhood would be less likely to be mooted than her womanhood is at present." Bell, "when she comes home in a state of questionable sobriety, the keeper of the house refuses admission (as he did last night,) and the only resource of Bell, or Bill, in such cases, is the watch-house."[21]

Smith's case, while entertaining to read, illustrates the problem of a chronic vagrant, a perpetual nuisance on the street. Not only is her femininity mocked, but the report also indicates that there was little sympathy for this type of vagrancy, thus calling for what may be assumed a prison commitment rather than a stay at the almshouse. These individuals needed to be supervised and put to work to reform their character. Habitual vagrants were blights on the city, outsiders who constituted a potential criminal class. Smith illustrates this societal fear. In addition, Smith's appearance takes center stage in the report, with the author focusing on her alleged manliness or lack of feminine beauty. In the eyes of the reporter, Smith challenged what it meant to look like a woman, thus perhaps coloring the reporter's attitude toward her, her femininity, and her offense.

Charges of public drunkenness and disorderly conduct in Pennsylvania's antebellum newspapers often overlapped with charges of vagrancy, suggesting that many of these offenders spent a great deal of time in public spaces. Intemperance- and alcohol-related crimes seemed to plague cities, but they were common across the state. Because women imbibed mostly in private places, it is difficult to ascertain the amount of consumption among women.[22] Newspapers, however, provide a glimpse into the commonality of the practice and offer examples of how women extracted sympathy from the court. On July 29, 1836, the *Ledger* recorded the case of Mary Jourdan, mother of three "for whom she yesterday went out to buy bread ... bought rum at the same time, and became very drunk, making much noise and otherwise deporting herself in a very unseemly fashion." She reacted to her sentence of a fine "with a world of tears" and "not having the money to pay her fine, she must of course go to prison."[23] Jourdan's situation illustrates the combination of several ills that society feared would lead individuals to a life of crime. Not only was she drunk and disorderly, but she seemingly was on the verge of poverty. Her inability to pay the fine, the imprisonment she subsequently faced, is representative of the ways the poor were historically victimized by criminal punishments, according to Jen Manion.[24] In this case, Jourdan's show of emotion did nothing to change the judge's mind. The report appears to portray her as a sympathetic character, and readers of the newspaper may have felt sorry for her, even if the court did not. The mention of her as a mother who went to buy bread for her children showed that she was trying to provide for her family but fell to the temptation of alcohol. Her tearful reaction demonstrates her sorrow or even panic at her situation, and although she faced criminal punishment, the newspaper framed her experience in such a way that the article provided a lesson to readers not to follow in the same path.

Beyond simply being a nuisance to society, women in the nineteenth century were often brought to criminal court to face charges of a sexual nature that broke societal moral codes. These offenses include adultery, fornication, and bigamy. The roots of prosecuting these types of crimes rest in the colonial, Revolutionary, and Early Republic eras of the nation. While colonial law in Pennsylvania was often structured to protect marriage, after the Revolution, new legal codes shifted focus to female purity and self-control. In addition, Clare Lyons argues that Philadelphian society in the post-Revolutionary period used "class and racial divisions . . . to constitute new constructions of sexuality" and thus "created the appearance of licentiousness of the rabble and restraint of the middle classes." As a result, women had the onerous task of being responsible for any sexual wrongdoing.[25]

Looking at this issue more closely in three counties I sampled, Adams, Cumberland, and York, the percentages for crimes of a sexual nature, particularly prosecuting for fornication and bastardy, were significantly higher than in the rest of the counties, where moral and petty crime were more on the order of public disturbance and alcohol-related offenses. This appears to be a holdover from the patterns in the colonial and Early Republic eras, as suggested by the works by Susan Klepp and Clare Lyons, because more than two-thirds of moral crimes were for fornication and bastardy, and these constituted one-third of all female crimes during this era in Pennsylvania.

Furthermore, it was not only concern for the moral tone of the community that drove courts to prosecute these crimes but fear that community resources would be taxed by having to support illegitimate children. Fornication and bastardy charges in Cumberland and Adams Counties accounted for approximately 70 percent of moral offenses, and in York County, 63 percent. Other counties had much lower numbers.[26]

These types of crimes captured the public's attention in the antebellum decades as well. In 1851 a Pittsburgh resident, Eliza Brunty, was charged with bigamy. She had married her first husband, James Brunty, in Ireland. He subsequently left her, immigrated to the United States, and married another woman. Eliza Brunty had then married a Mr. McNutt in April 1850, who was about eighty years old. He had since died. She showed the court a divorce petition from her first husband, but the court deemed that the document was "by no means conclusive." If the divorce was invalid, Mr. McNutt was an adulterer, and both Eliza Brunty and James Brunty were bigamists. Eliza Brunty was found not guilty when she admitted that "she had asserted she was his [Brunty's] wife for the purpose of inducing him to aid in the support of her and her child."[27] It is unclear from the records if she was charged with any crime for her falsehood. Eliza perhaps used her role as mother and needing to support a child to garner sympathy from the court. While we may never know for sure whether Eliza Brunty was indeed a knowing bigamist, she was able to demonstrate that her desire to support a child was at the forefront of the reasons for her actions. In trying to be a good mother, she got herself entangled in the legal system but also extricated herself.

Other women looked for compassion in the sentencing process, forgoing a fight altogether on their guilt or innocence. Elizabeth Green simply pled guilty to the charge of larceny of a significant amount of "wearing apparel" instead of going through a trial. She directed matters further by asking the judge to send her to Eastern State, "for she said she liked the quarters there better than at the Moyamensing prison." The judge honored her request, sentencing her to three years. She had only recently been released from Eastern State where, under the name Elizabeth Brown, she had already spent three years for larceny. The prisoner register described her in 1841 as an illiterate, twenty-one-year-old mulatto. Brown was married at the time of her incarceration and had worked as a servant in the past. She was released in March 1844, only to be sentenced again to three years, in July

1844. She was released in July 1847.[28] In addition to her time at Eastern State, Brown must have been imprisoned at Moyamensing at some point in her life to have requested that she serve her second sentence in the penitentiary. This exchange with the court demonstrates that while she did not fight the charges against her, Elizabeth Green or Brown played on the sympathies of the judge to influence the sentence, and demonstrated enough personal agency to advocate for herself.

EMPLOYING SYMPATHY IN VIOLENT CRIMES

In cases of nonviolent crimes, appearing sympathetic to play on the emotions of juries, judges, and the public may have been an easier task for accused women; yet, this approach was also used in cases regarding violent crimes committed by women. Exhibiting sympathetic characteristics appeared in various stages of the experiences of criminal women. While some perhaps utilized sympathy as a motivation for committing violent acts (some cases of infanticide examined in the next chapter might be viewed in this light), in other cases, trying to marshal sympathy might not play a role until the trial, during testimony, or even after a conviction. The case of Mary Jane Sebastian provides an interesting perspective to the idea of being a sympathetic defendant. Mary Jane Sebastian used poison to kill her husband, Henry Myers Sebastian, yet there is little evidence to suggest that extenuating circumstances existed to want out of this marriage, like another lover or abuse. Sebastian's crime and trial took place in November 1857, in Lancaster County, Pennsylvania. The defendant was young, only seventeen, a "light mulatto" and "rather good looking." Mary Jane had administered "white arsenic" to her husband over the course of several weeks. The prosecution stated that her motive was "a dislike for him, and the object to get rid of him." A local man, James Armstrong, who was identified as being African American, testified that Mary Jane had confessed to the crime, stating that she had poisoned him by dosing her husband's coffee. When Armstrong asked her if she was sorry, Mary Jane replied, "I was in a passion; I was angry at him at the time I did it." The pair had only been married a few months and did not really get along. Armstrong also stated that the "slow dose" (i.e., the poisoning over a period of weeks) was a "prevailing custom among the blacks—especially in the Southern country—to poison each other." Henry Myers Sebastian's sister also took the stand. She described her brother's physical condition the day before he died, stating that he "vomited green stuff" and when she told Henry's wife that he was dying, Mary Jane replied, "Oh s—t, let him die!" Mary Jane's mother, Nancy Patterson, testified that her daughter was "dumb" and "simple" probably because Mary Jane had "been living so long among the Dutch."[29]

Not only were Mary Jane's behaviors questioned, but physicians also discussed her mental status. At the time of her trial, Mary Jane was pregnant. Doctors Grove and Armor testified that sometimes pregnant women suffered from a short-term monomania—a brief lapse in sanity. The doctors recalled cases where women exhibited "extreme hatred" of their spouses while pregnant, which sometimes resulted in a mental break. In one case, the wife murdered her husband and proceeded to eat parts of his body. Other mothers suffering from monomania due to pregnancy murdered their children when they were born. The defense tried to establish that Mary Jane Sebastian suffered from a type of monomania which caused her to kill her husband, yet the prosecution declared that this "was not insanity of the mind, but insanity of the heart—human depravity," since she admitted to the crime.[30]

Mary Jane Sebastian was convicted of first-degree murder and sentenced to hang. While the verdict and sentence were read, the defendant betrayed no emotion, being "the only unconcerned person in the room." Her ordeal was not over, however. A year later, she was granted a second trial, during which many people testified to Mary Jane's mental instability, stating that she was "soft" since childhood and had "not got right wit." Mary Jane was found not guilty by reason of insanity, and was sent to prison to await removal to a local almshouse or hospital.[31] While Sebastian may not have portrayed herself as a sympathetic defendant, witnesses used their observations of her mental status to keep her out of prison. The defense of insanity or brief mental incapacitation provided enough sway to prevent Mary Jane from being cast to the public and jury as a monster. Instead, she was saved from a death or prison sentence to receive treatment at a hospital.

Several other factors may have led to this outcome for Sebastian. The trial took place in a small town.[32] It is likely that many people associated with the trial somehow knew the defendant, victim, or both. This knowledge shapes the way the community reacted to the proceedings and the defendant. In Sebastian's case, several people testified to the limitations of her mental capacity and spoke to the relationship between husband and wife, thus shaping the outcome of both trials. In addition, Sebastian represented a minority population, and in a period when racial tensions were growing in southeastern Pennsylvania, it may have been even more important for the defense to portray her as a sympathetic individual.[33]

For black women in the free North, respectability—or in Mary Jane Sebastian's case, appearing sympathetic—was a constant struggle. Jen Manion argues that in Early Republic Pennsylvania "the black community did not stand a chance of achieving legal or social equality," and Kali Gross suggests that although "Independence invigorated the antislavery movement . . . liberty also proved temporal, fraught with strife, and, ultimately, fleeting."[34] Mechanisms, such as the legal and criminal codes, were set in place to control and limit the upward mobility of free blacks, thus restricting black women's attempts to break into the realms society deemed respectable. The prevailing antebellum notion of womanhood was focused on white, middle-class life, which automatically excluded not only black women, but those women in the working classes as well as immigrants. So, as Barbara Cutter argues, black women approached this in two ways: they could try to live up to the standards and inevitably fail, or reject them altogether, providing the women with a liberating freedom to engage in the public sphere.[35] While we have little way of knowing how Sebastian felt about the gender ideology of the nineteenth century, what we can see from her actions and her experience in the legal system is that she approached her situation in ways similar to how white women did by trying to arrange character testimony on her behalf. Chapter 2 examines in depth other trials of female poisoners, but Sebastian's case follows a similar pattern of turning to poison to end her marriage. This pattern suggests that although she is of a different race than the other women discussed later, she, too, struggled with the legal limitations married women faced and showed initiative to extricate herself, albeit through a criminal act. In this situation, unity in their experiences as females overshadows the differences in race. Furthermore, although it took a second trial to set aside the guilty verdict, her mental status gave Sebastian the opportunity to be seen as a sympathetic character. She falls more into the category of "weaker woman" in this second trial, which ultimately saves her from the gallows. The fact that her crime was seen as a consequence of insanity plays into the accepted view of the nineteenth century that women were perhaps more susceptible to bouts of insanity, especially during pregnancy. By being placed within this more expected, albeit somewhat stereotypical, view of nineteenth-century women, it was perhaps easier for the jury in the second trial to be more lenient with Sebastian in their verdict.

RESPECTABILITY AS MOTIVATION AND COVER

While using respectability in court is one way that criminal women employed social standards to help their cause, other women used notions of respectability as a way to mask the commission of a crime or even as a motive to commit crime. Shoplifting represented one property crime that was often committed by women. It was a common offense in urban settings where, as cities expanded, more shops opened, and merchants proffered their goods to more people. In the counties sampled for this study, 28.4 percent of offenses were property-related, and counties that had larger urban centers tended to have higher rates of these types of crimes.[36] Women were often the perpetrators of this crime, perhaps because they did not look threatening to shopkeepers or because women often were the family's main purchaser, making it a crime of opportunity. In her study of late nineteenth-century shoplifting, Elaine Abelson argues that many of these offenders were respectable, middle-class women. A good number of women who were caught had in their possession when arrested both legally purchased as well as pilfered items, demonstrating that women sometimes participated in legal and illegal forms of consumerism simultaneously.[37]

While Abelson's study focuses on the large department stores of the later nineteenth century, judging from newspaper reports of antebellum shoplifting it appears that women did so in smaller, more local stores, and that many of the perpetrators were members of lower social classes. Kali Gross suggests that as Philadelphia tightened its laws regarding property crimes in the nineteenth century, race became a "liability" as law enforcement "targeted blacks and other segments of the urban poor."[38] In Philadelphia, Maria Stevens, an African American woman, was arrested "on suspicion of stealing a piece of mousseline de laine" from a local store in South Philadelphia. Stevens must have been a common offender, because the article noted that she had "done such things before." Mary Donnelly, presumably a white woman, was arrested for pilfering a piece of linen and twenty yards of another fabric, which she "concealed under her cloak." Another unnamed white woman was let off with a reprimand after attempting to steal a kettle from a stove store in South Philadelphia. She was known to have tried shoplifting in other area stores. Two African American women, Elizabeth Brown and Charlotte Fisher, were caught "in the act of stealing a piece of Calico" from a dry goods store in Philadelphia.[39] In these cases, they stole items that were commonly purchased by women, thereby delaying suspicion regarding their activities. Being female provided an opportune cover for these offenders due to the fact that they employed societal expectations of purchasing patterns and the gendered role of women as consumers to commit crimes.

Nineteenth-century citizens often had a difficult time considering shoplifting by women as a criminal offense, particularly when the crime was committed by a middle-class woman. Rather, they looked for a medical interpretation to explain the women's actions, such as describing shoplifting as an illness. Often, female shoplifters were deemed kleptomaniacs, and Abelson notes that physicians determined that they were "fundamentally irrational" and subject to the "'natural' constraints of the female sex." By doing this, legal officials sometimes accepted this criminal behavior as a mania that women succumbed to, thereby explaining away the criminal acts. As a result, all women were then considered to be possible shoplifters, since the rationale behind shoplifting was that women were the main shoppers in society, and women were weak and could not help themselves. Abelson argues that kleptomania was "a heavily value-laden, demeaning judgment about women and female sexuality"; although the term was a legitimate diagnosis, it also acted as another piece of evidence that women were viewed to be lesser beings than men.[40]

This idea that women suffered from kleptomania was focused on the expectation that the woman was of the middle or upper social classes. Although all women were seen as potential shoplifters, kleptomania as a reason for committing crimes was driven by class distinction. Women of the middle class were allowed the designation of shoplifter and were viewed to be experiencing the condition of kleptomania. Poorer women who stole were simply seen as thieves without any medical explanation for their crimes.[41] This categorization serves to apologize for and rationalize the behavior of middle-class women, while demonizing the behavior of those who were of a lower social standing, making it clear that class plays a role in being seen as respectable. This explanation of kleptomania does not account for the various motives of the women for committing the thefts.

While some may have suffered from a sickness, others who stole simply for material gain would negate the idea that they were proper women in the first place. Greed or selfishness are not characteristics associated with the socially driven expectations for nineteenth-century women. In a sense, propagating the idea of kleptomania helps to protect or maintain the societal framework about women's roles in society, when the evidence suggests that women are breaking that idealized notion of who they are and what their capabilities are. Take, for example, the cases listed above. Nowhere are these women defined as kleptomaniacs, even though they are designated as shoplifters. It is possible that for these women in these instances described, shoplifting was a necessary act for survival or a way to increase income, particularly in the poorer sections of the city, which may explain why many of those shoplifters mentioned in the newspapers were African American. As Philadelphia developed, the affluent classes moved out from the city center, allowing for the development of a shopping district in the city. While the shops along Chestnut, Walnut, and Market Streets catered to middle- and upper-class needs, the shops on South Street sold to a lower-income clientele since it was an artery through the southern, predominantly immigrant and minority neighborhoods. As the various shopping districts grew, so did the crime of shoplifting.[42]

Furthermore, considering the dominant views concerning black women at the time and the struggle they faced to fit into defined gender norms, African American women were less socially restrained and, either willingly or out of necessity, put themselves more directly in the public domain, at a time when women from across racial lines and classes were becoming more public figures.[43] In antebellum northern urban settings, free black women had the extra burdens of working to support their families, provide for them domestically, and try to be seen as respectable—at least in their own communities, even if their white counterparts do not hold that view. Few African American women were able to break through the belief held by many northern whites that black women could not be seen as respectable. Nell Irvin Painter argues that "black woman as lady" was an incredibly uncommon thought in U.S. society at the time, and only a few individuals, like Sojourner Truth, were able to claim a spot in this vaunted realm of "lady." Yet, as Barbara Cutter suggests, although whites often asserted that black women could not be part of their gender ideology, "African Americans could and did maintain that they were included."[44]

These particular black women who were designated as shoplifters were not given the opportunity to be seen as ladies who were victims of a medical or psychological condition. Instead, due to society's prevailing attitudes about race and class, these women were simply seen as criminals, sometimes repeat criminals, and these facts had significant influence in shaping the way they were portrayed to the public, and by extension, reinforcing racial and class stereotypes. Instead of having a single group of female shoplifters, the extra categorization of these women based on class and race ultimately separates the criminals into those that might receive more sympathy from the public and those that likely did not.

Swindling takes the use of womanhood as a cover to commit crimes to a new level—where women blatantly used feminine wiles on the unsuspecting. This type of criminal behavior is important to consider because these offenders understood that the social conception of women at the time, particularly respectable-looking women, allowed them the leeway to commit fraud without being suspected of wrongdoing. They exploited the definitions of womanhood and the social perception that women would not commit such crimes to their advantage: the ruse often allowed them to get away with criminal acts.

The tricks used by criminals on unsuspecting storeowners created considerable anxiety. The newspaper reports of these cases generally took the tone of warning citizens of the swindlers' modus operandi. The *Philadelphia Public Ledger* reported, "We are informed that there is a female, of tall and very genteel appearance, doing a pretty flourishing business in this city, in swindling and stealing." The paper stated that the offender gave a different name in each store she entered. In Philadelphia, the swindler went into a business to buy a hat, asked the storekeeper to watch an important package for her while she asked her friends' opinions of the hat before purchasing, and thus walked off with the hat. The package contained only worthless items.[45]

Other women exploited conventional notions of female respectability to pull off their scams. In 1841, the *Philadelphia Public Ledger* reported, "We have lately heard of numerous instances of bad notes having been taken from two or three very good-looking and well-dressed females." "In all the cases we have heard of," the author continued, "the passers are described as young ladies of genteel address and good appearance, and well calculated to allay any suspicion against them, even when the notes are detected and refused." In 1852, two women in Philadelphia, Jane Mullin and Elizabeth Teal, were arrested for stealing goods from stores by employing such a ruse. The two women "were in the habit of representing themselves as being sent by some well-known resident" for a "sample of goods." After they were given the goods, the women left and failed to return the items. These women were also in the habit, according to the newspaper, of asking to borrow from other ladies black dresses, shawls, and bonnets, for the purported purpose of attending a funeral and failing to return the "borrowed" clothing. These con women used the reputations of other citizens in order to make their actions seem legitimate. Not only did they steal from stores, they also threatened the reputations of women who were socially upstanding. In another case, a "genteely [sic] dressed" young woman with "very lady-like manners" went to a milliner's store, selected a silk material, and requested that the samples be sent to a Madame Gaubert's address. The swindler left, going to Madame Gaubert's to intercept the porter delivering the fabric. The porter then returned to the store, only to be sent back to Madame Gaubert's to find the woman after his employers realized the theft; the unknown female took off with the silk fabric, worth $100.[46]

What makes these cases even more disturbing is the fact that the offenders' appearances portrayed gentility, a characteristic that threw authorities and victims off balance because they did not expect to be duped by criminals taking the form of proper-looking citizens—especially females who dressed and acted decently. Such swindlers broke societal notions of what a female criminal was supposed to look like. A female swindler was not some monster, nor did she exhibit unfeminine characteristics; she dressed the part of a genteel, pretty woman and used the markers of her physical appearance to dupe others, making the crime of swindling particularly insidious.

In Pittsburgh, in June 1850, one woman caught the attention of local authorities. The unnamed woman had been "obtaining money of our citizens" by pretending to be representing "various charitable" organizations. The woman conned others for several months, representing herself as different ladies of repute in the city. The newspaper printed the story as a warning that because of her "elegant exterior" and manners, she "has been very successful in her impositions upon people's benevolent sympathies."[47] Once again, using the ruse of respectability by impersonating certain influential women allowed this offender to perfect her criminal craft. Furthermore, that she asked for money on behalf of charitable associations reflects not only the antebellum era's fervor in support of reform campaigns, but that it was also acceptable for women to be leading figures in the public sphere supporting various social movements. As it was not uncommon for women to be fund-raisers for charitable societies, this particular swindler perpetrated a con that protected her from being caught for several months.

Female swindlers threatened the structure of nineteenth-century society. Kathleen De Grave suggests that women were supposed to fit into either of two categories: the ideal of domesticity and purity or its antithesis—a "temptress, the brutal murderess." There was no place for these scamming women who broke the law because she was "too logical, too daring, too self-regarding, too independent, too selfish, too sordid, too calculating, too extravagantly greedy, too able to identify herself without reference to a man to fit in anywhere."[48] Thus, female swindlers became a subversive force, possibly explaining why newspapers were quick to write separate articles on these women's behavior as possible warnings to other citizens.

While female shoplifters and swindlers often used their feminine appearance or respectably styled clothing as a cover for their crimes, many women who committed property crimes fell into the category of larcenists.[49] On September 2, 1837, Mary Black, "a cognomen excessively appropriate, as she was dark as Erebus," was arrested for larceny, "having stolen a piece of carpeting from a private dwelling." Susan Edwards was sentenced to three months' imprisonment for "the larceny of one blanket, one chemise, and sundry bedclothes." The variety of goods pilfered was quite diverse. Larcenies of carpeting, clothing, stoves, work baskets, and tubs, resulted in convictions and jail sentences from thirty days to a full year. In Pittsburgh, Mary Brown was found guilty and imprisoned for stealing a shawl. Brown was part of a "gang of pilferers" which had harassed Pittsburgh for quite some time, until it was "successfully broken up by the arrest and conviction of 'Lady Bill' their captain, and Henrietta Douglass."[50]

The limited value of goods stolen and the seemingly practical nature of the items indicate that these women likely were driven to act partly out of necessity, and perhaps not habitually.[51] We have little way of knowing how the women felt about their larcenies. Due to the utilitarian nature of the articles stolen, it may be that these women saw their actions as a means to survive or improve their living situation in difficult times. For them, survival outweighed any apparent manipulation of social norms in the commission of their crimes.

The desire for respectability still played a role in many of these crimes, however, perhaps just not overtly. Some women used the trappings of decency to get away with crimes, while others stole because they wanted the material items that would make them seem like reputable women. When Mary Hildebrant, a young German girl of seventeen, was arrested in Philadelphia, authorities found in her possession "watches, jewelry, silk and satin dresses, coats, vests, pants, cutlery, and almost every moveable article mentionable." The reporter noted that "she is very good looking and always was very well dressed which prevented suspicion."[52] Like the female swindlers who used the guise of respectability to conduct their cons, Hildebrant used her beauty and seemingly wealthy-looking apparel to avoid suspicion by the authorities. It is in these types of cases where societal notions of what it meant to be respectable seemed to cloud some people's judgments about who could be seen as a criminal. At the same time, Hildebrant understood how the public viewed women and subsequently used society's blinders as a cover to commit crimes.

Likewise, Mary Beck, arrested for committing a series of thefts at houses where she was employed as a domestic, used her appearance to elicit sympathy from officials. Several families for whom she worked testified that their goods had gone missing. Beck was described as "a young woman of genteel appearance," which seemed to help her during her trial. Only a short time earlier, Beck had been convicted of larceny but had been "recommended to mercy" by the jury. Her good looks "created a good deal of sympathy for her and owing to the intercession of persons who felt an interest in her, she was liberated by the Judge." She was not so lucky the second time around and was committed to prison to await a trial.[53]

In 1855, a lengthy trial filled the columns of the *Pittsburgh Daily Dispatch*, as Emeline Keating was tried for grand larceny in the Court of Quarter Sessions. Keating was "a respectable young lady of rather prepossessing appearance, and owns a farm of land." During a visit to the Cadwalder Evans family home in Pittsburgh, Keating supposedly "purloined $1,600 from a bureau in Mrs. Evans' bed room." Keating, according to Mrs. Evans, was "papering a room" and had a box on the bed, in which were gold coins that belonged to the Evans family. When Mrs. Evans found the money, Keating "rushed towards where I was, threw me on the bed; and took the bag from me, saying she was ruined and that it was Mr. M'Lain's money." Mrs. Evans apparently believed her at first, and it was not until after Keating left the house when she realized her money was missing. Mr. Evans, who had died between the time of the theft and the trial, followed Keating to Washington, where she said she was going to get money from a Mr. M'Connaghy's estate that she was owed. After returning from Washington, Mr. Evans and Emeline Keating met with a judge who said Keating's story about the estate was a lie, since the executors claimed no money was willed to Keating and that it was clear the money she had in her possession belonged to the Evans family. Keating gave $350 back to Mrs. Evans, saying, "That's all I can account for now—that $350," having used the remaining $1,250 already.[54]

Keating told her side of the events in question when the Commonwealth finished their case. She claimed Mrs. Evans had invited her to visit, during which time Mr. Evans "made several indecent propositions to her." Offended, Keating threatened to tell Mrs. Evans of his conduct and, after leaving, told someone else how Evans "had acted towards her, and stated that he had frequently offered her large sums of money." Keating was advised to take the money if he offered it again. At a later date, Mr. Evans had again insulted her and offered $600 in gold to "purchase her silence." This was part of the money that Mrs. Evans had found to be missing and "Mr. Evans, not wishing to acknowledge what he had done, joined in charging Miss Keating with stealing it." Other witnesses for the defense testified that Mrs. Evans had mentioned that they had imprisoned Keating in their house since she had stolen the money. In addition, multiple character witnesses were brought by the defense to testify, and all stated that Emeline Keating's "general reputation as a lady of integrity and honesty has been good."[55]

Weighing the two conflicting stories, which was complicated by the absence of Mr. Evans due to his untimely death from cholera, the jury acquitted Emeline Keating.[56] It is possible that the stories of Mr. Evans's inappropriate advances toward Keating, reports of an illegal imprisonment in the Evans household, and her character witnesses allowed the jury to believe Keating despite the testimony that she admitted to Mrs. Evans she could only account for $350 of the missing money. Even with that admission of possessing the money, there was insufficient evidence to prove she had stolen it or whether it was given to her by Mr. Evans in exchange for her silence. The jury may have viewed Emeline Keating sympathetically as a victim. Reports of her respectability and good character may have played a role in the positive outcome for Keating. Keating's trial represents another case where the defendant's alleged respectability provided an advantage to her as she navigated the legal proceedings. Although we cannot know truly whether she stole the money, Keating's character and respectability was put on trial. Keating and her lawyers shaped the outcome of her situation by demonstrating her awareness of and engaging with societal norms of womanhood.

Several reports of larcenies indicate that some women stole because they desired goods that would make them appear wealthier. In a particularly long description of a crime of theft, the *Philadelphia Public Ledger* took the opportunity to editorialize on this trend in larceny. An unnamed girl, "respectably dressed," was charged with stealing items, including a ring, from her employer's home. Upon the stolen articles being discovered in her possession, the girl "confessed that she had committed a foolish act, and begged that they would not send her to prison." The judge, although recognizing that the girl was sorry for her deed, upheld the law and committed her to jail for an unreported length of time. What is most interesting about this case is the reporter's speculation on why the girl committed the crime:

> We should incline to the belief that the motive which prompted her to commit this act, was that love of finery which is too frequently displayed by girls in an humble situation, and which is as unbecoming the sphere they occupy, as it is impossible honestly to indulge in out of the wages received by them. To gratify this taste, petty larcenies, if not something worse, are not unfrequently resorted to, which, by being successfully practised at first, before suspicion is awakened, leads to bolder embezzlements and articles of more value are appropriated. Then it is that an exposure takes place, and the girl ruined in reputation sinks gradually from one crime to another until she is to be found in the lowest depths of inhuman degradation. A similar disposition to "show out" beyond what the means of the person will honestly allow, extends itself at present throughout every class of society, and is breaking down all the conscientious scruples which are usually the guide and test of conduct.[57]

This excerpt is particularly interesting because it illuminates the societal fears of class lines being breached, an anxiety over the growing desire for luxury which may lead to future crime, and also the general worry that individuals' spirals into crime, if allowed to continue, would weaken society. Such acts of larceny raised broader concerns that people were attempting to live beyond their means and in so doing were undermining established societal values.

Another example corroborates this sentiment. In December 1841, Hester Ann Anderson was committed "for the larceny of a lady's cloak, worth $60, and a pair of gum shoes, the property of a lady in whose family she was employed as a domestic." In the report, Hester claimed that she planned to return the items after church for she "had only borrowed them to look well in the congregation." The author judged her conduct as unbecoming: "If this story is true she was actuated by a motive prevalent to a lamentable degree in all classes of society, and which as in her case very often brings disgrace."[58] Coveting goods to indulge the desire for beauty and social uplift appears to be a similar problem for many nineteenth-century larcenies. Appearance and the need to impress play influential roles not only in the motivations to commit crimes, but also at the trial stage of female offenders' cases. While contemporary observers often lamented this trend, it reveals the fact that women used feminine appearance and proper dress not only as motivation to commit crimes, but to shape the way the jury, judge, and public viewed them.

The cases recounted above represent another trope of antebellum larcenies: that of thieving domestic servants. These young women seemed to be tempted by the luxury items in the homes of the families for whom they worked. While the temptation to steal may have been influenced by the desire to look respectable, it is also possible many viewed these purloined goods as compensation for poor wages and harsh working conditions. These examples represent only a few of the many cases of domestic servants who stole from employers. State penitentiary records suggest how common this practice was. Of those women sent to Eastern State Penitentiary who were employed in domestic service, 63.2 percent of them were convicted of larceny, robbery, or burglary. At Western State Penitentiary, that percentage was 74.6 percent.[59]

RESPECTABILITY AND FEMININITY AS DEFENSE IN COURT

In a variety of property crimes, the appearance of respectability or desire to be respectable in society provided women with motivation and cover for breaking the law. The issue of respectability and portraying femininity also was used by women as part of their defense at their trials. In this manner, the women used their knowledge of what mainstream society expected of them to aid their cause in front of the juries. Character witnesses painted the accused in a positive manner, attempting to persuade the juries of the women's innocence.

One case in particular demonstrates how extensively the characteristics of respectability and femininity could be used in the courtroom—for both the prosecution and the defense. In November 1840, Philadelphia newspapers reported on a female murder trial from the Court of Oyer and Terminer: "Sarah A. Coleman [alias Davis] . . . stands charged with the murder of a female, whom, it is alleged, she killed from jealous motives." She was accused of murdering Juliana Jordan in July of 1840. Jordan was found with her throat cut by a razor, with her sewing, shoes, and the razor lying in a pool of her blood. Davis claimed Jordan had taken her own life and insisted the blood found on her hands seen by eyewitnesses came from trying to stop Jordan from committing suicide. Other witnesses claimed to have heard cries of murder coming from the victim. Ann Norbury testified, "I first heard an awful screech; I first thought it was the screech of a pig in the hands of hog catchers, it was so shrill; it was a woman's; then the screech came 'murder.'"[60]

What is most interesting about this case is the way the witnesses regarded the victim and the accused. The witnesses testified about both women involved, and through their words, we observe how these individuals viewed the women and their character. Numerous people spoke about Davis during the prosecution phase of the trial. A man in the neighborhood, Joseph T. Vankirk, stated that "Mrs. Davis seemed very much excited; her lips quivered and she was pale and colorless; her conduct was not such as to excite any suspicion in my mind that she was guilty of the murder." William Bramble, a constable for the city, testified that the defendant "said 'I done it.'" When told she spoke like a crazy woman, Davis said, "She was not crazy, and I done it, I was obliged to do it or she would have thrown me downstairs." Others said Davis's demeanor was light and unconcerned about the death. One mentioned she was more concerned about hanging out her laundry. The witness continued, "I thought she acted very strange in being so calm; she had no respect for the woman."[61]

Although the prosecution depicted Davis in a colder, more distant manner, the defense witnesses painted Davis in a different light. Mary Louderbach stated that Davis boarded with her at one point and "she behaved herself respectably and decent, and I took her to be so." The defendant's sister Susan Hall had good things to say about both women. She stated that her sister and the deceased "were very friendly and affectionate, and appeared always to me like two sisters." She described her sister as "kind . . . her character among her acquaintances was considered of a kind nature; she was always called a good hearted soul who would wrong no one; her treatment to Julia was always kind."[62] Davis, in these testimonies, is portrayed in several different ways. For the majority of the prosecution's testimony, witnesses seemed a little disturbed by her aloof reaction to the death, commenting on her laughter and her desire to hang out her clothes. The character witnesses for Davis's defense spoke positively of her, considered her a respectable, decent, and a kind woman, someone seemingly incapable of such a murder and embodying virtues expected in an upstanding female.

The information regarding the victim Juliana Jordan's character and personality was also quite varied. The sister of the deceased, a witness for the prosecution, noted her dead sister's disposition to be "always lively, cheerful, full of jokes and fun." She noted that to her knowledge, she "never took laudanum or opium," a fact that Davis's defense exploited.[63]

The defense used Jordan's possible drug use to cast doubt on Davis's involvement in the murder. Mary Sutton's testimony is worth quoting at length:

> Knew the deceased, Mrs. Jordan, she told me she was in the habit of taking laudanum and opium . . . she told me she had taken laudanum once, and but for the timely assistance she got it would have killed her; she said she knocked and thumped against the partition, and the neighbors came in and rescued or relieved her; she didn't tell on what account she had taken the laudanum; I shouldn't suppose she wanted to die, or else she wouldn't have knocked for assistance. . . .
>
> Cross-examined. She never told me she took the laudanum or opium for the purpose of destroying her own life; she never told me that she wanted to take her own life; she was very lively, good natured, and kind; I never saw her low spirited at all; I didn't think she ever had any trouble; I always thought her health was very good; she appeared to me to be industrious and always behaved like a lady when she came to my house.[64]

By promoting the possibility that the deceased wanted to take her own life and used drugs casts doubt on who killed Jordan and provided an opportunity for the jury to question the guilt of Davis. It is important to note how the prosecution, on cross-examination of this witness, attempted to present Jordan as an upstanding, kind lady, who was not prone to suicidal thoughts. By promoting the possibility of suicide, the defense painted Jordan as unstable and disturbed, characteristics that blacken Jordan's reputation as a nice, calm woman. This trial illustrates how the testimony regarding the character and portrayal of women in such proceedings acted as a lens on how society believed women should act and whether the defendant and victim fit into the expected realm.

In addition to Jordan's supposed drug use, John Hoskins, witness for the defense, noted that Juliana owed him money. When he asked her to repay, she said that "she was poor and destitute; and that her husband had left her, and did not assist her." Hoskins testified, "I told her to return to virtue, that her husband was a clever man, and would perhaps forgive her transgressions." Hoskins admonished her to "go and do better."[65] By describing Juliana as a fallen woman, someone who had lost her "clever" husband and her virtue, the defense attempted to remove sympathy for the victim by showing she was not an innocent and kind, but a woman with vices who strayed from the path of respectability.

The trial closed on January 18, 1841. On January 23, 1841, the jury returned with a verdict declaring her guilty of murder in the first degree.[66] Five months passed between her conviction and her sentencing. Although the testimony plastered over the front page of the newspaper in January caused intrigue and sated morbid curiosity, the most dramatic report followed the sentencing of Sarah Ann Davis. The judge's speech, which addressed to both Davis and the courtroom, offers an interesting study of how authorities viewed female criminals: "Your protestations of innocence can now avail you nothing. They can but excite emotions of mingled amazement and compassion that, standing upon the verge of the grave, you should continue so blindly insensible to the awful condition in which your crimes have placed you."[67] The speech portrays Davis as a foolish woman who lacked reason by thinking that her innocence would be believed after all the evidence against her. Her blindness and lack of sense regarding her guilt appalled the judge, who did not hide his disgust for her in his statement.

One of the most interesting portions of the sentencing speech is the judge's admonition to Davis for being "driven, in the very desperation of your defence, to blast [the victim's] reputation and blacken her memory."

The judge made clear his disapproval of both Davis's and Jordan's immorality. He said to Davis, "You have proved that her life, like your own, was frail; that her means of subsistence were the wages of sin." He admonished Davis for taking the woman into her home and killing her out of jealously for thinking that Jordan was taking away Davis's husband. The judge continued, "Like the life of Julia Ann Jordan, yours has been one of guilt and shame."[68] Most striking in these passages, in an otherwise generic sentencing speech, is the articulation of the frailty of women's morality. The judge's words illustrate that stepping into a life of vice and crime leads to major consequences. Both women lost their moral footing in different ways, and both dealt with severe consequences.

Although in Davis's case her defense did not earn her an acquittal, the ideas of respectability, virtue, and femininity could have a positive impact on some cases.[69] In Philadelphia in 1841, a young African American servant, Harriet Aikens, was charged with poisoning several members of the family for whom she worked. One child died, while others merely became ill. During the trial, it was shown that Aikens got along well with the family. The mother of the children never suspected her of the crime. Aikens had brought home custard and a cupcake to share with the kids, which is what was believed to have contained the poison. It was later thought that Aikens made the custard as opposed to buying it like she claimed. Many people testified to the point that Aikens was a good, respectable woman. Witnesses stated that she was a "very honest and good tempered woman" and was an "inoffensive girl." Testifiers to Aikens's character seemed shocked that she could commit such a crime. A previous employer of Aikens's stated, "When we heard it was our little Harriet, we thought it impossible for her to be guilty of such a thing; we had a very good opinion of her."[70] The character witnesses may have helped in this case, as Aikens was acquitted.

Aikens had the characteristics of a doting nurse. She loved the children she cared for, got along well with her employers, and generally was a hard worker. Because Aikens was a servant, the characteristics of what made her a respectable woman might have differed from the overall middle-class view of upright antebellum womanhood as detailed at the beginning of the chapter. By demonstrating her ability to act respectably and professionally in her position of employment, Aikens had the power to work against racial stereotypes of African American women, as well as women from the lower classes. Her acquittal challenged the perception that African American women were not as virtuous as white women.[71]

Putting on the guise of respectability was one tactic female offenders used to try to convince juries, judges, and the public that they were not the monsters society assumed they were. Because antebellum Americans believed that outside appearances implied moral qualities, criminal women needed to portray themselves as virtuous, by wearing modest clothing, projecting a remorseful demeanor, or even crying to create doubt in her ability to be a murderer.[72] We see this at play with female shoplifters but also in the defenses of Davis and Aikens where the virtuous qualities of the accused were extolled. The use of respectability and virtue as a defense had varied outcomes—sometimes saving women from prison or a death sentence, other times failing to do so. Prescribed societal roles for women could be powerfully used in the court system. The issues of integrity and domesticity were wrapped up in the trial evidence and, in some cases, may have played a more important role in the case's outcome. The women themselves, through their appearance or behavior, tapped into these societal notions and used them to try to aid their cause.

Women who committed crimes threatened the order and stability of antebellum communities. Their actions and criminal lives brought to light the concerns held in antebellum society about race, ethnicity, crime, poverty, and the proper place of women. The portrayals and treatment of the female criminals in the local newspapers demonstrate these broader concerns. While the individual voices of the women mostly remain silent, their stories, often only told through newspaper columns, act as a specific medium through which historians can examine nineteenth-century life and help scholars begin to understand the reality of their situations and the motivations that led them to paths of crime. These sources also provide glimpses of how the criminal women navigated the world of these antebellum societal concerns as well as the world of crime and the justice system.

While some observers viewed these criminal women as failing to live up to socially imposed expectations, the women themselves demonstrated an ability to use such expectations to their own benefit. The women who entered the legal system knew what characteristics society expected proper middle-class white women in antebellum America to have. Although few of the women criminals fell into this social category automatically, as many were racial or ethnic minorities or were of the working class, they marshaled those traits of passivity, respectability, and propriety as well as they could to try to sway the juries, judges, and the observing public. Furthermore, some of these women used the cover of femininity and respectability to get away with their offenses in the first place, particularly in the cases of larceny, shoplifting, and swindling. Respectability sometimes took center stage in trials of murder as well, as defense lawyers painted the defendant as respectable or feminine while denigrating the victim and the prosecution tried to prove the opposite. Other women who became entangled in the legal system looked to the courts for mercy, portraying themselves and their situations as sympathetically as they could to secure a reprieve or a light sentence. By using the traits of idealized femininity to their advantage, these women demonstrated ingenuity and social awareness, as well as an ability to help themselves as they navigated the intersecting layers of the antebellum legal system and societal standards.

CHAPTER 2

"She Would Have a Divorce at the Risk of Her Life"

Women and Crimes That Challenged Social Limitations

On September 27, 1853, J. Simpson Africa, a notable citizen of Huntingdon, Pennsylvania, noted in his diary, "Samuel Harris made complaint before my father against Elizabeth Harker for poisoning Mrs. Harris, his wife." Making the situation even more suspicious was the fact that John Harker, Elizabeth's husband, had died mysteriously in May of 1853. While Elizabeth Harker sat in jail awaiting trial for the murder of Mrs. Harris, several doctors and other members of the community disinterred John's body for an examination. Africa wrote in his journal that on November 8, 1853, his father along with the physicians made "an examination of the stomach of John Harker deceased, who, it is supposed, was poisoned by his wife who is now lying in our Co. jail awaiting her trial for poisoning her sister Mrs. Harris, wife of Samuel Harris."[1]

Harker, aged sixty-five, stood trial for the murder of Mrs. Harris in Huntingdon County in November 1853. As the *Huntingdon Globe* reported, the closing argument of the prosecution presented a "most appalling array of facts against the prisoner" which would "overwhelm every objection, and sweep away every reasonable doubt of her guilt." Harker's countenance made the news as well. During the early portion of the trial, "the prisoner seemed but little affected by her awful situation; but as proof after proof was elicited, fastening the guilt unmistakeably [sic] upon her, her courage gave

way, and her tears, and sobs, added not a little to the painful and embar-
rassing duties of the Court."[2] Harker is painted by the local press as almost
emotionless at the start of the proceedings, portraying her to readers and
observers as unfeeling, perhaps as a way to shape public opinion against
her. What is also shown by the reporter, however, is that the impact of her
actions seemed to settle in to Harker as the trial continued, changing Harker
from a stoic defendant to one whose emotions apparently betrayed her
guilt. The descriptions of Harker serve to shape opinion against her, and
while her emotions may have garnered sympathy from some observers, the
evidence of her calculated measures outweighed emotion in the eyes of the
judge and jury.

Harker was found guilty of first-degree murder, a crime that carried the
death penalty according to Pennsylvania law.[3] The judge's sentencing speech
tells a great deal about how the community viewed Harker, and suggests
how antebellum society, more broadly, viewed other female murderers.
"Your crime shocks us, and shocks all" the judge declared, "it is MURDER—
murder by POISON; deliberately and cruelly administered." He suggested
that Harker, motivated by jealously and greed, visited Harris "having first
provided yourself with poison for the purpose of destroying her life to make
that home yours." The judge recounted the events of the crime, including
the prolonged sickness and slow death of Mrs. Harris due to arsenic poisoning, while Harker plotted how she would manage the home and possessions
after Harris passed away. According to the judge, Harker hid "the horrid
secret" in her "depraved bosom," and others should learn from Harker's
experience that crimes committed with "the very utmost wickedness and
depravity of heart" warranted death by hanging. Harker showed emotion
and anxiety over her situation, but as she listened to the sentence she "acted
the part of the most hardened wretch, and received the sentence with a
smile."[4] The trial reporting portrays Harker as coming full circle in behavior
from the start of the proceedings to the end of the sentence. She began the
trial seeming resolved, became seemingly anxious and upset over her situation, but by the end had returned to a strong character, this time described
to observers as hardened.

Two months later, it was finally concluded that John Harker, aged
sixty-six years, had also been killed by arsenic poisoning, probably administered through a meal of stewed greens that he had asked Elizabeth to
prepare for him. She never stood trial for this second murder, most likely

because she was already sentenced to die for killing Mrs. Harris. The evidence that she killed both her husband and sister suggests strongly that she intended to marry Mr. Harris and take over that household. Harker spent the rest of her life in prison but was never hanged for her crime. She died of illness in her prison cell in November 1855. According to local sources, Harker had the freedom to leave the jail during the day and return to her cell at night.[5]

Harker appeared to be motivated to commit the crimes to extricate herself from a marriage she no longer wanted. Using poison allowed her a common method that might, but in her case ultimately failed, to hide her crime.[6] Although the judge showed his disgust at her actions, citing jealously and calculating planning of the deeds, and one might presume he was not alone in his sentiments, particularly in a small community, this case demonstrates that some women turned to crime when other means of changing their life circumstances failed. For many women who entered the criminal record, particularly for violent crimes, they turned to crime because they had limited options available to them.[7] Harker, from the limited evidence provided in the trial, was likely not going to be able to acquire a divorce from her own husband and thus turned to poisoning as a way to achieve her goals. She understood the limitations of the legal system as it applied to her situation and looked for other means, albeit criminal ones, to achieve what she wanted. Through her crime, she challenged antebellum society and the legal and social boundaries within which women were expected to stay.[8]

Often, these criminal women—those who directly challenged society's limits placed on women or challenged their accusers or the court officials overtly—were categorized as wretched, almost inhuman, and unfeminine. The local press description of these women helped to cement these designations in the minds of the local community, thus shaping how these women were viewed as their trials progressed. Almost a third of the crimes sampled for this study were violent offenses, yet the vast majority of those cases involved assault and battery charges.[9] See the table below for a break down of violent crimes. This chapter focuses on the roughly 6 percent of offenses committed by women that produced a more robust archival record—murder and infanticide cases.

Women who committed infanticide demonstrate this trend of turning to crime as a response to circumstantial limitations of freedom, mobility,

TABLE 2. Violent crimes committed by women

Crime (indictment)	Number of indictments (of the 1,930 violent crimes)	Percentage of indictments (of the 1,930 violent crimes)
Assault and battery	1,817	94.15
Infanticide	7	0.36
Murder of bastard child	11	0.57
Murder of bastard child and concealing death of bastard child	9	0.47
Concealing death of bastard child	33	1.71
Murder	44	2.28
Poisoning	7	0.36
Attempted murder	1	0.05
Accessory to murder	1	0.05

Source: County Quarter Session Dockets.

or finances. In Philadelphia in February 1837, an infant was found "wrapt in a blanket, which was frozen to it. . . . [It] came to its death by the neglect of its unnatural mother." Two days later, the same Philadelphia newspaper reported that a lady noticed suspicious movement in a cemetery and upon investigation found pigs eating the corpse of a newborn child. This infant was covered in only "two shirt sleeves, in which it had been wrapped when thus murdered by its unnatural mother." Women were often the perpetrators of infanticide, as evidenced by the prevalence of the crime in local newspaper coverage. On August 7, 1837, the *Philadelphia Public Ledger* wrote about an unknown infant boy whose "inhuman mother or other monster who left the child at the place where found, was so lost to all sense of decency as to leave it exposed entirely naked." In rural Lewistown, Pennsylvania, twin infant girls were found on the banks of the Juniata River, "who had no doubt been destroyed by their inhuman mother" who likely tossed them from a bridge. It is striking that in all these reports, the identity of the mother is unknown. The anonymity of the perpetrator possibly frightened and destabilized the community when the public and authorities knew a killer was in

TABLE 3. Breakdown of types of crimes against children

Crime (indictment)	Number of indictments (of the 1,930 violent crimes)	Percentage of indictments (of the 1,930 violent crimes)
Infanticide	7	0.36
Murder of bastard child	11	0.57
Murder of child and concealing death of bastard child	9	0.47
Concealing death of bastard child	33	1.71

Source: County Quarter Session Dockets.

their midst and could not be identified. In addition to the reason above, the fact that the infants were easily hidden, and that people who found infant corpses could not always determine whether the baby had been born alive or stillborn, made it incredibly difficult to prove an infanticide case.[10] Table 3 indicates the small number of offenses dealing with the deaths of babies that made it to court and demonstrates the nuances of Pennsylvania law related to crimes against children.

In Pennsylvania in the 1790s, penal code reforms altered the laws against infanticide. The statute in place for most of the eighteenth century put the onus on the mother to prove that the dead child was stillborn and not killed. It was generally thought by the public that since most women who committed infanticide were unmarried, they would resort to killing their child to protect their own reputation. Thus, a hidden corpse was sufficient to convict a woman of infanticide. In the colonial era, women could be prosecuted for infanticide and for the concealment of a bastard child, both of which were capital offenses. Juries sometimes had trouble convicting women of the crime of infanticide or concealment, or at least felt the penalties were too harsh. As the eighteenth century progressed, Susan Klepp notes that "prosecutorial standards became increasingly restrictive as standards of evidence changed to favor the accused." This shift, however, was not enough and William Bradford, attorney general of Pennsylvania and later of the United States, helped immensely in getting further changes made to the legal code. Revisions to the laws in 1786 and 1790 required that the prosecution show that the child was born alive for the woman to be convicted.

Then, in 1793, only first-degree murder was made punishable by death. After these changes, women charged and convicted of infanticide were convicted of second-degree murder, which entailed a prison sentence of up to five years, rather than facing execution. Furthermore, concealment of the death of a bastard child could also result in a five-year prison sentence. Although some women could still be found guilty of first-degree murder in infanticide cases, it became much more difficult to prove. The new tiers of laws and corresponding punishments allowed juries to convict for the crime but generally on the lesser charge of concealment.[11]

Even though the numbers are quite low for this type of crime, these women radically challenged notions of how women, particularly mothers, should behave. Descriptions of infanticide cases shocked newspaper readers and communities. The adjectives "inhuman" and "unnatural" used to describe the mothers of these infants confirm that the authorities, reporters, and most likely the community found these crimes to be appalling and illustrate that they viewed these women as unfit mothers. The motivations of these women to commit the crime, however, were often more logical or practical than newspapers led people to believe, despite their actions remaining criminal and disturbing to their peers in the community.

Sarah Walton admitted to killing her baby by strangulation, saying that "trouble had caused her to commit the crime." In a different incident in Carlisle, Pennsylvania, "a colored woman, a resident at the Poor House," gave birth to a child and "adopted the cruel and inhuman resolution of destroying its existence." The mother cut the child's throat and placed the dead infant in an outhouse. When she confessed to the crime, she told authorities that the father of the baby, who was also a resident of the poorhouse, told her to kill it. The motivations for this crime and that of Sarah Walton, while not overtly clear, illustrate that sometimes necessity or other pressures drove women to this type of crime. It could be that these mothers felt that the best thing they could do for their children was to not let the babies suffer from poverty or the instability of single motherhood, a struggle that working-class women of earlier generations faced as well.[12] These women indirectly challenged the social system that limited the ability of the lower classes or racial minorities to rise out of their current social status. The women likely did not view their crimes as a challenge to social norms and the economic system, and more likely acted as a result of their current economic or social situation; yet, the fact that some women appeared to want to protect their children from poverty suggests that they resisted continuing the cycle of poverty in a future generation.

Other newspaper articles on infanticide indicate the occupation or ethnicity of the perpetrators, which also speaks to the motivations for these women to commit the crime. In Pittsburgh, Barbara Kean, a young German woman of twenty, killed her child and placed the body in a privy. In Philadelphia, a sixteen-year-old domestic servant, Mary Craft, from Scotland, gave birth to an illegitimate baby boy and nearly severed his head to kill it. Margaret McDonough, who had only been in the United States six weeks since she arrived from Ireland, was also a servant who killed her illegitimate child.[13] These cases speak to the issue of young immigrant women, new to the United States, who could not support a child and wanted to hide their situation as unwed mothers from employers or judgmental others. Like the case from the Carlisle poorhouse, these instances indicate the level of desperation that some of these mothers must have faced when deciding that committing infanticide was the only way forward. Economic condition, occupation, or status as a recent immigrant to the United States influenced some mothers to commit infanticide to some extent. Although these cases represent unfortunate circumstances, these women perhaps viewed their crimes as a means of protection, possibly shielding their children from future hardship, or protecting themselves from losing employment. These women demonstrated awareness of their situations, realizing that they could not support a child or did not want one at that point in their lives, and took matters into their own hands, consciously choosing to commit a crime to remedy their situation. Through the commission of such crimes, these women resisted social and economic structures that limited their mobility and freedom and chose a path that probably seemed to them to be the only viable option in the moment.

COMMITTING MURDER: POISON

Like those women who committed infanticide, female murderers directly challenged not only how women were expected to behave, but also the legal system that limited the choices of women, particularly married ones. By taking matters into their own hands and committing murder, these women provided themselves with the (potential) opportunity to start new stages of their lives or begin new relationships that otherwise seemed out of reach through legal methods.[14]

In May 1847, Mary Myers and John Parker faced trial together for the murder of Mary's husband, John, in Venango County, Pennsylvania. According to several testifying doctors, John Myers had died of arsenic poisoning in January 1847. Once the cause of the death became established, the testimony turned to why he had been poisoned and by whom. Dr. George Meeker testified that Mary said she "would willingly buy a barrel of liquor if he would drink it up and kill himself."[15]

Mary made it clear she was unhappy in the marriage and wanted out. Mary's sister-in-law, Nancy Myers, testified that Mary came to her house to ask Henry Myers (John's brother) about getting a divorce. Nancy Myers stated that Mary desperately wanted a divorce but that Henry said it would be difficult to procure one if John treated her well and wanted to stay married. Mary was undeterred, declaring that "she would have a divorce at the risk of her life." The issue of divorce came up in other testimony as well, as did the fact that Mary Myers asked around town for someone who could write a will for her husband, even though her husband was, at the time, in perfect health.[16] With this testimony regarding divorces and wills for her husband before he was sick, Mary Myers was transparent in wanting her husband to grant her a divorce. The lengths to which she went to inquire about a divorce, and ultimately to poison her husband to get out of the marriage, can be seen as acts of last resort, defiance against both her husband and a legal system that limited her options.

In addition to the blatant attempts to get out of the marriage, testimony about Mary Myers's demeanor during her husband's sickness and subsequent death raised red flags for the jury. When Mary Myers tried to laugh off the suggestion that her husband had been poisoned and said he was a drunkard, Dr. C. Klotz testified that he told Myers "he was poisoned with arsenic; I told her this repeatedly." Another physician, Dr. W. E. Bishop, told the court, "She said if John Myers got well and heard the story [that he was poisoned], she had better be dead; she had lived in hell all her life-time" and it would be worse if her husband survived. Furthermore, he noted that Mary Myers said to him, "I wish you, or they would contradict the story" of her husband being poisoned.[17]

Witnesses outside the medical field also mentioned Mary's attempts at playing the sickness off as a drunken frolic. Henrietta Mays said that Mary confided that her husband "had been in the habit of spreeing . . . and he had taken his last spree now." According to Mays, Mary "appeared very anxious that the thing should be over" and kept blaming the sickness on alcohol. Mays stated that "she shed tears on one occasion, when talking about the property being taken away from her, but at no other time."[18] There was apparently no love lost between husband and wife as Mary seemed to be little grieved by and more annoyed at her husband's illness.

What was the role played by Mary's co-defendant, John Parker? He boarded at the Myers residence sometimes, although he was married. Evidence from the trial suggests that there may have been a love affair between Parker and Mary Myers. Parker spent a great deal of time around the Myers property, although doing what remained unclear. While John Myers was ill, Dr. Bishop testified that Mary and John Parker conversed with each other and that after Parker had left, John Myers "called to Mrs. Myers to go to bed; he said she had been courting long enough." Rumors swirled in the community regarding Mary Myers and John Parker, but both denied the affair. Fueling the rumor mill were several encounters that took place between Parker and Mary Myers. Many community members saw the two supposed lovers dancing at a frolic and observed them talking secretly in the days before John Myers's death. All signs pointed to an affair and potential murder plot. To make matters worse, only a few weeks before Myers's death, Dr. Meeker testified that Mary came to him and asked for an abortion, which he refused to do, leaving Mary pregnant while on trial. With the rumors that she and John Parker were lovers, the timing of her pregnancy, and her husband's quick demise, it is little wonder that the community thought Parker and Mary Myers were having an affair. Finally, evidence came to light that John Parker purchased arsenic, ultimately sealing his fate, as well as that of Mary Myers.[19]

On May 31, 1847, the jury found both John Parker and Mary Myers guilty of first-degree murder. Ten days later, they were both sentenced to hang. In his sentencing speech, the judge told the defendants and the courtroom that the crime was committed by "hearts desperately wicked" and is "an instance of such a cold-blooded, deliberate, and wilful murder as the annals of human depravity seldom furnish." The judge stated that although the pair of murderers used "secrecy, caution and ingenuity" in the perpetration of the crime, they could no longer hide from God and they would have to deal with His punishment for their crimes.[20]

The case of Mary Twiggs parallels those of Harker and Myers in many ways. She enters the historical records in late spring 1857, when a pair of mysterious deaths in Montour County, Pennsylvania, captured the small town of Danville's attention. Catherine Clark, wife of William Clark, died of poisoning, according to her autopsy. Her death prompted local officials to exhume David Twiggs, who had died three weeks earlier. Both corpses had arsenic in their stomachs. Their spouses, William Clark and Mary Twiggs, were alleged lovers, and the pair was arrested for their spouses' murders.[21]

William Clark stood trial first, in February 1858, and his attempts to cover up his guilt quickly became apparent. In a letter written to an out-of-town friend, Clark asked, "If you would be so kind as to buy the following amount, it would save my life and enable me to reward ten-fold for the said trouble and expense: that is, to buy me three ounces of arsenic and eight grains of strychnine. Get two and a half ounces by itself, and half an ounce by itself." Clark then asked his friend to deliver the poison to him in jail so that he had the exact amounts on his person that the local druggist claimed to have sold him. In that way, Clark would try to counter the evidence against him. Clark's ploy failed, the jury convicted him of first-degree murder, and he was sentenced to hang.[22]

After a delay in the attempt to find unbiased jurors, Mary Twiggs went on trial for murdering Catherine Clark in May 1858. She entered the courtroom "with a smile upon her countenance, and exhibited other outward signs of a stout heart." The *Danville Intelligencer* reported Twiggs as having a full face with coarse features, but that the reporter was "prepared to see a woman even less devoid of beauty." Many of the same witnesses who testified against Clark also testified against Twiggs, noting her romantic relationship with Clark and her appearance at Catherine Clark's deathbed. Twiggs "frequently brushed tears from her eyes" during the trial, which was over quickly, resulting in a guilty verdict and death sentence.[23]

William Clark hanged in September 1858. Twiggs was scheduled to die in late October. While in jail, she attempted to escape, digging a tunnel using "a small iron spike, and a rib bone," being very close to completing her task when the jailer caught her and found heaps of dirt under her bed and loose stones in the wall. While she awaited the gallows, local ministers met with Twiggs, urging her "very pressingly to make a frank confession, quietly assuring her, that if she died with a lie on her lips she would be condemned in another world." During her last nights in prison, "several kind and sympathizing ladies stayed up with her" to comfort her, and her children were allowed to spend the last night with her in jail. Twiggs showed "maternal feeling too deep for utterance" and shed many tears over her children and her impending fate. She maintained her innocence, even on the gallows.[24] By this point, any use of emotion or attempt to evoke sympathy to aid her cause was too late. Her circumstances, however, must have touched some of the women in the community to take the time to visit her while she awaited execution. While we do not know exactly what was done or said to prompt these ladies to do so, the fact that they spent time with Twiggs demonstrates that she portrayed herself or was portrayed in the press as a sympathetic character, even though she was headed for the gallows for murder.

The cases of Harker from the beginning of the chapter, Myers, and Twiggs demonstrate a level of desperation to escape from troublesome marriages. Myers was vocal about wanting a divorce and having a will drawn up for her husband. In Harker's case, there is no evidence in the records that her marriage was unhappy. That she killed her sister and her own husband to free herself to marry her sister's widower suggests wanting out of the marriage for selfish reasons. Twiggs plotted with Clark to rid themselves of his wife in order to foster a new romantic relationship. For these three women, poisoning their husbands seemed like the only permanent solution easily available to them. In some respects, their actions raise the issue of how socially trapped some women felt during the antebellum era. In Pennsylvania, a 1785 law allowed the Pennsylvania Supreme Court to issue divorces, but in 1804 a revision granted Circuit Courts and county Courts of Common Pleas that same authority. Actions that would most likely allow a couple to get a divorce and allow the parties to remarry legally included such reasons as evidence of adultery, bigamy, or desertion, for example.[25] The situations of Twiggs and Harker did not fit the legal parameters, nor was Mary Myers's situation dire enough for her to be granted a divorce. These women turned to murder as the best option available to them.

While some women might have used murder to end a marriage when a divorce was not easily accessible or to gain control over an aspect of their life, the case of Lena Miller reflects an example of using murder as a means of preemptory self-preservation. In July 1866 Lena Miller, a German immigrant living in Clearfield County, confessed to poisoning her husband. She tried a variety of natural poisons such as laurel leaves, filings of a brass buckle, quicksilver from a mirror, laudanum, even the secretions from a boiled green grass snake. When none of those attempts worked, Miller said that she was consumed with the thought of killing her husband and went to a store to procure rat poison. Having been told by the shopkeeper that rat poison would not kill a human, she purchased arsenic instead. On the evening of June 30, 1866, Lena Miller began administering the poison in her husband's food and drink, dosing him two or three times a day until she ran out on July 10. She purchased more, as well as ingredients for a mustard plaster to help her now-sick husband, as a doctor had instructed. He died on July 12, without ingesting any more of the arsenic. As for a motive, Lena Miller stated that "he treated me badly and abused me so." She continued, "He made me work hard outdoors on the farm. He would sometimes get mad and knock me down, and the marks of abuse could often be seen on my body." Lena Miller argued that she was motivated to kill because she had been physically abused by her husband but could not bear to leave her children behind. In fact, this was her second abusive marriage; she had deserted her first husband.[26] She was executed on November 13, 1867, stating that she was ready to die because she trusted in the mercy of God.[27] The evidence against Lena Miller was beyond reproach in the eyes of the jury, and the letter of the law was carried out; yet, in her testimony on why she committed the crime, her motivation reflects a desperate, dangerous situation, one that may have pulled at the heartstrings of some contemporary observers. In a period when divorces were difficult to obtain, women were sometimes left with few options to get out of violent situations.

All of these women carefully planned their murders, seeking out poison and slowly administering it to their victims.[28] Poisoning was central to many of the cases of female murderers in this period and a weapon of choice of many of the murders committed by women in Pennsylvania. As demonstrated in the table at the beginning of the chapter, in my sample, there were forty-four murders and seven poisoning cases. If the poisoning victim died, the crime was designated as murder rather than poisoning. These were not crimes of passion, but rather calculated, reasoned actions that required patience on the part of the women committing the deeds. The victims become sick, making the deaths look accidental, diverting attention from the perpetrator—at least at first. Poison offered a way for women to overpower their victims, particularly men who were most likely physically larger, stronger, and, perhaps in some cases, violent toward their wives. The use of poison is a seemingly passive, nonaggressive way to kill, allowing the women murderers to use some traditionally feminine characteristics or behaviors in the commission of the crime. N. E. H. Hull contends that it was common for women to use poison because they seized "weapons available to them" and "poisoning food was consistent" with expectations of women's domestic responsibilities.[29] While this notion of using female responsibilities to cover up a crime is similar to the shoplifting and swindling cases, in these extreme instances of murder, there is a more drastic motivation at play—little legal recourse for women to end undesirable or abusive marriages. Furthermore, some of these women even acted as caregivers to their victims! To the casual observer, these acts may have looked on the surface like compassion; but for the women themselves, caregiving offered a way to keep an eye on the progress of the murder and adjust course if necessary. These women remained active in the process, demonstrating an awareness of the need to keep the trappings of femininity in place to avoid suspicion. Yet, to many observers, some who testified at trials, this false compassion was viewed as disturbing and manipulative after the victims had died and evidence of crimes emerged.

Just as noted in chapter 1, the local community structure plays a significant part in these cases. The trials of Harker, Myers, Twiggs, and Miller took place in smaller towns, thus making the court proceedings even more of a spectacle.[30] In all the cases, community members were involved in the trial itself as witnesses and jury members, as courtroom observers, and as a reading public through newspaper and pamphlet publication. Local citizens testified to the defendants' behavior and words or discussed community events in which they interacted with the accused to shed light on their actions. Through the communities' involvement in the trials, one can see how influential their opinions and observations could be in shaping the outcome of the trial and the ways the defendants were portrayed to the public. In these cases, the women radically challenged social expectations of being dutiful wives and demonstrated their individual choice and power to separate themselves from marriages they no longer wanted. To that end, the women were often painted by the prosecution, judges, and newspaper reporters as monstrous, inhuman, and depraved—all for failing to adhere to, or willfully ignoring, their place in antebellum society as wives and women.

Even the physical appearance and demeanor of the defendants affected how these women were viewed, thus placing them in a category of unfeminine or unsympathetic. At her sentencing Harker was painted as a "hardened wretch," and Twiggs was not viewed as pretty or feminine.[31]

These observations illustrate some level of distrust or dislike of the accused by the community, purely based on their looks, demonstrating an attitude that women are supposed to be feminine and pretty. Lena Miller provides another example of this issue. She was reported to be "a large, strong well developed woman" with a "rather masculine" face. As to her demeanor, she was "sullen and revengeful under provocation, cunning and deceitful in her purposes." Furthermore, she was "addicted to falsehood, vulgarity and profane swearing and had a slavish appetite for strong drink."[32] Miller and Twiggs, with their unfeminine looks and behaviors, had not only challenged their limited place in the legal system with regard to their roles as wives seeking an escape, but they shattered the communities' expectations of what they believed constituted an ideal female citizen of their counties—specifically, white, middle class, pretty, and tending to her domestic responsibilities dutifully.

COMMITTING MURDER: PHYSICALLY AGGRESSIVE CRIMES

As already discussed, nineteenth-century women were thought to be inherently virtuous, suited for the domestic sphere, and to embody characteristics of gentleness, compassion, and piety. Yet, nineteenth-century observers also noted women's frailer physiognomy and proneness to irrational behavior and emotional responses. Carroll Smith-Rosenberg and Charles Rosenberg suggest that, according to nineteenth-century medical tracts, a woman was seen as "frailer, her skull smaller, her muscles more delicate. . . . The female nervous system was finer, 'more irritable,' prone to overstimulation and resulting exhaustion." It was also thought that the female reproductive system affected women's physical and mental state. Rosemarie Zagarri notes that nineteenth-century observers believed that women's "more vivid emotional life constricted their intellect," making them irrational.[33] Women were trapped in their own weaker physicality and mentality according to nineteenth-century society and therefore were prone to double standards. In the crimes detailed above, the use of poison might suggest the women's physical weakness, but the determination, patience, and logic that caused them to commit the crimes is evidence of the bias women criminals faced in terms of their own physical and mental development. The calculated, reasoned approach to the crimes undermines the commonly held notion in the nineteenth century that women were ruled by excessive emotionality.

While the women who committed murders using poison seem to fall directly into categories set up by nineteenth-century society regarding women's inherent physical and mental nature, what does one make of women who committed violent crimes of a more physical and aggressive quality? The case of Charlotte Jones and Henry Fife in McKeesport (right outside of Pittsburgh) in 1857 provides one such example. The two were convicted of killing George Wilson and Elizabeth McMasters, who were brother and sister.[34] The murder occurred late on the night of April 30 into May 1, 1857. Suspicion soon fell on Jones and Fife for several reasons. Dr. William Penney said he noticed the pair out on a street in McKeesport at 3:00 a.m. on the morning of May 1. It struck him as odd that a woman should be out at that time. Many people noticed the strange woman, Jones, around town in the early hours wearing a distinctive red calico dress and sunbonnet. Furthermore, Jones was seen visiting the victims a week before the murder in the same red calico dress.[35] Jones was not from the area, which is why people seemed to notice her and her male companion and to suspect them of the murder.

Several weeks after the murder, the *Pittsburgh Daily Dispatch* published a long article summarizing the evidence of the crime before the start of the trial. Interestingly, the article illustrates that public opinion had already solidified against the suspected offenders. The victims were elderly individuals "whose years and feebleness alone should have been a protection against the violence" perpetrated on them. The public learns that Jones was the niece of the two victims, that she and Fife were lovers and sometimes passed as husband and wife, and that Jones had confessed to some part of the crime. After Jones was found with blood on her bonnet and dress, the author of the article stated, "Of *her* connexion with the crime, there can be no doubt. It will be a matter for a jury to decide whether she was a passive or active instrument in the murder." Jones, however, did not act alone. The author could not believe that the murders were committed by only one person "and that one a woman." The author and the public believed that Fife was an accomplice, and that they "are *all* guilty."[36]

The local newspapers provided full coverage of the trial proceedings on a daily basis. Readers learned of the gruesome beatings of the two victims, particularly Elizabeth McMasters. Wilson, who suffered three stab wounds, was found on his back, lying in front of the door frame, while Elizabeth McMasters was found facedown in a large pool of blood by her head and a bloody fire poker nearby. On the third day of the trial, the motive for this crime emerged when one witness said that Charlotte Jones knew the elderly pair had a great deal of money. Charlotte implicated herself further with a confession made to the mayor of Pittsburgh, H. A. Weaver on May 3, 1857, which stated that she was present at the murder scene when Henry Fife and another accomplice, Monroe Stewart, killed the two victims. Although cautioned by the mayor not to incriminate herself, she stated, "I will state the truth and the whole truth, if I am to hang for it." This confession, entered into the evidence by the Commonwealth, made her, at the very least, an accessory to murder. It is possible that she made the confession in hopes that she might be used as a witness against the other two defendants. Even so, blood found on the clothing of Fife and Jones connected the two with the crime.[37]

Even after the trial concluded on July 12, 1857, resulting in guilty verdicts against Fife and Jones, discrepancies regarding who really committed the murders circulated. In her initial confession provided during the trial, Jones claimed not to have actually committed the murders, perhaps believing that this approach would place the blame on the men, and possibly free her from the gallows. In addition, her jailer apparently suggested to her that she would be a sympathetic witness for the state, perhaps due to the fact that she was a woman. This may have motivated her confess in the first place. In providing this first confession, she used her position and the information at her disposal to try to protect herself from death—even the defense lawyers in closing statements suggested as much. Furthermore, information on the jury's balloting in deliberations revealed that they struggled to determine whether Charlotte Jones was guilty of murder—it took at least ten secret ballots to convict her.[38] The defense requested a new trial, in part based on Jones's potentially compromised confession, which they argued was procured when she was tricked into believing that confessing would make her a protected state's witness. The Pennsylvania Supreme Court disagreed, deciding that the jailer had made Jones no promises. Fife and Jones failed to receive a new trial. A change of story then occurred in the period after the Supreme Court decision: Charlotte Jones made a new, final confession, in which she exonerated Monroe Stewart and claimed that she and Fife were the two murderers. As their fate on the gallows was sealed, it appears that Jones decided either to come clean about her true involvement in the murders, or to perhaps take into her own hands the power to shape how the public would view her and her actions. In either case, she wrote her own history.[39]

This confession, described in the newspapers and published in 1857 as *The Confessions of Henry Fife and Charlotte Jones, Under Sentence of Death for the Murder of Geo. Wilson and Elizabeth M'Masters: Together with a History of the Case and Statement of Monroe Stewart,* provides further information on the crime and a likeness of the criminals (fig. 1). The pamphlet recounted the earlier confession of Jones, in which she implicated only Fife and Stewart with the murder, suggesting that the two men forced her to take them to her aunt and uncle's house to steal their money. She claimed she begged them not to kill her relatives. The second confessions of Fife and Jones after their convictions shed more light on their relationship and what caused them to commit the murders. Fife stated that after Jones had visited her aunt and uncle in McKeesport, the subject of robbery arose as Charlotte relayed that her relatives had $1,100 in gold in their home. She told Fife that "she would have that money." Jones continued by telling Fife that "if she did get it, she expected to get it by *poisoning* them." Fife then asked Charlotte if she could kill them, to which she replied that "she *hated her aunt,* and could kill her." A few days later, Charlotte told Fife she could not obtain the poison and that they would have to kill Wilson and McMasters by some other means. Jones claimed that "she was able to kill the old woman, if I was able to kill the old man." Henry Fife had a knife with him, and the two proceeded with their plan. Fife quickly killed the old man by stabbing him three times and Charlotte tried to strangle her aunt. She failed to finish the deed, and Fife became angry and "stamped upon her head with the heel of my boot; but failing to kill her, I seized the poker and beat her until I saw her brains oozing from her head."[40]

Charlotte Jones's confession corroborated much of Fife's in terms of the execution of the crime. Other aspects of her confession tell more about her specific motivations. She stated that her "parents were poor" and her "education was neglected." She had fallen in love with Fife the first time she saw him, and they often would pass as husband and wife.[41] Her desire for money is evident in the crime, in that she told Fife she would get her relatives' gold and was willing to kill for it. That she grew up poor may have had something to do with this ardent desire. Furthermore, her love for Fife added to her motives. Love and the need for money were therefore linked. Although the pamphlet is highly sensationalized and certainly provocative reading, the source remains important in providing at least a version of Charlotte Jones's voice and reasoning for committing the crime. The local newspaper

FIGURE 1 Frontispiece from *The Confessions of Henry Fife and Charlotte Jones, Under Sentence of Death for the Murder of Geo. Wilson and Elizabeth M'Masters: Together with a History of the Case and Statement of Monroe Stewart* (Pittsburgh: Hunt and Miner, 1857).

was skeptical of this confession, stating that it is difficult to believe because "so many and so conflicting have been the statements of this unfortunate woman, that it has become impossible to determine what may be truth or falsehood in them."[42] Although the reporter is correct in stating the fact that it is difficult to know what parts of the story surrounding Jones's life and involvement in the murders were true, the conflicting statements do show the process by which Jones deals with her situation. In the confession made to the mayor, one that she thought may have made her a witness for the state, her words and actions suggest that she tried to save herself from prosecution with a seeming willingness to blame her co-defendants. The pamphlet publication certainly shifts gears, as Jones tries to portray herself (or is portrayed) as a victim of poverty and lack of education, a young woman swayed by love, rather than a brutal murderess. When her fate on the gallows was sealed, this shift to appear sympathetic is a way to empower herself as a way to control the story and her legacy.

Fife and Jones went to the gallows on February 12, 1858, in the courtyard of the Allegheny County Courthouse. Inside the prison, Charlotte Jones's demeanor was said at times to be "equivocal," but that she was prepared for her spiritual reckoning after death even though her "spiritual convictions were not very deep." In her scaffold speech, Charlotte tried one last time to set the record straight about her motivations and involvement in the crime—taking one last opportunity to control and influence the situation and her public persona. She addressed the crowd with the following words: "Any statements that I was not sorry are untrue; because I have suffered continually since the perpetration of that offence." She believed her punishment to be just, and she hoped to make peace with the Lord after her death. Her composure failed as the moment of her demise approached. She was reported to have been "lamenting, hysterically, praying audibly. . . . It was with the greatest effort that she maintained anything like composure. . . . Fife attempted to reassure her, embracing and kissing her." The two died within minutes of the floor of the scaffold dropping away.[43]

In this case, one sees a woman committing a violent murder with a male accomplice. Although she tried to obtain poison to commit the deed, in the end she resorted to physical violence. The bloody affair may have made it easier for the jury to convict the two. Although Fife was more involved in the killings than Jones was, she helped to mastermind the plan and took an active role in the murders. While people viewed her as a fiend for committing such a horrid crime, her motivations illustrated that she was guided by and perhaps led astray by selfish reasons: desiring material wealth to create a proper home with her lover, Henry Fife. Furthermore, it is possible that the love she had for Fife influenced her to be part of this plan for robbery and murder. That the murders were committed in a small town on the outskirts of an urban area and that the perpetrators were outsiders may have made it easier for the community to convict them in the newspapers and the jury to convict them in the courtroom. Whereas other female murderers turned to crime because they felt legally constricted in their situations, Jones's crime does not fit the pattern. She willfully eschewed the law and societal standards for passive women and followed a bloody path for material gain. Jones does, however, try to use her womanhood—through the narratives of her confessions—to shape both the outcome of the trial and ultimately how she was perceived at her execution.

In addition to the story of Charlotte Jones, a case from Philadelphia also sheds light on the overt challenge that some female murderers mounted against societal norms.[44] Tamar Filbert was murdered by Marian Wilson on July 28, 1840. Wilson fatally beat Filbert after the two became embroiled in a lawsuit over an altercation. The doctor who examined Filbert before she died testified that "the skull was broken in a horrible manner." We glimpse Wilson's character from courtroom testimony. The landlady of the house "heard Mrs. Wilson say, three times successively, 'I'll beat you,'" and Filbert told the landlady directly that Wilson had "been beating me with my own broom." The landlady later found the deceased on the stair landing laboring on account of her wounds. Another tenant in the house stated to the court that Wilson said "that she would trammel the bones out of Mrs. Filbert's body, and that she felt as if she could whip any man."[45]

Wilson's trial in the Court of Oyer and Terminer commenced on November 12, 1840, and lasted for three full days. Witnesses spoke at length regarding the temperaments of the two women involved. Margaret Horner testified that she told Wilson "to cool down her temper," in response to which she "raised both arms above her head and clenched her fists, and said she felt as if she could crush a strong man; she said if I get hold of that old woman, I'll beat her flat as the broom, I'll leave no life in her." Mary Ferrell, another tenant, noted that as people attempted to save Filbert, authorities knocked at the door of Wilson, who "looked unconcerned" and denied the charge of murder. On November 13, 1840, the landlady, Catharine Steele, took the stand, testifying that Wilson was querulous and that she did not like her. For the victim, the descriptions are more positive. Maria Becker, an acquaintance of the deceased for sixteen years, stated that Filbert "was a calm, mild, religious woman. . . . I never knew her to quarrel, and never knew her to say an angry word to any one."[46]

Most of the testimony of the three days corroborated the witnesses' testimony in the initial investigation and developed a thorough timeline of the events, but these few examples of the women's temperament and character show how victims and perpetrators were portrayed to the public and how the community perceived their womanhood. Filbert, who was described as being calm, industrious, mild, and religious, embodied the idealized traits, while Wilson's strength and anger challenged these expectations, especially in her repeated declarations that she felt she could kill a man. While she was likely aware of the fact that her actions and behavior were seen as unseemly, it is possible that she did not care. In her actions and words she was comfortable enough with her place in society to challenge what the community held as expectations for her and for women at large. At the close of the trial Wilson was convicted of second-degree murder and sentenced to ten years in Eastern State Penitentiary.[47]

DEFYING AUTHORITY: NONVIOLENT CRIMES

Instances of murder, with longer trials, extensive newspaper coverage, and a more elaborate paper trail, more easily lend themselves to analyzing female criminals' behavior and demonstrating the ways women challenged societal institutions or individuals who wanted to limit their power and freedom. With cases of nonviolent crimes committed by women, the evidence is still there to show that women continued the historical trend of not being content to simply follow societal expectations and boundaries.[48] Female criminals were consistently challenging these limitations, not just in committing a crime, but in the way they reacted to their crime and experience in court. In October 1847, a girl was picked up off the streets of Pittsburgh as a vagrant by a "humane lady" who had "the intention of effecting a reformation" in her behavior. The young female vagrant was a frequent notation on the police records for Allegheny County and had been, for years, "walking over the path that leads to the devil." The benevolent woman provided the girl with clothing, cleaned her up, and supplied her with other comforts in order to effect a change in her behavior. After only a few hours in the home, the girl fled—presumably returning to a life on the streets.[49] This case illustrated the perpetual problem of vagrancy, which was a major concern for urban centers, but it demonstrates something else as well. The girl who was picked up by this "humane lady" had no desire to be molded or controlled. By fleeing and returning to her own life, the young girl demonstrated her individual power to shape her experience, to keep her freedom, even if it meant homelessness, and challenged the idea that she needed to be reformed or that this woman was really best suited to aid the young girl.

Other cases of minor crimes demonstrate similar reactions by the female perpetrators. On March 7, 1837, Mary McLaughlin and Mary Levering were arrested by the city watchman. One woman was found "lying on the pavement, and the other holding onto a door, most gloriously drunk, and so full of fight." At their trial the next morning, their attempts at garnering sympathy from the mayor failed. He stated that "a woman that would get drunk would steal, or do anything else." The two were sent to Moyamensing Prison.[50] Mary Blackburn, "a roaring sun-burnt *critter*, from Virginia, apparently an Irish woman," was arrested for public drunkenness. When in court the watchman stated that she had been drunk and that "she exclaimed, stamping her foot upon the floor, 'You are a liar, sir—you are a vagabond.'"

She was imprisoned for thirty days.[51] Blackburn directly challenged the authority of the watchman in court. She did not acquiesce to the accusations, but took power into her hands to defend herself. The issue of the offenders' ethnicity is raised again since at least two of these three women seem to be Irish. Furthermore, the fact that Blackburn was described as a "critter" suggests that at least the reporter, but likely other readers as well, saw this woman as less than human, and certainly less than feminine. It was common practice across the state to link the Irish and intemperance. In Pittsburgh, Catharine McNelly ran a boardinghouse and whiskey shop. According to the local newspaper, her patrons were "mostly sons of that green Isle of the Ocean about which the Know Nothings are supposed to have gone crazy." She supplied her customers with "liquified [sic] corn" and the men subsequently caroused about the city. She was arrested for selling liquor on a Sunday and fined fifty dollars. McNelly, not having the money or assets worth the price of the fine, spent thirty days in the county jail.[52] While she herself did not carouse about the city, she was an accessory to disorderly conduct in promoting the conditions by which the city was disturbed.

Habitual drinking not only hurt the person but could lead to a life of crime, which were some of the concerns that temperance advocates took up in the nineteenth century.[53] Although many temperance advocates were worried about the potential crimes men would commit as a result of drinking too much, in particular domestic abuse, women who drank could also end up in front of the local courts. This is evident in cases of repeat offenders. Ann Dougherty, along with three other women, was "charged with the old offence of drunkenness in the street" and spent twenty-four hours in jail. While leniency might be applied for first offenses, repeat offenders received harsher punishments. Dougherty, quite a mischievous woman, appeared in records on May 14, 1840, and August 8, 1840, and, most likely, numerous other times. In May, the *Philadelphia Public Ledger* reported that she had "been out of prison yesterday but two hours, when she committed sundry acts of disorder and indecency, and actually came very near reducing Mrs. Borlang to a state of nature, by her manipular dexterity in the way of tearing clothes." She was sent to Moyamensing Prison for thirty days. In August, she "was charged with raising a row about a man's house. . . . Ann pleaded her cause *manfully*, and strongly and earnestly promised never to do the like again."[54] This time, she was fined $200. Ann did not limit her types of crime, being collared for different offenses each time. In addition, the last entry, emphasizing that she pleaded her case "manfully," appears to show the biased perspective of the reporter, implying, perhaps, that she had lost her feminine virtues. Furthermore, she was able to testify on her own behalf, demonstrating that she knew she had the power to defend herself in court. In this respect, pleading "manfully" could be seen as a positive attribute—portraying personal strength and courage, which ultimately challenges the way society expected women to act.

Disorderly conduct, in which public drunkenness often played a part, also plagued the nineteenth-century city. Cases of this crime usually took the form of spewing profanity, making noise, and general mischief. Margaret Williams, arrested and sentenced to thirty days at Moyamensing for swearing, "told the officer, with an oath which should have blistered her tongue, that 'she was on a spree, and would see it out.'" The variety of actions that constituted a crime in this category according to nineteenth-century judicial authorities is striking. Hannah Williamson was committed for thirty days for "entering the churches during service, and crying out suddenly in a loud voice." Ringing bells during the night, exposing themselves in public, and imitating other individuals also caused women to be brought before the mayor.[55] These seemingly minor acts of mischief threatened the peace of the city and breached propriety. Although not overly criminal in nature, the fact that these actions were punished so severely demonstrates the determination of city officials to crack down on disturbances in order to rid the city of its growing criminal and mischievous elements. What these actions tell us about women in the antebellum city is that they are, at times, very public figures, behaving in ways that defied societal expectations, following in the tradition of women of earlier eras.[56] While these women may not have been aware of or cared that they challenged standards of antebellum womanhood, their behavior shows that women were active participants in the life of the city. Whether their more public life was a personal choice or due to economic circumstances, these women showed that they were neither content nor inclined to assume the mantle of domesticity that middle- and upper-class citizens set as the custom for women.

———

Criminal women exhibited a level of control through their actions that served to thwart the expectations of idealized womanhood that antebellum society placed on them, as did other groups of women in the era. This is a significant statement concerning a time when society sought to limit and control women. Several cases detailed in this chapter demonstrate the extreme circumstances married women found themselves in when they determined to kill their husbands to end their marriages. Although the judges often saw these crimes as depraved, the women's actions and motivations suggest additions to that narrative. These women were constrained by a civil legal system that severely limited their ability to obtain divorces. For many of these women, without cause for a divorce (such as extreme abuse or neglect), they had no legal means to escape an unwanted marriage. Instead, they turned to murder, often in the form of poisoning, to achieve their goals. These represent calculated crimes, deeds that took time and patience on the part of the women, yet what this shows is not just cold-hearted murder, but also women demonstrating awareness of their social and legal situation and looking for ways to fix their circumstances on their own. They challenged the social limitations placed on them by marriage and find their own way out. These women demonstrate an independence and confidence to commit heinous acts, and those actions defied social conventions.

Other women challenged society and its prevailing expectations of them by being visible and disorderly in public. In a period where women were slowly moving into the public sphere in limited ways, some female criminals stormed their way into public in loud, distracting, and aggressive ways. These women, who committed mainly petty crimes, represented a changing public domain, one where women were more commonly a part. The fact that these acts crossed into the legal system represents not only the struggle that officials had not only with disorderly conduct in their communities, but the fact that women were a part of that problem. These crimes bring the issue of women in the public sphere to the forefront, forcing communities and local officials to confront broader issues of women's place in society. Women who committed crimes had the power to challenge authority, and while in some cases they were likely cognizant of the fact that they were challenging society's limitations on them, others were perhaps unaware of the influence their crimes might have on the way women were viewed.

CHAPTER 3

"Amazonian Outbreak"

Antebellum Women and Political Crime

On March 1, 1850, a mob of women, numbering anywhere from sixty to one hundred individuals, interrupted the working rhythm of a rolling mill in Pittsburgh. Armed with "stones and other missiles [*sic*]," they attacked and injured out-of-town puddlers and boilers brought in to replace strikers, drove them from their work stations, and proceeded to throw "coal and dirt into the furnaces, ruining the iron" and damaging the furnaces. In a second wave of attacks, the mob targeted a nearby rolling mill but was stopped before they could do any harm. The attacks were acts of solidarity, the result of rising frustration over wage reductions put into effect at the beginning of the year, which had prompted many mill workers to go out on strike. One month later, four of the female ringleaders of the mob were tried in the Allegheny Court of Quarter Sessions for their participation in the Rolling Mills Riot and ultimately fined and sentenced to thirty days in the county prison.[1]

Riots such as these were political and social statements, the result of economic pressures on mill workers. These women embraced their capability to resist power structures put in place to limit their liberty and that of their loved ones. While the women in the previous chapter challenged social structures and restrictions through more traditional forms of crime, which also demonstrated their worth, self-awareness, and power, against a society built to subordinate women, female rioters took this individual power a step further. Their actions in the public sphere took on decidedly political overtones. These women assumed the problems their husbands and other male family members faced as industrial workers and sought change through violent action. Therefore, the women's rioting offered them a way to demonstrate political behavior, even though, if arrested and convicted, they could face a fine or imprisonment.[2] Women rioters used this form of criminal behavior to work for social change, delving into the generally male-dominated realm of politics. The term "political" used in relation to the crimes these women committed is defined broadly here. Political crimes are not limited to offenses dealing directly with government, political parties, or acts of treason, but could include any criminal activity in which women's participation demonstrated an oppositional viewpoint on a social or political situation in order to effect some change in society or to rebel against a disliked policy. Many times, women appeared to be motivated to riot in order to protect their families, homes, and communities; their actions ranged from simply reflecting frustration over issues to borderline treason. Whatever the motivations or outcomes of the riots may have been, women's participation demonstrated political behavior and gave them a voice.[3]

At times it is difficult to determine the social class of female criminals, though in the case of this chapter participation in riots and political crimes appears to be more clearly dominated by those of lower classes or demographic groups with less social and political leverage, such as immigrants, free blacks, runaway slaves, and factory workers. Rioting may have been one of only a few ways for them to have their voices and concerns heard by the larger public. The groups that these rioters opposed constituted those who often had more economic and political leverage, were of higher social standing, or were considered to be members of more mainstream demographic groups. This chapter examines three types of riots as examples of antebellum political crime: nativist riots, fugitive slave riots, and labor riots.

Rioting and mob action have a long history, and much scholarly work has dealt with the issues of collective violence. Terms like "mobs" or "riots" need to be carefully defined before delving into the workings of collective violence in order to avoid stereotypical distinctions. Historians, George Rudé argues, have designated them as "the people" or "the rabble," both being stereotypes that "present the crowd as a disembodied abstraction and not as an aggregate of men and women of flesh and blood."[4] This is true not only for the work done by Rudé on European riots, but also for the antebellum American riots discussed here. By focusing on the various groups involved in riots, and by extracting the role of women in these uprisings, I attempt not only to recover women's roles from obscurity, but also to demonstrate how diverse these groups were socially and economically.

Eighteenth- and nineteenth-century European rioters resisted changes in industry, capitalist markets, and politics to protect their traditional ways of life. They had specific targets and goals for their action; the mobs were not without control.[5] American rioters similarly protested the established order and worked for social and economic change during the antebellum period. Frustrated rioters opposed the policies of factory employers, slave-holders and pro-slavery politicians, and American nativists—all of whom represented the social status quo, espoused more popular political beliefs, or were economically more stable than the rioters. The women in this chapter act for themselves, for male loved ones, or in conjunction with men to push for significant change in their communities. Historian E. P. Thompson argues that, often, mob participants believed they acted in the name of a cause which benefited the wider community, which gave them a "notion of legitimation." Furthermore, Thompson contends that riots occur "among those groups who sense that they have a little power to help themselves."[6] Therefore, collective action, and by extension, collective violence, was deemed to be political activity. This is true for antebellum Pennsylvania's riots, on both sides of the conflicts. People from lower social classes represented one side of the riots and in some cases instigated them, clearly having realized that rioting provided them with some power to effect social change, or at the very least to demonstrate their social and economic frustrations. Their opponents, those defending the status quo, also believed they were protecting their community. These different perspectives on the right course of action within a single community led to the riots detailed here and brought political issues to the forefront of the community's consciousness.

Nineteenth-century American mobs took on a more violent character than the rioters from the previous century.[7] The mobs used as examples here mainly represented the lower classes of American society protesting the policies of more established orders. While they had direct purposes in mind for their collective action at the outset of the demonstrations, the directions their actions took tended to be more spontaneous and quickly formed an energy of their own, which propelled riots to become violent. For instance, the 1844 ethnic riots of Philadelphia started peacefully but rapidly took a deadly and destructive turn. Fugitive slave riots, however, stemmed from a quick reaction; the violence and riots were not calculated but were opportunistic and driven by necessity. In this respect, antebellum riots differed from those of the previous century, which were much more restrained. Furthermore, the antebellum riots focused on here had motivations that dealt with social issues of the day, which centered on ethnicity, race, religion, and labor. For that reason, the antebellum rioting was of a more overt political nature.[8] The participation of women, both white and African American, native-born and immigrant, in collective action became an articulation of political behavior and a demonstration of their beliefs, even if they were not considered part of the polity and were expected to remain in the domestic sphere. While many women of various racial, ethnic, or socioeconomic backgrounds were stepping into the public sphere during the antebellum period, some women, usually more of the middle- to upper-class ilk, limited their public personae to becoming involved in civil society and participating in benevolent societies and social reform movements. In their involvement in antebellum riots, other women fashioned a more explicit political role for themselves, one that demonstrated their awareness of their capabilities to participate in the public arena and to push for change.

Women in the antebellum era followed a precedent set by earlier generations of women activists in the political realm. During the American Revolution, women wrote speeches, wore patriotic symbols on their clothing, and participated in economic boycotts. Numerous historians have considered women's political behavior in the Early Republic, noting that women were present in many political functions celebrating the young nation.[9] In the Early Republic, women's participation in party and electoral politics had serious repercussions. Women, many insisted, could better serve the country by staying in the domestic sphere. By the time Andrew Jackson's election this shift had occurred more fully, removing women from the political sphere almost entirely, while it had expanded for men.[10] During the antebellum period, some women fashioned a more overt political role for themselves, one that may have been more acceptable for females in the Revolutionary and Early Republic eras, by participating in public demonstrations. In any case, women found a way to exhibit their political beliefs in an era when their participation in party and electoral politics was discouraged.

Women staked their claim in the political realm during the antebellum decades in ways other than riots and benevolent associations. According to

Carol Lasser and Stacey Robertson, their "public identities" were shaped actively by the women themselves as "notions about civic identity and activity" developed from being tied close to domestic roles, to wage earners, to "*passionate partisans*," where women became more openly tied to political issues.[11] Women employed a variety of methods to establish their public character in the antebellum era. S. J. Kleinberg suggests that women led much of the initial labor unrest in the first decades of American industrialization, which was certainly the case in the Pittsburgh labor riots discussed in this chapter. Women seamstresses went on strike in northeastern cities in the 1820s and 1830s and began to form unions in the 1840s. The women's rights' movement grew during the 1840s and 1850s, sparked in many ways by the abolitionist movement, in which women saw correlations between their oppression and that of slaves. Between the 1848 Seneca Falls Convention and the Civil War, women's rights meetings occurred almost annually. Furthermore, women petitioned state legislatures for married women's legal rights.[12] Women were in no way fully separated from the political realm during the antebellum era, yet rioting provided a more violent, urgent method of working for change.

While much of the literature on women's political activism in the nineteenth century focuses its attention on white women's struggles, black women also became politically active. Gayle Tate chronicles the evolution of their participation in politics. She argues that this occurred in two stages: "the origins of the politicalization of black women" in looking at women's resistance to slavery, and "the political maturation of free black antebellum women" as these women redefined "themselves in freedom." She maintains that through local efforts, black women—those who were free as well as those were still slaves—demonstrated a level of influence and could advocate for others who were voiceless.[13] Her arguments can be seen in action by free black communities that came together to defend runaways, in which women openly participated in violent occurrences or enslaved women took it on themselves to escape to freedom.

PROTECTING AMERICA: PHILADELPHIA'S 1844 NATIVIST RIOTS

In the first half of the nineteenth century, the rapid growth of urban centers led to disorder and violent riots. While anti-Irish tensions had existed in Philadelphia during the eighteenth century, the arrival of large numbers of Irish Catholic immigrants to the city in the antebellum decades exacerbated urban tensions as the Irish created a huge unskilled labor force that threatened the livelihoods of already-established Protestant and free black populations.[14] The city had seen a series of riots involving Irish immigrants between the 1820s and the 1840s, including an 1825 brawl between Irish Catholics and Protestants who were fresh off the boat from Ireland and an 1828 riot between natives and some of the city's Irish weavers. Then, in 1831, Irish Protestants and Catholics rioted in the city after the Protestants put on a parade to celebrate the Battle of the Boyne. This resulted in a violent clash between the groups and a subsequent trial in which the Protestants brought the Catholics to trial for riot, and the Catholics countered by taking the Protestants to court for the same reason.[15] Tensions between the Irish Catholics and nativists in Philadelphia reached a breaking point in May of 1844 resulting in two waves of riots that summer.

The tensions behind the uprisings in 1844 not only stemmed from these past riots, but also from controversy over the Bible in public schools. Native-born Protestants wanted the Bible to be interwoven throughout the curriculum as a means to promote virtue and protect civil liberty. As a result of the Catholics' demand for freedom of conscience, which should have been protected by America's tradition of religious liberty, religious nativists turned their anger toward Catholics. In 1842, the Philadelphia school board ordered that only the King James Bible be read in the public schoolrooms. Feeling that Catholic children would be inculcated with Protestant notions, Catholic bishop Francis Patrick Kenrick asked for Catholic students to be allowed to read the Douay Bible. As a compromise, the two sides agreed that Catholic children would be excused from the classroom while the Protestant Bible was being read, even though the Catholic Bible was still excluded.[16]

Louisa Bedford, a young Protestant teacher in the working-class neighborhood of Kensington who had both Protestant and Catholic pupils, became directly involved in the conflict, growing frustrated at the disruption in her classroom when the Catholic children were excused. When she voiced her concerns in early 1844, Hugh Clark, an Irish Catholic school controller, suggested she suspend all Bible reading until a new plan could be instituted. His suggestion was immediately deemed insidious, as opponents claimed he wanted to "kick the Bible out of the schools." Protestant citizens in Philadelphia seized on this suggestion, thereby worsening tensions between the religious and ethnic populations and fueling the organization of

American nativist groups in the city, run by middle-class, respectable men. They believed that Catholics planned "to make the schools Bibleless, irreligious, and a breeding ground for a Catholic conspiracy to capture the souls of America's Protestant youth," forcing Bedford, against her wishes, to remove the Bibles, when in reality she had made the choice to do so in order to regain control of her classroom. As the matter was further investigated, Miss Bedford testified that she had never been ordered to stop the reading but that Clark told her he would take responsibility if she decided to do so.[17] The public, however, paid little attention to the nuances of the issue and the various conversations among teachers and administrators. This incident served to fuel ethnic and religious tensions, which reached a tipping point in early May.

On May 3, 1844, the nativist group known as the American Republicans held a rally in Kensington to show their determination not to let the Irish Catholics control their schools or city. A second demonstration, on May 6, drew three thousand protestors. The crowd was quickly driven to Nanny Goat Market in the heart of Irish Kensington when a rainstorm erupted. Locals became infuriated at this encroachment in the heart of their neighborhood and began shooting into the crowded marketplace. A nineteen-year-old protestor, George Shiffler, was killed, and nativists retaliated by returning fire and breaking into Irish homes using brickbats and stones.[18]

Contemporary sources indicate that women participated actively in the riot, particularly on the side of the Irish, who desperately tried to protect their community from nativist intruders. A writer for the *Philadelphia Public Ledger* reported that Irish "women and boys joined in the affray, some of the women actually throwing missiles [*sic*]." Even women who did not wield weapons "incited the men to vigorous action, pointing out where they could operate with more effect, and cheering them on and rallying them to a renewal of conflict whenever spirits fell or they were compelled to retreat." Another observer, John Hancock Lee, wrote, "The conduct of the Irish women in the early part of this battle, was no less fierce than was that of the men; for they were seen urging the men on to deeds of violence, and running in all directions, with their aprons filled with stones, rendering all the assistance in their power. One woman was knocked down with a brickbat, but she instantly regained her feet, and shouted at the top of her voice for the men to maintain their ground and give it to the natives."[19] These accounts, although not from the mouths of the women themselves, still serve to demonstrate the ferociousness of these women who were defending their homes, their families, and their community landmarks. Through their actions, they established their right to be part of the city, regardless of whether nativists considered them worthy of a place in American society.

Even a fictional version of the account described the passion of the Irish women of Kensington, writing that "no tigress ever fought more desperately or frantically for their prey, than these did for their foreign masters." The author continues, imagining the scene and putting words in the women's mouths: "'By the Holy Virgin!' they yelled, as their unbound hair streamed around their hideously distorted visages, 'we will this night, wash our hands in your hearts' blood, and send every heretic soul of you to purgatory.'"[20] Although this account is laced with anti-Catholic sentiment, it does demonstrate the intensity with which the women protected their neighborhood.

The following day, nativist crowds marched on Kensington to avenge the death of Shiffler. Most of the Irish had fled the city the night before, but those who stayed were ready for a fight. As a result, nativists changed their approach and started to set fire to inhabited homes. Those under assault fled the city. Nativists then turned their rage on the symbols of Catholicism, torching St. Michael's and St. Augustine's churches, destroying the structures in a matter of minutes. As a result of the rioting, the city was placed under martial law by governor David R. Porter.[21]

Philadelphian Sidney George Fisher, who volunteered as part of the local guard to protect the city against further rioting, noted the women's roles in the disorder. While "the boys were the most active," he confided in his diary, women, "too, were busy, as in the French Revolution, cheering on the men & carrying weapons to them."[22] While it is unclear whether these women were nativists or Irish, they played an active role in the rioting, corroborating reports of Lee and the *Philadelphia Public Ledger*. Women participants on both sides of the conflict would have believed their actions were in defense of their respective communities. While the Irish women were literally defending their property in the Kensington riots, nativist women would have been defending the broader idea of their American home and who belonged in it—two perspectives on the same theme.

According to Michael Feldberg, the Kensington riots shared the general characteristics of Jacksonian riots: only a few combatants were armed, the rioters showed a good deal of restraint (at least initially, waiting to embark on mass destruction until the third day), and those involved were not "the poorest or most oppressed." He contends that most rioters were young men who had steady employment and that many of the older participants were longtime members of their respective neighborhoods. Feldberg reasons that the rioters were driven by "a deep commitment to their ethnic heritage and their political cause" rather than hopelessness.[23] It is true that both sides were committed to their heritage and politics, and it is in this sense that women's involvement was clearly political.

While these characteristics may be true in some respect, Feldberg's analysis is not nuanced enough. Saying that the rioters were restrained may be giving them too much credit. By taking their cause into the heart of Kensington, the nativists seemed to be spoiling for a fight. While they may not have intended to attack the Irish community, their actions were provocative, so much so that the Irish felt threatened and therefore shot in self-defense. The initial events quickly escalated to extreme violence and mass destruction. If the rioters were truly restrained, would they not have simply ended their attacks on the first day, without provoking more citizens to riot on the subsequent days?

Though not all the combatants were from the poorest classes in Philadelphia, the Irish certainly represented a disadvantaged social group who were seen as unskilled, brutish, and a threat to stable American society, even though they wanted to be American citizens. The nativists were drawn mainly from Philadelphia's "middle-class journeymen artisans and members of the working class" who were aiming to limit citizenship for immigrants.[24] In these riots, class dynamics as well as immigrant status played a significant role as a catalyst for the violence. The Philadelphia elite did not condone the violence and did step in to ensure peace after the riots subsided, maybe in part due to the "personal shame and guilt" they felt for allowing the situation to get out of hand.[25]

Even after the rioting in Kensington had subsided, ethnic and religious tensions remained. On May 27, 1844, the *Philadelphia Public Ledger* reported that "a very genteelly dressed woman, named Isabella Hamilton" had been held to the bail of fifty dollars, by the Mayor "for attempting to incite a riot by using threatening and denunciatory language against Catholics and the Pope."[26] A murder case that went to trial on June 6, 1844, in Philadelphia's Court of Quarter Sessions further demonstrates the heightened suspicion of religious differences. Caroline Sweeney was charged with killing her husband, Dominick Sweeney, six months earlier. Evidently, Caroline was motivated by the fact that Dominick was Catholic. It was charged that she was intoxicated when she stabbed her husband seven or eight times with a shoemaker's knife. She initially claimed that Dominick had "threatened to kill her, that she had given him one stab, but did not kill him." During the trial, it was revealed that Dominick was from Ireland and Caroline from England. It is possible that Caroline was Anglican, possibly exacerbating tensions between the couple or between the husband and his in-laws who lived with the Sweeneys. Furthermore, witnesses testified to hearing Caroline say, "Now you—Catholic" or "There, Sweeney, you—Catholic, take that." Another witness stated that Mrs. Sweeney had told him that they "had a discontented life . . . that he [Dominick] was a Catholic and did not like her not being of the same religion." On June 10, 1844, the *Philadelphia Public Ledger* reported that Sweeney had been convicted of manslaughter, was "sentenced to five years imprisonment in Eastern Penitentiary," and would have to take her infant with her to the prison.[27] These cases demonstrate the continued role of women in speaking out or acting on political views in both public and private, and reflect women's awareness of the city's political, religious, and ethnic tensions, using them as justifications for their behavior. The strong response to these cases by city officials reflects the need to limit the chances of further rioting in the city, especially so soon after the Kensington affair.

Alas, city officials would not be so lucky. A second wave of rioting hit the city in early July. While both sides were determined to let the July 4 holiday pass peacefully, they were also prepared for possible violence. This time the rioting would occur in the Southwark district, another historically Irish Catholic neighborhood. It was rumored that rifles were being taken to St. Philip de Neri Catholic Church on July 5 as a prelude to an attack by Irish Catholics on nativists. To quell the crowd, Sheriff McMichael hauled the guns to Commissioners Hall. Even so, crowds continued to gather in Southwark. General George Cadwalader, who had helped to stem the violence in Kensington, told the crowd to disperse, but few listened. He returned with troops and three cannons. The crowd finally dispersed and twenty protesters were arrested.[28]

The following morning, nativists arrived at the church, demanding the prisoners be freed. To avoid violence, the prisoners were released and the church turned over to the nativists. Outraged by this decision, Cadwalader used his troops to clear the streets. The crowd responded by throwing rocks, bricks, and other objects. The soldiers fired into the crowd, dispersing most of them. Some returned with a confiscated cannon from the nearby navy dockyards and shot at the soldiers, leading to a battle that lasted through the night and into the morning. Once again, martial law was imposed in the district, as soldiers, the new objects of nativists' hatred, lined the streets.[29]

While it does not appear that women had as much direct involvement in this phase of the riot, one contemporary report noted that they "seemed more earnest than men, in their conversation upon these most exciting topics, and some of them used language most bitter and inflammatory." This indicates that women were at least in the crowd surrounding the church in Southwark, onlookers to any potential excitement. It also appears that women were vocal in their opinions of what was going on, suggesting some level of participation or at least influencing the direction of the proceedings. In reaction to the violence that erupted in Southwark on July 6 and 7, one newspaper article reported that "females were seen running distracted through the streets, wringing their hands and uttering the names of brother, husband, father with the wildest gesticulation."[30] In this instance, the women were seen as helpless, victims of the rioting as their male family members were attacked by the militia.

Following investigations of the riots by the city, several of the ringleaders were held to account in criminal trials. Throughout the remainder of July 1844, the *Philadelphia Public Ledger* published testimony of the proceedings, in an attempt to understand why the militia had fired on civilians and why the situation had spiraled out of control.[31] General Cadwalader testified after the fighting in Southwark that his troops had been assailed, that they had buckets of water thrown on them, and that "the women were our greatest foes," implying that nativist women had played a more significant role than initially assumed. It is unclear exactly what role the women played here— whether they physically attacked the militia, provided weaponry and support to men like the Irish women had done in Kensington, or simply spewed verbal abuse.[32] In any case, the nativist women demonstrated their views toward the violence of the riot and protected their families and homes as best they could.

In the wake of the riots in Philadelphia, nativist women found a voice and were inspired to further anti-immigrant action in the city, making banners, marching, and organizing mass meetings. A nativist newspaper, the *American Woman*, geared toward women and edited by a woman, Harriet Probasco, began publication. While it only lasted for about a year, beginning in August 1844, it certainly wanted women to know they had a political role to play in protecting the United States from foreign influences.

Articles taught women how to behave patriotically, telling them they should "impress upon their children the truth, that the exercise of the elective franchise is a social duty, of as solemn a nature as man can be called to perform; that a man may not innocently trifle with his vote. . . . It is in the inculcation of high and pure morals such as these that in a free Republic, woman performs her sacred duty, and fulfills her destiny."[33] While this article told women to offer their political influence from the home rather than in public settings, that the periodical focuses its political attention on the nativist cause demonstrates that women had a distinct political role and could choose a particular group or ideology to support.

On August 31, and continuing into September, riot cases were taken up in the Court of Quarter Sessions. Some of the ringleaders were tried on charges of arson and murder, others on charges of rioting. In October, the Court of Oyer and Terminer took up more serious cases of murder. Some who recalled what occurred in Kensington noted women's involvement. Peter Albright testified that "I saw three Irish women picking up stones in their aprons" with the intent on using them against the nativists.[34] No women were brought to trial, suggesting that while they participated in the riots, defending their loved ones' property and their communities as a whole, they were not ringleaders. While the crowds involved in these riots were quite large, the vast majority of the participants, including all the women, were not prosecuted for the violence and destruction.

Although women were not the instigators, they were, without a doubt, active participants. While mental images of nineteenth-century "mobs" might conjure up a large group of males, women and, in some cases, children were active participants as well. The 1850 Rolling Mills Riot in Pittsburgh is one antebellum incident where women took the lead in violently assaulting the factories. In the fugitive slave riots detailed below, women again were again active participants, but should not be considered the leading instigators of destruction.

RUNNING FOR FREEDOM: FUGITIVE SLAVE RIOTS

As the nation hurtled toward the Civil War, more tensions arose regarding what to do about runaway slaves. Pennsylvania, bordering the slave states of the Upper South at the Mason–Dixon Line, was an important locale for slaves attempting to reach freedom, and free black communities developed

TABLE 4. Southeastern counties population

County	1840	1850	1860
	Free black population / total population	Free black population / total population	Free black population / total population
Adams	690/23,044	555/25,981	474/28,006
Cumberland	996/30,953	957/34,327	1,340/40,098
Franklin	2,033/37,793	1,948/39,904	1,799/42,126
Lancaster	3,003/84,203	3,614/98,444	3,459/116,314
York	973/47,010	1,125/57,450	1,366/68,200

Source: "Historical Census Browser," University of Virginia Library Geospatial and Statistical Data Center.

in southern areas of the state, as indicated in the table below.[35] When slave catchers and owners became more aggressive in their pursuit of runaways into free territory, black communities rallied around their friends and neighbors in order to protect them from being captured. This is particularly true along the border between slave and free states, and the shifting black populations in these counties over the decades may reflect the tightening of fugitive slave laws, especially after 1850. The southern border region of Pennsylvania was a volatile place, dating back to the late eighteenth century, but by the middle of the nineteenth century it had become "the most dramatic and influential scene of forceful black resistance" according to Stanley Harrold. Communities in south-central Pennsylvania witnessed the fight over slavery and freedom, fought out in civic and personal arenas.[36]

The importance of these black communities in the region is key to understanding the violence that ensued as the nineteenth century progressed. Population growth in general grew outward from Philadelphia since the colonial era. Furthermore, as the urban areas in southeastern Pennsylvania developed in the antebellum decades, so did the rural areas. In fact, rural populations from the Pennsylvania census from 1790 to 1850 seemed to increase more than urban areas did.[37] Southeastern and south-central Pennsylvania have elements of both rural and urban areas, allowing economic and social opportunities for growing free black communities in larger towns and cities, but there were also rural areas in which these individuals could live quietly in their communities. This region of Pennsylvania became a significant population center for free blacks in northeastern United States. Much of Pennsylvania's slavery had been concentrated in this region, and following the Act for the Gradual Abolition of Slavery of 1780, which among other provisions enabled children born to slaves to be freed from their mother's master at age twenty-eight, many of the former slaves remained in the area, thus laying the groundwork for established free black communities that developed in the nineteenth century and enticing other free blacks and fugitives to come. While this region was dangerous for free blacks, residing in this borderland allowed individuals to more easily stay in communication with family who might be enslaved and to act as intermediaries in their relatives' quests for freedom.[38] At the same time as the region provided community and easier communication with those still enslaved, southern Pennsylvania also became more tempting to slave catchers and kidnappers.

South-central and southeastern Pennsylvania, then, became home to vibrant, active population pockets of free blacks. The people in these regions built communities based on shared experiences and cultural heritage. Kinship networks and bonds between friends and coworkers also helped to create tightly knit societies. James and Lois Horton argue that these communities and networks "provided mutual support and created the foundation for political action."[39] Furthermore, as Jane and William Pease suggest, northern free blacks had "a distinctive group consciousness" due to the shared experience of a slave heritage.[40] This inherent commonality, whether they themselves had been slaves or close friends or relatives had experienced enslavement, gave these growing communities a bond that white neighbors did not have. The bond perhaps heightened how protective they were toward one another, particularly when their communities were threatened by outside forces. The fugitive slave riots in this chapter provide cases in point for how vital these black communities were to resisting laws that sought to limit their freedom.

Due to its early efforts to end slavery in 1780 and its critical geographic location between slave territory and free, Pennsylvania was constantly in tension with competing laws trying to limit freedom from slavery. Pennsylvania made several attempts to circumvent the federal Fugitive Slave Act of 1793, which made it legal for slave owners to recapture runaway slaves in any territory of the United States, regardless of whether the state or territory recognized slavery. In addition, there were penalties for anyone caught helping a fugitive slave. Pennsylvania passed legislation to regulate the process of reclaiming runaway slaves. In 1826, the state's Personal Liberty Law required documentation that proved the slave status of slave catchers' claims as well as requiring that a judge hear the cases, not lower court officials. By the 1840s, the focus on how to use the legal system to deal with fugitive slaves changed. Before then, the emphasis was on freeing Pennsylvania's own slaves; now lawyers used state laws to aid runaways and those living in free black communities. This shift in legal strategy demonstrates the growing tension and violence that plagued the region. The 1826 law was not enough to stop slave catchers, and in the 1842 *Prigg v. Pennsylvania* case, the state was deemed to have "unconstitutionally interfered" with the federal 1793 law.[41] This did not stop Pennsylvania legislators, who enacted another law on March 3, 1847. This statute prohibited officials' assistance in upholding the Fugitive Slave Law of 1793 by holding them liable for returning fugitives back to their owners. The act was meant to prevent fraudulent kidnapping, to keep the public peace, and to limit the powers of the local judiciary.[42] This 1847 law would prove important considering the pro-slavery sentiment that was sometimes popular in southern Pennsylvania.

On June 2, 1847, a case in Carlisle, Pennsylvania, would put the new law to the test. Three fugitive slaves, Lloyd Brown and his ten-year-old daughter Ann, and Hester, a woman known to be married to a free black man in Carlisle, escaped from Hagerstown, Maryland. All three slaves were captured near Shippensburg, Pennsylvania, and transported with their captors to Carlisle, where the owners showed proof to the justice of the peace that the slaves belonged to them. The owners were issued a certificate giving them legal custody of the fugitives. Furthermore, Carlisle law enforcement allowed the owners to keep the slaves in the local jail until they could be returned to Maryland.[43]

Local free blacks were angered by this turn of events. George Norman, the husband of Hester, "tried to snatch her away" as the sheriff was taking the three slaves to jail. Norman failed, leaving "a group of blacks, mostly women," who "milled around the jail in an angry mood while the prisoners were taken inside."[44]

As the afternoon wore on, more trouble brewed. The crowd shifted from the jail to the courthouse awaiting a habeas corpus hearing at 4 p.m. At the trial "a large crowd of infuriated negro men and women gathered in and about the Court House, who evinced, by their violent conduct, a disposition to rescue the fugitives by force."[45] Judge Samuel Hepburn ruled that the slaves should not have been under the custody of the sheriff after the slave catchers had been arrested for forcibly entering the house where the slaves were found, but he also ruled that the owners still had rights to the slaves. Seeing an opportunity, members of the free black community became "increasingly agitated and incensed" and tried to rescue Hester from the prisoners' box. The sheriff and his assistant threatened to shoot anyone who attempted to help the slaves escape, which quieted the courtroom chaos.[46]

Dickinson College professor John McClintock, who was present at the trial, realized that the judge and lawyers were unaware of the new 1847 law, which they had just broken. Even after McClintock gave the judge a copy of the law, peace was not achieved, as local free blacks attempted to rescue the hostages, resulting in a riot. In the trial testimony, one witness stated that "Norman & some women grabbed hold" of Hester in an attempt to free her. McClintock warned a law enforcement official that he would be held accountable if he arrested Ann Garver, who had attacked one of the slave owners. One regional newspaper article noted, "A general rush was made on the slave owners and the constables by the negro men and women, and a frightful melee ensued in the street, in which for some minutes paving stones were hurled in showers and clubs and canes used with terrible energy."[47] Hester and the little girl Ann escaped, but Brown was taken back to Maryland. As a result of the melee, John McClintock, along with twenty-eight others (including nine women), were charged with causing a riot (the historical record is a little unclear as to the actual number of people arrested, indicted, or those actually tried).[48]

The trial testimony recounted the alleged action of McClintock in urging on the riot as well as the active role played by women. Much of the testimony pointed to the women's direct action. Willis Foulke, a young doctor in the town, stated that he saw "4 or 5 colored women and several young colored men coming up the steps, one after another, in Indian file," coming toward the courthouse with "a firm step & an apparently determined countenance." Foulke continued that he knew well Hannah Decker, one of the rioters, and testified that "she had a stick in her right hand, two or 2 ½ feet long," which she held "in such a position as to hide it." Another witness, Samuel Smith, stated that outside the courthouse, "there was a woman near [the] carriage with a club," whom he identified as Elizabeth Boon. Soon after, one "wench rushed" the carriage. Susan Hunter held a door closed "doing all she could" to protect the fugitives. Hunter was seen "with stones in her hands" and was heard to say that she would "fight in blood up to her knees for her color." Other women were also vehement about their cause. Sophia Johnson was heard to have said that she would knock down the first man who came into the alley. Witnesses had no doubt those women who were in the thick of the fighting played a critical role in the escape of Hester and Ann.[49]

Deputy sheriff Robert McCartney also testified that the women were considerably troublesome, even going so far as to threaten *him*. There was, he recalled, "a great deal of warmth used by the colored women towards myself—by Clara Jones, Seeley Lawson, Ann Garver, & a number of others." Susan Hunter and Elizabeth Cribbs were seen to be "busy with their tongues."[50]

Interestingly, several African American women took the stand in this trial, providing their direct voices and perspectives on the event. Most women who testified downplayed the roles of other women in the riot, perhaps as a way to limit the legal consequences for their actions. For instance, Violet Johnson, Jane Jefferson, and Elizabeth Warfield recalled that Mrs. Garver was frightened of going into the crowd and was simply in the area looking for her husband. They argued that Ann Garver had not done anything wrong and had no weapons on her person. In fact, they claimed that the "negroes did nothing" at all and that the "negroes did not strike, throw stones or do anything else." These women claimed that the escapes were of the fugitives' own doing. Other women said that Susan Hunter was with them, inside the Snodgrass house, close to the courthouse when the riot occurred and was not an active participant.[51] It is possible that these women may have been trying to protect their neighbors and friends, particularly the females on trial, with their testimony. Help from their community would be of the utmost importance considering the fragile freedom of free blacks in areas near the Mason–Dixon Line in the 1840s and 1850s. Unfortunately, there is no way to determine exactly why the women said what they did or what exactly occurred at the Carlisle courthouse. The discrepancies in the testimony prove only that there was much chaos at the scene, that some violence occurred, and that Hester and Ann made their escape.

The rioters' defense counsel alluded to this in his closing speech to the court. Ann Garver, he insisted, "was very much excited, & well she might be, believing as she did that the colored women about to be carried away, were *free* women." With such contradictory evidence and testimony, he doubted the jury could rightfully convict Garver. On August 30, 1847, the jury returned with its verdicts: thirteen men were found guilty; McClintock and the rest of the defendants were freed.[52]

That women played such a central role in this riot, even being taken to trial for their actions, indicates a strong community of free blacks in Carlisle. Although they could not participate politically at the polls, this community, through rioting, demonstrated their political beliefs and attempted to right moral wrongs by protecting the fugitives from having to return to slavery. They laid bare the injustice of the system and tried to thwart the power of the southern slaveholders to retake their human property. Their actions speak directly to their views on the federal and state justice system with regard to fugitive slaves. By challenging slavery through riots, these freedwomen continued the resistance movement that their enslaved brothers and sisters started on the plantation. Together, this resistance pushed the fight for emancipation forward.[53] What is more telling is the fact that no women were sent to prison for their actions, even though trial testimony demonstrated often how involved numerous women were in the fracas. They were obviously part of the riot, yet none was convicted. The lack of convictions speaks to juries finding it difficult to convict women of crimes during this period—in this case, even though the women were African American. It raises the question of whether the lack of convictions for women was based on evidence or motivated by wanting to avoid further violence. In these riot cases, only a few women saw jail time for their participation in demonstrations, and those were mostly for labor riots, suggesting that female rioters may have stood a better chance of getting away with their actions in the eyes of law, thus making them more valuable participants in trying to effect social change. In this riot in particular, the women's involvement demonstrated broadly that all could play an active role in the fight for freedom.

The McClintock riot, only one such event that took place in southern Pennsylvania, was not the first in the state that marked increasing tensions over slavery and fugitive slaves prior to the passage of the Fugitive Slave Act of 1850.[54] While running away from slavery can be considered a form of political action, aiding runaways was equally political. Women also became involved in an organized effort to prevent the return of fugitives. The Female Vigilant Committee, an auxiliary of the Vigilant Committee of Philadelphia, was formed in 1838. The parent committee, organized in 1837 by black and white abolitionists, provided runaways with material items and financial assistance. It also helped the fugitives navigate the legal system. The Female Committee devoted much of its time and energy to raising funds to aid runaways.[55]

After the passage of the 1850 Fugitive Slave Act, the stakes were higher for runaways and those willing to help people escape to freedom. Free black communities united to protect their neighbors, or even strangers who were fleeing slavery.[56] One of the most nationally renowned fugitive slave riots was the deadly showdown in Christiana, Pennsylvania, a small town in Lancaster County, on September 11, 1851. The saga began two years earlier when four slaves from Maryland left the plantation owned by Edward Gorsuch after illegally selling their owner's grain. The slaves took flight to Pennsylvania, settling in Lancaster County, near Christiana. In 1851, Gorsuch and a posse of relatives and friends procured the necessary paperwork to obtain his slaves, and headed north.[57]

Throughout the nineteenth century, the free black and fugitive population in Lancaster County had been growing; while numbers remained relatively small compared to the white population, the rate of growth caused locals to fear that racial violence was imminent. Making matters worse, local newspapers had taken to reporting acts of violence by blacks, fueling fear and distrust of the growing black community.[58] Those who fought at Christiana, however, were not merely victims; rather, they showed initiative and were willing to face dire consequences, hoping their actions to protect friends and neighbors would effect a positive change in their free lives in the North.

Gorsuch's four slaves made their way to this growing black community. One survivor of the riot, Peter Woods, stated, "We knew that these new colored fellows were escaped slaves. . . . We colored fellows were all sworn in to keep secret what we knew and when these fellows came there they were sworn in too." The mutual support found in this African American community is evident, and similar to that found in Carlisle and other places in the southern part of the state. William Parker, an escaped slave from Maryland, acted as the informal leader of this community, and made it his life's work to protect others being returned to slavery.[59]

On the day before the riot, the fugitives from Maryland went to Parker's home for help in defending themselves against Gorsuch and his men. Seven blacks, including two of the fugitive slaves, stayed in Parker's home the night of September 10, 1851, and used the house as a fortress against the slave catchers. At daybreak on September 11, 1851, the fighting began. They told the slave catchers to go away, "as they would rather die than suffer any of their number to be carried off; also that they would not fire unless the whites made the first attack, and if they did fire first they were dead men."[60]

Once the assault began, Eliza Parker, William's wife, blew a horn to summon support. Hannah Pinckney, Eliza Parker's sister, wanted the inmates of the house to surrender, fearing that they would lose due to the growing number of whites coming to aid Gorsuch. In response, Eliza "seized a corn-cutter and declared she would cut off the head of the first one who should attempt to give up." While Hannah was cautious, Eliza was determined to resist the slave catchers and protect their family and home, and by extension, the lives of other fugitives in the area. These women helped lead the resistance against Gorsuch and his agents. Those under siege in the farmhouse were reinforced by the arrival of blacks from the surrounding communities. They came with "stones, rails, canes, clubs, rifles, revolvers, pistols, pitchforks, scythes, and corn cutters. Their everyday means of work were taken up as weapons."[61] The black community's arrival turned the tide in favor of those in the farmhouse.

At the end of an hour of fighting, Edward Gorsuch laid dead, and his son and nephew were badly wounded. The other white fighters retreated. Isaiah Clarkson, one of the African Americans who responded to the horn call, witnessed "infuriated women, forgetful of all humane instincts," rushing toward Gorsuch and "with corn cutters and scythe blades hacked the bleeding and lifeless body as it lay in the garden walk." While it is unknown who killed Gorsuch, Parker noted in his autobiography that "*the women put an end to him*" after the battle was over, but he does not go into detail about their actions.[62] The motivations behind these accounts of the brutality done to Gorsuch's body remain unclear. What is clear, however, is that women were active, militant participants.

Once it became apparent that a death had occurred at their hands, Parker and a few others left hastily for Canada to avoid arrest. Eliza Parker stayed behind but went into hiding. Over thirty people (a conservative estimate) were arrested for the riot and murder of Edward Gorsuch. While the majority of these were black men, several white men—including Castner Hanway, who was unsuccessfully tried for treason—and six black women—Elizabeth Mosey, Susan Clark, Tamsy Brown, Eliza Brown, Eliza Parker, and Hannah Pinckney—were also arrested for their participation. Some of those prisoners who were charged with treason were taken to Philadelphia's Moyamensing Prison to await their trial while others were kept at the Lancaster County Jail. Locals were questioned as to what they knew about the riot. One of these was Tamsy Brown, a child, who claimed she was at school during the riot and that her grandmother, Susan Clarkson (presumably Susan Clark), with whom she lived, told her about the death of Gorsuch. She admitted to knowing Eliza Parker and Hannah Pinckney, but did not seem to be present at the riot. It is unknown why she was arrested if she was not involved. Perhaps she was merely a victim of circumstance or held because she knew others who were more directly responsible. Eventually, all the women and a few of the men were discharged before any trial occurred. This is an interesting turn of events considering that several men in the slave catchers' posse identified Eliza Parker as an active rioter, and she could have been charged at the very least with violating the Fugitive Slave Act. Ultimately, Eliza Parker made it to Canada.[63]

There are several possible explanations for why the women were released and not charged with treason like some of the male rioters. The lawyers for the prosecution may have figured it was too difficult to find a jury that would convict these women of a capital crime, and perhaps believed that arresting the men would be punishment enough for their families left behind. Taking Eliza Parker and Hannah Pinckney to trial may have triggered political outrage in an unstable and volatile political environment. It was already going to be difficult to prosecute the men for treason at the federal level, but the possibility was still there to try the rioters for murder in Pennsylvania court.[64] Because the trial became political propaganda surrounding the Fugitive Slave Act, the prosecution may have believed that trying a white man for treason first would demonstrate the seriousness of the federal law and serve as an example for others not to follow. The Christiana trial echoed the McClintock trial in a way, where a white man was put on trial and the mass of rioters acted in supporting roles. As was evidenced in the McClintock trial, the women put on trial in Carlisle had their actions downplayed by witnesses and were ultimately acquitted. The lawyers in the Christiana trial may have decided that putting women on trial was not worth the effort for a potential legal loss.

The lawyers may also have viewed the women as merely pawns in their husbands' actions, caught up in the crossfire of being in the house when the riot occurred. Yet, as other instances in this study have shown, women from all backgrounds in the antebellum period were acting on their own volition and breaking down societal norms. In this case, the women were fortunate in the outcome, Eliza Parker in particular, because it is clear, even from accounts of the male rioters, that they had participated in the violence by their own free will—and in so doing, they openly defied the law that could send them and others back to slavery. While the women's voices in this case remain relatively silent in the historical record, their actions on that September morning and in the days that followed indicated their sentiments on slavery and the rights they believed they had as free blacks in a free state. They willingly risked criminal charges to protect their community and challenged their discriminated social status by opposing the posse of slave catchers. James Horton and Lois Horton suggest that in a period when few women "questioned their place in the American polity . . . black protest against the growing political exclusion of African Americans was widespread."[65] What is demonstrated in the events at Christiana and Carlisle is that not only was black protest growing, but black women were taking a central and active role in the proceedings. They were aware of the limitations of the laws protecting themselves and their loved ones, and still challenged them with violence.

Both of these possibilities speak to the nineteenth-century attitudes toward black women. Freed African American women faced an immediate roadblock to the assumption of women's virtue and morality because of their skin color, since standards of virtuous womanhood of the time were based on expectations for white women. Black women abolitionists faced this stereotyping consistently in their work.[66] That being said, it is possible that these stereotypes shaped the prosecution's view of the black women involved in Christiana who chose to protest and employ violence. The lawyers ultimately viewed the women as either not important enough to try or simply followers of their husbands; and in their quest for a conviction, perhaps the lawyers decided that the women would not be the best face for the trial, thus putting Castner Hanway on trial first. These women, however they were viewed by the lawyers, eschewed the social standards set by white society, and ultimately created their own, choosing action and self-defense as a mechanism for change.

By October 6, 1851, thirty-eight men, mostly black, were indicted for treason in the U.S. Circuit Court. In the end, only Hanway was tried. Two weeks later, the jury returned a quick verdict of not guilty, after deliberating for only fifteen minutes. Subsequently, all remaining charges of rioting were dropped against the accused. Although their actions defied a federal law, the Christiana rioters simply defended those in their community against the institution of slavery. Treason against the United States was an extravagant charge, impossible to prove.[67]

In the two fugitive slave riots in Carlisle and Christiana, free black women joined men in taking major risks to help fugitive slaves escape bondage. By their actions, they demonstrated their capabilities as political actors. While black women in cities had more opportunities to join antislavery organizations or mutual aid associations, the women in Carlisle and Christiana became foot soldiers on the front lines of the fight, allowing them to take a more direct, violent role in resistance against slave catching and kidnapping. They also illustrated the strength, determination, and organization of free black communities. In these riots, the free black communities resisted both state and federal laws. Furthermore, these two events demonstrate how important women were to these communities; they were vital players in collective action, taking on just as much responsibility as did male rioters. Without other means of political participation, these women turned to the avenues available—namely, rioting. Furthermore, because society already held them in a lower regard, perhaps the women felt they had less to lose and more to gain by their active, militant performances.

LABOR UNREST IN ACTION: THE 1850 ROLLING MILLS RIOT

As detailed at the start of this chapter, in March of 1850, a group of women participated in demonstrations that turned into violent attacks on iron mills in Pittsburgh. While it appeared that women were the main demonstrators-turned-rioters, they were not alone, nor were their actions made without the provocation of poor labor conditions. A crowd of men and boys "followed the women and encouraged their proceedings." Some observers believed that the women were "only put forward as a feint, to provoke resistance, and thus give some pretext for far worse violence by their backers." Still, only women employed violence at first. Historian James Linaberger argues that the women met little resistance because law enforcement and the strikebreakers were unsure of how to resist the women without provoking the men in the crowd.[68] This gave the women a better chance at early success. On March 2, more threats of riots occurred, this time with men and boys joining the women directly in attacking the mills.

Newspapers took up the story of the riots and opined vociferously on the central role of the women. The *Saturday Visiter*, a Pittsburgh periodical edited by Jane Swisshelm, noted that the factory workmen "were not prepared for this Amazonian outbreak." The editorialist continued, "We [presumably Pittsburgh society] regret this occurrence because of its effect upon the position of the outstanding workers. The men, however, should bear no blame, if we may believe their own protestations."[69] The tone here is decidedly sarcastic. While it is possible the strikebreakers may not have been expecting women to be involved in the riots, particularly at the forefront of the collective action, the author is also not convinced that the men were simply following the women's lead. Furthermore, a sense of judgment looms over the men for putting the women on the front lines in a struggle that was not necessarily theirs to fight. In any case, the women played a central role in the action, demonstrating the willingness to take up the cause for their friends and family, perhaps as a way to protect loved ones from the potential harm that men may have endured if they instigated the riots.

Other articles "apologized" for the rioters' actions. Pittsburgh, one author wrote, was "sorry for this proof that the working men are not able to take care of themselves—are not fit for freedom. We look upon this whole affair as an insurrection among slaves." The employment of such phrasing in an environment of rising sectional tension regarding slavery was not only meant to provoke discussion about the actions of the rioters but is suggestive about the social attitudes toward the city's working class. Freemen, according to the author, would not have "been brought to commit such excesses on such slight provocation." The rioters, consisting of working-class men and women, were "slaves of centuries." In this article, an implicit link between societal injustices arises—connecting women's treatment in antebellum society with the poor working environments laborers faced. These demographic groups, subjugated for years, had seemingly reached a breaking point that necessitated the drastic action that played out in these types of riots. "Woman," the same author continued, "is every day proving her humanity—proving she is not an angel, but of the genus homo—governed by human passions, liable to human wants, and in great want of human rights." While men were able to effect change through politics and legal means, women had "been taught to succumb to brute force, to resist it in kind, and rely upon noise for victory."[70] While comparing this riot and the workers to slaves and slave insurrections might have turned some public opinion against the women rioters, it speaks more broadly to the struggles that women and the working classes have faced over the generations. These female demonstrators exhibited not only their capability of pushing for social change, but also the desperate need to alter the status quo—in this case, for the working classes. Although the female rioters were likely directly linked with the mills and the striking workers and their initial motivation was to change the working conditions, their actions represent a broader aspiration during this period to change the status of women as well. Their political activism in the form of riots constitutes a step in this direction, perhaps an unintended result of their action.

The *Saturday Visiter* was not finished editorializing about the actions of these women. The riot became a catalyst for a discussion of women's place in society. A week after the first articles on the riot, an anonymous piece suggested that not all Pittsburgh females were of the same stock as the rioters, yet "it does appear a little strange, that the only two serious riots that have ever occurred in our city have been headed by women." This fact raises larger issues about why women participated in these events. The author noted that the "Amazonian tendency" among some Pittsburgh women was a result of "the general belief of woman's inferiority." Did women act in these aggressive ways to demonstrate that they were not, in fact, inferior? Was it because they and their loved ones had been subjects of an unfair economic and social system for so long that they had simply reached a breaking point? Perhaps it is both. The article noted that while Pittsburgh's male population had "too much respect for themselves to violate the laws they have made . . . they will incite women to do what they themselves would not or dare not do."[71] Women who participated in the riot seemingly got "a fool's pardon" for their actions. At some level, they were viewed as pawns in a larger scheme conceived by men. Whereas rioting men may have been resisted more quickly by the strikebreakers and law enforcement, placing women in the front ranks allowed the rioting to go further because no one really expected them to be so aggressive. While not outright condoning the actions of the rioters, the articles in the *Saturday Visiter* sympathized with the women to some extent and placed blame for these riots at the feet of community institutions and societal systems bent on keeping the working class and women in their place.[72]

The way in which the newspapers portrayed the female rioters in Pittsburgh represents a trend that continues into the twentieth century. Although the women acted in the public sphere and in a political manner, the press downplayed the importance of what these women were doing. Nan Enstad, in looking at female shirtwaist makers in early twentieth-century New York, argues that the press, in their focus on middle-class views on women, ultimately "precluded taking striking women seriously as political actors." Furthermore, the press, in their coverage of these shirtwaist strikes, "undermined women's legitimacy as political actors by representing them as an irrational mob."[73] In these instances where working-class women step into the public arena in ways unexpected by contemporary society and the press, whether as rioters or strikers, the women remain unable to effect serious political or economic change. Although their actions make a statement, the way the press publicizes the events ultimately shapes the public's reaction and often limits to what extent such women are taken seriously. For women involved in the Rolling Mill Riots, the fact that they were relatives of the striking workers serves to undermine their political statement to an extent, as they appear to the public to be pawns in the schemes of men. The expectations of how women were supposed to behave, even working-class women, are evident in the way these riots were presented to the public.

If the newspaper coverage and denunciation of the women's activities were not enough, the trial of the mob's ringleaders illustrated that the city would not tolerate such behavior from women, especially those from the lower classes. The Rolling Mills Riot case started in the Allegheny Court of Quarter Sessions on April 8, 1850. Four women—Ann McDermott, Margaret Graham, Mary Reeves (alias Catharine Riley), and Eliza Morgan—faced indictment for rioting along with several men. The trial testimony came solely from employees at the mill; none of the defendants took the stand in their own defense, which offers a skewed portrayal of events. Many employees testified to the central role that women played. F. L. Griesheimer, manager of the mill, testified that "ten or twelve women came with stones and coal in their hands. One of them had something like a mace hanging to her hand." They threw "as hard as they could throw, brickbats, coal and cinders. I was struck twenty times, I suppose." Others testified that men in the crowd encouraged the women to action; they spoke of the injuries they sustained at the hands of the female rioters but often observed that they "saw no men throwing" bricks and stones.[74]

A second day of testimony continued the accounts of those victimized by the rioters. The trial ended the following day, and the jury began deliberations. Partway through the afternoon, the jury returned, stating that "they could not agree that there had been a riot." The enraged judge told them that the fact that "there *had been* a riot was as clear as that the sun shone" and that "he would starve with the jury till they did agree." When the jury returned that evening, they had found two men and all four women guilty of rioting. While the men—Patrick McDermott and James Bratt—received eighteen months in the Western State Penitentiary, each of the four women was sentenced to thirty days in the county prison and fined fifty dollars.[75]

Outrage at the sentencing of McDermott and Bratt was voiced immediately. The eighteen-month sentence struck observers as absurdly harsh considering that all the testimony had been clear that the men were not active participants in the riot—at least not initially.[76] The lack of commentary on the women's sentences suggests that the author of the article believed the punishments to be just. The lopsided sentencing in this trial demonstrates that convicting women of crimes was difficult for some juries, even when evidence went strongly against them. Perhaps the severe sentences for the men were meant to send a message that they should have done more to stop the women from taking such a destructive, unfeminine approach, or that they should have encouraged them not to riot in the first place.

The day after the sentencing, a member of the staff of the *Pittsburgh Daily Dispatch* visited the women in the county jail. One learns that the McDermotts (Ann and Patrick) were Irish and considered "noble spirited" and intelligent. The author of the article seems to feel sympathy for Ann McDermott, who had her infant in the jail with her as her husband began his long sentence at Western State Penitentiary. Mrs. Reeves was said to be keeping "up her spirits bravely" while Mrs. Graham and Mrs. Morgan were less brave, perhaps due to the fact that they were also mothers and were now separated from their children. The women served their sentences, but their fines were dismissed.[77]

The Rolling Mills Riot case is of great interest because of the central role played by women. Furthermore, the fact that it was a labor riot, one in which the women were not the employees on strike, makes the case even more significant. It could be that the men felt they could get more accomplished by allowing the women to take the lead. Perhaps the men believed their efforts would have been more readily quashed if initiated by them. By all accounts, the police had difficulty stopping the women for fear that if the women were attacked, the men in the crowd would hurry to protect them. The wives of the workers must have felt that it was necessary to riot in order to protect the livelihoods of their husbands, which in turn supported their families at home. It is quite possible that the women took the initiative to riot, although there is no way to know what motivated them. These women demonstrated their views on a socioeconomic situation that had a direct impact on their quality of life. Their actions reveal frustration and a deep desire for improvement. While their methods were aggressive and unfeminine in the eyes of some contemporary observers, their motivations to protect their families and livelihoods took on a maternal, womanly cast.

The Rolling Mills Riot was not the only labor unrest Pittsburgh faced. Only two years earlier, at the end of July 1848, another series of riots occurred at cotton mills in the city over the reduction of work hours from thirteen to ten per day. These are presumably the other riots headed by women mentioned by the *Saturday Visiter*.[78]

Trouble loomed in July 1848 when some female workers at Penn Mill who wanted to work their traditional longer shifts in order to receive their normal wages, demanded that those employees already at work under a new ten-hour regulation be discharged from their jobs in order to push for a return to the old law. Witnesses recalled "a large collection of females, and some men" at the front of the factory, "*hissing those who were going to work*" and calling them "*slaves*." When the workers entered the factory anyway, those protesting, including "several little girls," threw eggs, stones, and potatoes at the factory, while those inside threw bobbins from the window at the rioters. A police officer on the scene, Joseph H. Scott, identified three women by name: Mary Lynch, Joanna Brown, and a girl with the surname of Stewart. This action continued for some time, drawing larger crowds, which encouraged the women to keep standing up for their rights. Others corroborated these actions, naming other female rioters, including Miranda Holander and Rosetta Richards, as well as an unnamed woman who attempted to chop down the front gate. When the gate broke, the mob rushed inside, with one female rioter stating, "*It is not our intention to destroy property; we want to get at the girls.*" At the trial, two women, Mary Fulton and Elizabeth Haggerty, testified to this effect, saying they just wanted to remove the girls from the factory who were following the new ten-hour law, and that they rioted to protect their rights as workers to earn their full wages under the longer shifts. As a result of the collective violence, seventeen faced indictments for riots, including twelve men and five women.[79] What we see here is an interesting dynamic between the two groups of women workers, demonstrating that they were not all united in their attitudes toward the workplace and the conditions they faced. Some women who continued to work under the ten-hour law "appeared to accept and even to cooperate

in reproducing the conditions that oppressed them."[80] The women rioters, on the other hand, perhaps believed their cause to be undermined by
those women who worked for fewer hours. The lack of solidarity among
the women could have helped to escalate the riot and demonstrated the
wide spectrum of views women held toward work and wages, where each
woman made an individual decision about what course of action was best
for her—working or striking.

At the trial of the rioters, counsel for the Commonwealth argued
against the women's actions, stating that "females should be peaceful and
law abiding, and when they engage in mob violence against their own sex,
they lose all title to consideration and pity." This moral indictment against
the women's action at Penn Mill demonstrates the prevailing social norms
that women should not take part in the more traditionally male-dominated
realm of violence and aggression. Yet, as workers themselves in the public
eye, these women had cause to protest changes to their working conditions.
The fact that they were factory workers differentiates their collective action
from those women at the Rolling Mills Riot, who were wives and relatives
of the employees. Census records indicate that these cotton mill women
comprised both immigrants and native-born Americans. That they were of
the working class may have contributed to their motivations, feeling, perhaps, that they had little recourse but more violent protest. They leveraged
what they could, in their own words, "to see our rights."[81]

Even so, the women's violent actions, including the use of an axe to
break down the gate, were viewed as socially problematic in that they were
unfeminine. The judge opined on the plight of the female defendants in
his charge to the jury, suggesting that because they were women, they
might expect "an unusual share of your sympathy." He continued, "They
enjoy our respect so long as their conduct is consistent with the delicacy
and modesty of the female character. But . . . when they play the part of
ringleaders in a destructive mob, and are guilty of acts that would disgrace
the greatest ruffians of the opposite sex—they forfeit all claim to any peculiar degree of respect." As far as the judge was concerned, when someone
broke the law, as these women did, they should be punished accordingly,
and not be given sympathy because of their sex. The jury agreed, returning
a guilty verdict for all five women and eight of the twelve men. Two years
later, in July 1850, women at the Eagle and Hope cotton mills rioted due
to the same issues.[82]

Women in these and the Rolling Mills Riot demonstrated political action in protesting what they viewed as negative changes to their or their family members' working conditions. They represent important agents in labor history. Female laborers organized and resisted in ways that responded to their desired goals within a framework of their various work lives. The women rioters in Pittsburgh showed this as they used violence and striking as means to resist the oppression they or their male family members faced. Ava Baron suggests that communities in which women socialized, including work and neighborhood associations, "helped to forge solidarity and formed the basis for collective identity and labor militancy."[83] While the courts viewed their actions as unfeminine and inappropriate, the women, with power in numbers and unity, saw their collective violence as necessary in order to secure changes in the prevailing labor conditions.

————————

Although these three types of riots stemmed from different motivations and had very different outcomes in the courts, several commonalities emerge. These examples were part of the larger riotous atmosphere in antebellum Pennsylvania and the United States. The rapidly changing economy and widespread industrialization, population makeup, burgeoning cities, and national tensions over the institution of slavery led to numerous riots in the United States in the decades leading up to the Civil War. Furthermore, these events were not limited to male participation. In the riots analyzed here, women took part to varying degrees. In the nativist riots in Philadelphia, although a woman may have been part of the initial debate over Bibles in schools which led to the rioting, women also participated in the mob activity by hurling stones, wielding weapons, and cheering on their male family members. They were not instigators of the demonstrations—men took that role—nor were women taken to trial for the deaths that occurred in the riots' two waves. In this instance, women acted among the anonymous rioters, blending into the crowd that caused so much destruction in the city.

In other cases, women played a much more distinct role. During the fugitive slave riots in Carlisle and Christiana, Pennsylvania, women were named specifically for their actions. This is most likely because of the more modest nature of the activities, whereas in Philadelphia, thousands of people participated in the riots, allowing women to remain anonymous. In both cases, women were actively violent, wielding weapons and risking their physical well-being to help fugitives evade a return to slavery; were arrested for their participation; and faced potential incarceration. Although the women were only held in prison awaiting the trials and their cases ultimately dismissed, these women exhibited their willingness to participate in criminal activity to express their views on political and social issues.

As with the fugitive slave riots, the women who instigated the Rolling Mills Riot and the cotton mill riots in Pittsburgh faced a criminal trial for their actions. Unlike the women in the fugitive slave cases, however, the wives of the strikers in the Rolling Mills case actually had to endure a trial, were found guilty of their crimes, and faced jail time, as did those who rioted at the Penn cotton mill. It could be that because women in these cases were leaders of the riot and appeared to be in control of the activities, the court was willing to try and convict them, while those involved in the fugitive slave cases only sometimes faced trial.

Women participated in these riots to protect their families and their homes as part of their domestic responsibilities. Their actions also demonstrated a love of their community and a desire to protect it. In doing so, they challenged expectations of women's behavior and ventured into the male sphere of public, aggressive, and violent action. Women's participation in riots demonstrated their political beliefs and provided them a way to address social wrongs and oppressive policies, particularly because these groups of women were often members of lower economic and social classes or racial and ethnic minorities in their respective towns and cities. Whereas traditional roles may have kept some women from having a strong political voice, these groups of women were freed in various ways from the constraints set forth by the middle-class gender ideology and thus played a more active political role. Rioting gave women a type of voice in the political realm, one of direct action, rather than speechifying or simply casting a vote. Although contemporary society sometimes trivialized their involvement by only mentioning their participation in passing, women's riotous activity was important. They achieved a level of political power through their criminal activities, showing strong community bonds, a desire to protect family members and their homes, and sometimes brute Amazonian strength against oppressive antebellum institutions and political notions that strove to keep certain populations powerless.

PART 2

In Prison

CHAPTER 4

"Disturbing the Other Prisoners"

Female Inmates in Pennsylvania Penitentiaries

In the spring of 1862, Eastern State Penitentiary inmate Elizabeth Velora Elwell wrote to another inmate, Albert Green Jackson, "My dear I am most dead every night When I come up to the old Sell and leave you my dear honey . . . may we see the time my dear that we will not have to go to the cole seller to talk one word [*sic*]."[1] This excerpt from a series of letters from Elwell to Jackson reflects a budding romance between the two inmates, conducted within the prison's walls. By the 1860s, according to this letter, the rules of total isolation appear to have been lessened in Pennsylvania's premier penitentiary, an institution developed with absolute silence and solitary confinement at the heart of its disciplinary regime.[2] This excerpt and the rest of the letter collection demonstrate that Elwell was not content to simply waste away in the penitentiary. She found ways to avoid being silenced or forgotten in an institution bent on anonymity and isolation. The treatment and incarceration of most female inmates in Pennsylvanian state prisons in the nineteenth century was not a positive experience. Incarcerated women faced inequality and their rehabilitation was sometimes neglected, mostly due to their small population. However, these women were not passive cogs in the prison machinery. They made their presence known by resisting, whether it was complaining to the prison visitors, writing letters, vandalizing property, or attempting self-harm. By these actions, female inmates kept their personal identity alive and refused to succumb to anonymity.

The women in Pennsylvania's penitentiaries and county jails, the subject of chapter 5, continued to demonstrate their individualism, self-worth, and personal power even when incarcerated. Like their counterparts in the earlier chapters who harnessed notions of womanhood either to hide the commission of crimes or to possibly influence the outcome of their trials by appearing sympathetic and unthreatening, and those who used criminal activity to extricate themselves from situations where no legal recourse was easily available, the women who were convicted were not willing to become victims of the prison system. Instead, they continued to manipulate the system in various ways to alleviate their incarceration, rebel against disciplinary protocols, influence reformation efforts, and, ultimately, shape their own experiences in prison.

In its purest form, the Pennsylvania system of total isolation and silence would be able to treat all inmates, regardless of sex, race, or type of crime, in exactly the same fashion. In theory, incarcerated women could be treated in the same manner as male inmates in the Pennsylvania prisons. Mark Colvin argues that Pennsylvania separated females from the outset and "equitable treatment of women prisoners" continued in the state, even after it adopted the separate system.[3] The evidence from prison records and reports that discuss female inmates indicates that this contention is not entirely correct. While in some prisons women were placed in a separate section of the institution and in isolated cells, they were not treated the same as men. Women were often not subjected to or resisted the prison protocols of total silence and isolation. Prison employees actively treated women inmates differently. This may reflect their discomfort with having women in an institution that was designed predominantly for men, an attitude that the women were unthreatening and did not need to be subjected to the same prison rules as men, or even reflecting a belief that women criminals, due to their small numbers in prison, were not worth the effort to be reformed. Whatever the reason for the different treatment of female inmates, the women prisoners often found that they could access forms of freedom or flexibility in their incarceration, and many took advantage of this to exert control over their own imprisonment.

At some level, prison officials neglected these women. While the idea of neglect may hold a passive connotation for some, the differential treatment and the ignoring of female inmates' rehabilitation was an active form of neglect on the part of the employees. This inconsistency in discipline spawned the increased work of female prison reformers in the antebellum decades and ultimately drove the need for separate facilities for women—female reformatories—at the end of the nineteenth century and the beginning of the early twentieth. Furthermore, consistent female resistance added to the need for a revised plan for the incarceration of women.

In the antebellum decades, when the penitentiary movement took off in the United States, female inmates constituted a significantly smaller prison population than did male offenders. Mark Kann argues that the small number of female inmates led to a dire existence in prison. There was a strong double standard at play, where women criminals were viewed with disdain and distrust because societal expectations had created high standards for them. These women inmates "were often treated as unsalvageable human refuse to be buried rather than human beings to be rehabilitated." He suggests that because there was such a small population, prison officials could not justify the expense necessary to provide separate staff and provisions for female inmates, which "subjected women to institutional neglect." Kann is not alone in his observations. He and other scholars are correct in contending that the small population of female inmates in most prisons created dire consequences for those individuals.[4] Nicole Hahn Rafter observes that women's experiences in prison varied. While some prisons instituted strict protocols for women to follow, just like male inmates, in other penitentiaries this was not a priority. This inconsistency led to women being incarcerated in neglected, sometimes dangerous conditions.[5]

The idea that female inmates constituted refuse to be hidden away is decidedly harsh. In the case of Pennsylvania, however, the female inmates *refused* to be buried. The women's experience in prison was one where prison officials did not always adhere to their own rules for inmates when it came to dealing with female prisoners. What took place behind the walls of Pennsylvania state prisons indicates that officials wanted to, or felt they needed to, treat these inmates differently, sometimes more leniently. As a result, punishment was inconsistent. There was also little rehabilitation. Yet, the women rejected the idea that they were to be forgotten. They resisted being ignored. This tradition of resistance was evident in earlier generations of women prisoners as well as those who were incarcerated in the later decades of the nineteenth century.[6] These women used whatever means necessary to let their presence be known, to work for better situations for themselves, or to reform the system entirely. They continued to influence the system with their actions, just as their counterparts did at the court-room level.

Some contemporaries of the early American penitentiaries homed in on the specific issue of female inmates and were ahead of their time in their observations. In his introduction to Alexis de Tocqueville and Gustave de Beaumont's *On the Penitentiary System in the United States*, published in 1833, political theorist and prison reformer Francis Lieber asked, "Are separate penitentiaries for females required?" He answered his own question, stating, "I believe they are, if the Pennsylvania penitentiary system is not adopted."[7] In other words, if officials of the Pennsylvania system upheld its style of discipline with the rules of total isolation, silence, and anonymity, female inmates could be treated side by side with male inmates without needing special facilities. Theoretically, the Pennsylvania system of discipline could treat a wide variety of offenders in the same way, all promoting individual rehabilitation through silent reflection and hard work. In essence, inmates would disappear into anonymity and reemerge as rehabilitated citizens. Evidence of the way female inmates were treated by prison officials and their consistent resistance made Lieber's prediction of needing separate female penitentiaries come true in the late nineteenth century. Because incarcerating female inmates caused almost immediate problems for prison officials and subjected female inmates to institutional neglect, and at times exploitation, this decision to put women in the same penitentiary would lead ultimately to the failure of this system of punishment and necessitated separate female institutions around the turn of the twentieth century.

In Pennsylvania's two state penitentiaries, female inmates sometimes received special treatment and did not have to follow prison protocols during their incarceration, particularly in the early years when the female population was quite small. Female prison reformers, the subject of chapter 6, observed this differential treatment as neglect. In their eyes, the women were not fully participating in rehabilitative programs, which included isolation, silence, reflection, and religious teaching. Their reformation was being neglected, as if prison officials felt female inmates could not be rehabilitated or believed they did not belong in prison at all. Female prison reformers ultimately took up this cause as their own. But how did the female inmates themselves view their treatment in prison? Evidence from the records of the state penitentiaries demonstrates that women took advantage of the freedom or privileges to which they had access. One can glimpse incarcerated women manipulating the rules of the institution and sometimes being aided by the employees in thwarting prison protocols. Female inmates were allowed out of their cells, interacted socially with employees, and wrote letters. While the women might have manipulated the prison system to ease their incarceration or gain privileges for themselves, prison employees often looked the other way when it came to upholding prison rules and enforcing rehabilitation protocols for female inmates. The actions of the prison employees and the behaviors of empowered female inmates rendered the Pennsylvania system a failure.[8]

A TALE OF TWO PENITENTIARIES: THE DESIGNS AND RULES OF WESTERN AND EASTERN STATE

Before turning to the disciplinary issues that arose in the state's prisons, it is necessary to understand the architecture of these institutions, the reasons why these penitentiaries were constructed, and the early rules established for them. It is within these institutions, which were often flawed, where women, now lacking their freedom, still found means to challenge protocol, make their presence known to officials and reformers, and manufacture ways to improve their incarceration. The development of the Pennsylvania penitentiary system stemmed from a perpetual problem of inadequate jails in which inmates lived together in one room without classification according to crime or any hope of rehabilitation. Early prisons acted as holding pens for these offenders, but also often included witnesses for trials, debtors, vagrants, and those awaiting trial themselves. Reform groups originating in Philadelphia, such as the Pennsylvania Society for Alleviating the Miseries of Public Prisons (now the Pennsylvania Prison Society), worked to better the prison system in the state. These reformers wanted to separate inmates from one another, which would create healthier living conditions and provide less opportunity for prisoners to be corrupted or influenced by others. Prisoner separation, reformers believed, would allow for rehabilitation.

In the Walnut Street Jail in downtown Philadelphia, which later became the state's first penitentiary in 1790, inmates were grouped together according to the offenses committed in order to encourage repentance and rehabilitation efforts. The penitentiary system, beginning with Walnut Street and continuing with Eastern and Western State Penitentiaries, promoted a style of punishment that combined isolation and rehabilitation. This plan represented an innovative, more humane way to punish offenders. It attempted to deter future criminals without the commonly used physical punishments of the eighteenth century.

With the opening of Walnut Street, where male and female inmates were housed in separate quarters, judges from across the state could choose to send convicts there as opposed to holding them in their respective county jails.[9] When Walnut Street failed to serve as an adequate penitentiary, the Pennsylvania Prison Society advocated for new penitentiaries "in different parts of the State, so that the convenience of the interior and western counties might be promoted." The Pennsylvania legislature, in 1818, passed an act to build the Western State Penitentiary, located in Allegheny (Pittsburgh), Pennsylvania. While the construction of Western State eased the burden on Walnut Street, the growing number of inmates in the Philadelphia prison necessitated the need for a larger penitentiary in the city. In 1821, the state legislature passed an act to build Eastern State Penitentiary in Philadelphia, promoting "separate and solitary confinement at labour."[10]

These new penitentiaries ushered in a new era of penal discipline. Alexis de Tocqueville and Gustave de Beaumont best describe the shift in punishment between Walnut Street and the new penitentiaries on either end of the state: "The principles to be followed in the construction of these two establishments were, however, not entirely the same as those on which the Walnut Street prison had been erected. In the latter, classification formed the predominant system, to which solitary confinement was but secondary. In the new prisons the classifications were abandoned, and a solitary cell was to be prepared for each convict. . . . Thus absolute solitary confinement, which in Walnut Street was but accidental, was now to become the foundation of the system adopted for Pittsburg and Cherry-Hill [Philadelphia]."[11] These two state penitentiaries would act as large-scale trials for the use of the separate system and put to the test Lieber's query regarding female inmates to the test. From the early days, women inmates caused disruption and chaos in these institutions, ultimately forcing the need for reformers' interventions and wholescale reforms to the system toward the end of the century.

The Penitentiaries' Design
The original designs for the penitentiary at Pittsburgh were influenced by the Maison de Ghent and Jeremy Bentham's imagined Panopticon. No

original floor plans for this design survive, but the building failed miserably to uphold the Pennsylvania system of isolation and silence. One description noted, "The prison as constructed consisted of an outer octagonal wall, within which were placed a front building for administrative purposes and a single large ring-shaped cell building. The latter consisted of a double row of cells, back to back, each cell fronting on an open vestibule in such a way that the adjacent vestibules formed a continuous covered passageway around both the inner and outer sides of the ring." The cells only received light from a narrow slat in an iron door, and it was planned that a central observation tower was to be placed inside the ring. The observation building was never finished, thus leaving the penitentiary without any means of central surveillance.[12]

Western State received its first inmate on July 31, 1826, even before construction had been completed. The portions completed at the beginning of July 1826 included "the exterior walls and gates, the front building, two of the towers, the northwest section of cells, separate cells for 'female convicts,' and the kitchen." The Board of Inspectors believed they could begin admitting inmates without jeopardizing the silence and isolation required by the Pennsylvania system while the construction was not yet finished.[13] Why the designation of female convicts is put in quotation marks in the contemporary sources of the Commissioners Proceedings and Board of Inspectors' Minutes should be considered. The quotation marks make it seem as if women's presence in the prison is an annoyance or a joke that officials simply had to tolerate. Alternatively, the author may not have viewed these women as "feminine" at all and that the use of quotations demonstrated a judgment of their loss or lack of feminine virtues from committing crimes. Either case indicates that the women were not seen as equal to the male convicts either in terms of a threat to society or importance to prison officials. This posture toward women sets the stage for disciplinary problems when it comes to female inmates.

Problems quickly arose at Western State. The Pennsylvania penal code indicated that inmates needed to be put to hard labor, which was difficult to achieve when the inmates were also supposed to be subjected to solitary confinement in small cells. Any hard labor would have to be performed in groups, undermining the idea of isolating prisoners. Furthermore, the goal of silence was not achieved at Western State. Tocqueville declared that the prison's construction "is so defective, that it is very easy to hear in one cell

what is going on in another; so that each prisoner found in the communication with his neighbour a daily recreation."[14]

In 1830, warden John Patterson also noted the architecture problems at
Western State, declaring that, "the cells being arranged in a circular form,
only a part can be seen at one view, and when several convicts are unlocked
for the purpose of labour or exercise . . . some of them are necessarily a
part of the time out of the view of the overseer," which presented a major
problem in controlling the inmate population. The warden got permission
from the state legislature in 1833 to reconstruct the prison along the lines of
John Haviland's radial Eastern State Penitentiary, which had opened in 1829,
using Haviland as the architect for this new structure. The new cells allowed
for better light and ventilation and provided enough space for the inmates
to be employed in labor in their cells.[15] Once completed, the new penitentiary worked more efficiently as an institution of solitary confinement.

Eastern State Penitentiary must have learned from the early tribulations
of Western State as their architectural design was much different. An imposing building, Eastern State dominated the landscape of Philadelphia. The
building's exterior design was meant to "impart a grave, severe, and awful
character."[16] Imposing stone walls, which surrounded the cell blocks, left the
public curious and fearful of what happened inside. To those condemned
to experience the penitentiary as inmates, the prison became a monument
to terror and the unknown.

The outside wall was approximately thirty feet high and the walls and
floors were made of stone, two feet thick in order to prevent escape. Inside
the walls, in the "centre of the great courtyard is an observatory, whence
long corridors, seven in number, radiate. On each side of these corridors,
the cells are situated each at right angles to them, and communicating with
them only by small openings, for the purpose of supplying the prisoner with
food." The radial design allowed one "to command a view of every prisoner
without his knowledge or observation." Each cell, for light and ventilation,
had a narrow skylight, known as "dead eyes" or the "eye of God." One might
view these skylights as tantalizing for the inmates, always having a view of
freedom, but never being able to reach it while incarcerated. Furthermore,
the religious connotation of the moniker "eye of God" symbolized God's
omnipresent observation of the inmates. Each prisoner was also provided
with "a yard attached to each cell on the ground floor . . . [and] in the second
story each prisoner is allowed an additional cell or bed room" to provide

FIGURE 2 Exterior facade of Eastern State Penitentiary. Photo by author, July 2008.

FIGURE 3 Cell in Eastern State Penitentiary with "dead eye." Photo by author, July 2008.

exercise space.[17] Great pains were taken in the design of this prison to give inmates a chance to reform through the isolated and sparse accommodations. Even so, women in Eastern State Penitentiary figured out ways to use the penitentiary's design to their advantage and thwarted prison protocols.

Inmate Daily Life

From the outset of the prisons' existence, protocols were put in place to order the daily lives of the inmates. Little is known about the daily lives of those at Western State. One description of the penitentiary notes that male inmates wore coarse linen shirts, trousers, and roundabouts (a type of short jacket) in the summer and woolen or linsey garments in the winter. Women wore clothing "of the same materials." Furthermore, their diet included one pound of bread and one pound of coarse meat broth on Sundays and Wednesdays, one quart of Indian meal mush with a quarter pint of molasses on Mondays and Fridays, and a pound of bread and a quart of potatoes on Tuesdays, Thursdays, and Saturdays.[18]

Detailed descriptions of the rules at Eastern State Penitentiary provide a more comprehensive portrait of the inmates' experiences, especially at the outset of one's incarceration. Upon arrival, the inmate was examined by the prison physician for health concerns, and then the warden and overseers examined the new inmate to familiarize the officials with the inmates' stature, appearance, and background as well as any physical marks that may serve as identification. After this initial admission process, the inmate was "then clothed in the uniform of the prison, a hood or cap is drawn over his face," and his is taken to his cell where "the bandage is removed from his eyes, and he is interrogated as to his former life." The inmate learned the prison rules and was "then locked up and left to the salutary admonition of a reproving conscience, and the reflections which solitude usually produce."[19] The steps toward rehabilitation started immediately for the prisoners, as the process of admission had the effect of stripping the inmate's former life, even including their wardrobe.

The food at Eastern State consisted of one pint of coffee or cocoa for breakfast; "¾ pound of beef or ½ pound of pork, one pint of soup," and potatoes or rice for the midday meal; and for supper "as much Indian mush as they please to take, one half gallon of molasses per month, salt whenever asked for, and vinegar as a favour, occasionally. Turnips and cabbage in the form of crout [kraut] is sometimes distributed. The daily allowance of bread is one pound of wheat or rye. This is certainly an ample ration, and more than can be consumed by the majority of convicts."[20] Unlike the excerpt for Western State, which described only briefly the clothing of female inmates, similar reports of Eastern State do not describe the clothing of women. Furthermore, often only male pronouns were used to describe inmates. Although there was a growing, but still small, population of female inmates at Eastern as the nineteenth century progressed, they were almost invisible to those individuals describing the prison and its protocols. Female inmates remained an afterthought in the prisons throughout the century, yet records reveal that women played an active role in shaping their incarceration, making the jobs of prison officials quite difficult.

EARLY PENITENTIARY DISCIPLINARY BREAKDOWN

While it may seem from the architectural designs and strict rules of the penitentiaries that prison officials allowed for solid control over inmates, especially after Western State worked to rectify its initial failings, prison officials of both institutions were not ready to deal with a female population, however small. In the prisons' descriptions, the female inmates were merely afterthoughts to the larger male population, indicating that prison officials had not really considered what to do with women who were sentenced to their institutions or were uncomfortable with having women in the prison—which explains in part why female offenders' treatment was so inconsistent across the state. Almost everything was described in terms of the male inmate, with only rare references to the female convicts. Even passing comments regarding female inmates, like Western's "separate cells for 'female convicts,'" seem almost derisive.

Prison records indicate that efforts were made from the outset at Western State Penitentiary to provide cells for the female convicts, illustrating some level of awareness of the need to treat them differently. Isolation, in theory, could enable officials to treat female inmates in the same manner as the males without having to designate separate cells. In practice, however, this was not the case. Less than a year after Western State opened, on April 2, 1827, convict Hiram Lindsay escaped from its confines. It was later discovered that Lindsay was aided by a "colored woman" who from "feelings of humanity, on the part of her Keepers was not confined to her cell." Only one woman was in the prison at the time: Maria Penrose, twenty-one, born in Huntingdon

County, Pennsylvania, and described as having a yellow complexion with black hair and eyes. She arrived at the Penitentiary on September 6, 1826, on a sentence of two years for larceny committed in Bedford County. She served a little over one year and was discharged on December 1, 1827.[21]

Penrose was a typical female convict in Western State Penitentiary: she was young, African American, born in Pennsylvania, and convicted of larceny. Penrose's action illustrates not only the early failings of the penitentiary's design, but also the issues employees had dealing with female inmates. In this case, the woman appeared to evoke sympathy from the keepers or did not post much of a violent threat to the keepers or the security of the prison and was allowed the privilege of being out of her cell. The special treatment demonstrates the struggles prison officials had enacting the harsh discipline of the Pennsylvania system on female inmates because they may have not have appeared threatening in the eyes of the employees. Furthermore, since she was the only female inmate at the time, the employees may not have felt it necessary to lock her up. In any case, it was an active choice of the prison employees to let her out of her cell. The fact that she was out at all presented a major problem to the institution when she facilitated Hiram Lindsay's escape and indicated a failure on the part of the keepers to help Penrose reform her behavior by keeping her in a cell for individual reflection.

In a place where anonymity and isolation was to be the norm, this escape can also be interpreted as Penrose's showing pity and compassion toward a fellow inmate. Maybe she felt that her quasi freedom in the prison enabled her to help Lindsay in his escape and provide him with his own freedom. Penrose manipulated her privilege from the keepers to help thwart the system. While we do not know whether she aided Lindsay out of compassion for him or whether she had intentions aimed at hindering penitentiary discipline further, such as letting more inmates free or escaping herself, her actions indicate that some prisoners had the opportunity and the capacity to work against their punishers. Penrose used her advantage of being the sole female inmate to act against the prison system.

The evidence that penitentiary officials across the state struggled to know how to deal with female inmates becomes more defined when examining the 1835 legislative investigation into practices at Eastern State. The investigation looked into several issues that had arisen in the early years of the institution's existence, including the main indictment of cruel punishments inflicted on inmates. A different charge, however, is of interest regarding female inmates: "A frequent and illegal practice in the treatment of convicts by the warden, of departing from, and in effect disregarding, the sentences of the courts of justice: relaxing their severity, commuting their inflictions, or evading their real meaning; thus substituting his individual caprice or discretion for the decisions of the law, and defeating the regularity and precision which ought to characterize the penitentiary system."[22] This particular charge and the testimony regarding the offenses implicated females more so than male inmates, suggesting again that penitentiary officials struggled to deal equitably with women prisoners, leading to disorder in the prison and an unruly existence for the women.

This issue of differential treatment of female inmates is ironic, considering that prison officials and reformers discussed the plight of female inmates and were well aware of the problems that might arise in treating them differently than their male counterparts. Thomas McElwee, a representative in the state legislature from Bedford County, in his report on the investigation discusses what to do with female offenders and critiques the criminal justice system: "The disproportion of male and female convicts defies calculation when it is supposed the number of offences committed by females, are nearly equal to those committed by males—and the atrocious nature of those offences altogether on a parity. The omission to convict them must be attributed to the misplaced and criminal sympathy of courts and juries."[23] This passage indicates a sense that not only did prisons have a difficult time treating female inmates the same as men, but so did judges and juries.

McElwee argued that "sex or condition should not sanctify crime" and that the actual offense should be the sole reason for conviction or acquittal. The author declared, "I have no faith in the ethereal qualities of the feminine gender, and believe much evil has accrued to society, by stuffing their heads with the idea, that they are angels, goddesses . . . when their faults, their follies, and their vices drive men mad, and produce fatal disruptions in families." It seems that since the prevailing social thought was that women were paragons of virtue and morality, many people had a difficult time believing that they could commit serious offenses. This struggle to comprehend the actions and motivations of female criminals translated to difficulties in punishing them when convicted. McElwee was clearly frustrated with this general sentiment toward women. His call to treat female offenders equally to men demonstrates a progressive view of women in the antebellum decades. McElwee suggested that society should not "under any circumstance, justify a crime in a female which we condemn in a male."[24] The fact that there were only four women incarcerated during the investigation at Eastern State seems to prove his point. The table below shows the annual admissions of males and females.[25] It is interesting that this discourse on female offenders precedes the testimony of the investigation, because what happened inside the walls of Eastern State indicated that female inmates, particularly in their limited numbers, did not experience the penitentiary in the way the original developers had intended and often took advantage of their situation to either improve their lot or make trouble for the keepers. Just as women strove to influence their courtroom experience using notions of propriety or committed crimes to challenge social limitations that women faced, women in prison used their wits, personality, and behaviors to wield some power over their incarceration. They refused to be viewed as weak or powerless.

The testimony of the investigation provides details of the experiences of the first four female inmates. Amy Rogers, inmate 73, and Henrietta Johnson, inmate 74, were admitted in April of 1831 for manslaughter. Rogers was sentenced to three years, and Johnson was to serve six years. In December 1831, two more women entered Eastern State. Inmates 100 and 101, Ann Hinson and Eliza Anderson were sentenced to two years each for manslaughter. It is possible these two women worked together to commit the crime since they had the same sentence and entered on the same day.[26] All women were of African descent. Amy Rogers was a washerwoman. Ann Hinson and Eliza Anderson were married and each had children, and Henrietta Johnson and Ann Hinson were noted as being able to read. All four were relatively young, only in their twenties.[27] Aside from their crimes, these women represented typical female inmates. The crime of manslaughter sets these four women apart as few women were sent to the prison for violent crimes; most were incarcerated for property crime.

Several employees gave testimony to the charges, and many noted the involvement of these four women in actions that helped lead to the investigation. The women's central roles in the charges indicate a breakdown of prison discipline and demonstrate that the female population was not treated the same as the male inmates. The investigation reveals that women, when they could, took advantage of this more lenient, differential treatment

TABLE 5. Admissions to Eastern State Penitentiary

Year	Total admitted	# of females	White females	Black females
1829–30	58	0	0	0
1831	58	4	0	4
1832	24	0	0	0
1833	77	0	0	0
1834	118	0	0	0
1835	137	18	—	—
1836	143	11	3	8
1837	161	3	1	2
1838	178	14	6	8
1839	179	8	3	5
1840	139	7	2	5
1841	126	7	1	6
1842	142	3	3	0
1843	156	7	2	5
1844	138	12	7	5
1845	143	12	6	6
1846	117	7	3	4
1847	124	6	1	5
1848	121	5	2	3
1849	128	4	2	2
1850	150	10	5	5
1851	147	18	12	6
1852	126	5	4	1
1853	117	6	5	1
1854	124	5	2	3
1855	146	12	11	1
1856	146	11	9	2
1857	237	15	8	7
1858	207	6	3	3

Source: Annual Reports of the Inspectors of the Eastern State Penitentiary of Pennsylvania, 1829–58.

to have some control over their experiences as inmates. Although they likely had little choice in what they were asked to do by prison officials, the women still could shape their experience by using these opportunities to improve their time as convicts. One gatekeeper, James Torry, told the investigating committee that the warden, Samuel Wood, used as "his own housekeeper, one colored woman, a prisoner," likely Ann Hinson. Other female inmates also cooked in the warden's private kitchen.[28]

The fact that the only four women incarcerated in the penitentiary were central to the investigation raises the issue of prisoner agency. Because the prison records were written from the keepers' and reformers' perspectives, the documents do not indicate whether these four women manipulated the employees into receiving their special privileges. Suggesting this in the records would indicate a failure of the prison system to control the inmates or a prevailing attitude that women inmates were unthreatening. By focusing the charges on a few individuals, such as the warden and Mrs. Blundin, the official records make it seem that the inmates were treated more like pawns of these few individuals as opposed to the inmates wielding power over their own imprisonment. To this point, Leslie Patrick suggests that "it might be argued that misogyny converged with racism to render Hinson invisible and therefore even more depraved in the historical imagination than Mrs. Blundin or any of the other individuals charged in the scandal. The neglect of Ann Hinson's presence in the penitentiary and the testimony condemning her behavior have perpetuated the belief that female inmates in predominately male prisons were inherently culpable and beyond the pale of reform."[29] At the same time, however, it is entirely possible that the women did manipulate the system in some way, but that the details of the manipulation are simply silent in the records. Even if they did not scheme to receive this special treatment and were simply told what they would be doing to aid Mrs. Blundin or the warden, the women likely would not have complained about their lenient treatment. They were savvy enough to understand that they should take advantage of these privileges however they arose. Because of the employees' choice to treat the women differently, inmates like Ann Hinson experienced a less stringent incarceration. It was to their benefit to go along with how the employees treated them. As a result of their lived experience in the prison, these female inmates enter the historical record through the legislative investigation, albeit briefly.

Ann Hinson was not the only female inmate to be named in the investigation. Another employee, Leonard Phleger, noted that Rogers and Johnson each had special privileges, such as being allowed out of their cells to cook. Phleger stated that Rogers received extra provisions, including "apples, eggs, roast beef, ham, apple butter, preserves, milk." She was also seen out of her cell, doing washing for the warden and other prison employees. Considering that she was noted in the descriptive registers as having been a washerwoman, this may not be surprising. That she was out of her cell and interacting with prison employees to perform personal tasks for them on a consistent basis goes against prison protocols.[30]

In other instances, female inmates drank liquor and attended parties. Inmate 100, "a black woman by the name of Anne . . . a convict, was present when I [employee William Griffith] went down. She appeared to be sitting looking on—dressed in a calico dress with a turban about her head." He later noted that after one of these parties, a different inmate, "a black woman by the name of Eliza . . . was so much intoxicated that she was scarcely able to walk alone—I put her into her cell—continued to be a good deal troublesome all the time I stayed up, knocking and crying." The acquisition of liquor seemed to be a continuing problem. Griffith noted that on one occasion, Ann was found "lying drunk in the kitchen, when they went for the supper or dinner . . . there was some stir about this—the watchman's wife was charged with giving her the liquor."[31] By allowing these women to acquire liquor and to attend social gatherings, prison officials were not breaking the vices of these inmates and instead were providing them with special privileges, which ran counter to the path to rehabilitation laid out by the penitentiary system.

While many of the instances detailed in the investigation show the women going along with the prison employees' expectations or requests, Amy Rogers complained to inspectors about the prison. She told judge Charles S. Coxe that "she had been compelled to wash clothes of the officers that were soiled with venereal matter, and medical substances, designed for that disease . . . that she was apprehensive that the disease might be communicated to her—if there was a fracture of the skin while she was washing." The complaint continued that Mrs. Blundin, the watchman's wife who was supposedly in charge of the washing and was informally in charge of the female inmates, went to Amy in her cell, "exhibited to her her person with the mark of the disease and asked her to assist her in washing it, and in applying the remedies."[32] These requests went beyond individual, artisanal work that all inmates were supposed to complete. Not only was she asked to do personal laundry for employees, which was an abuse of the system, she felt her health was being put in danger by Mrs. Blundin's requests regarding venereal disease treatments. On a later date, Judge Coxe visited Amy again. Once he arrived at her cell, he testified:

> She was very much affected—in tears and crying—she alleged that she had been taken out of her cell, and put into this one without a yard, and that it all arose from her having communicated those facts to me—that two men had come into her washing apartment to put up a stove, that one of them was a first cousin of Mrs. Blundin's, and that they had contrived to make a quarrel with her—had attacked her about the charge she had made—had roundly taken her to task, and so on—that she answered them pretty sharply—they had complained to Mr. Wood, and Mr. Wood had had her locked up in this cell.[33]

Amy Rogers's complaint suggests that officials punished her for her insistence that she was being treated unfairly. Her discussions with Judge Coxe imply that Rogers knew her rights as an inmate. She was aware that what was being asked of her could be seen as unethical, dangerous even, and used the opportunity to make her claim to Judge Coxe, who was charged with making sure that the prison was run in an ethical manner and to "listen to any complaints that may be made of oppression or ill conduct of the persons so employed, examine into the truth thereof, and proceed therein when the complaint is well founded."[34] This is one of the rare occasions of an inmate initiating action against the prison system, as opposed to simply following orders or taking advantage of privileges given to them as women by the keepers. One must consider the possibility that she may have been trying to manipulate Coxe in the hopes of reducing her sentence or receiving extra privileges for her troubles, yet the fact that she realized that she was being treated unfairly and took it on herself to make the complaint demonstrates individual power and agency. The prison employees, no matter Rogers's intentions, did not approve of her discussions with Coxe and punished her, suggesting that they realized their actions may have been unethical and went against the procedures of the Pennsylvania system.

Interestingly, although details of Rogers's experiences made it into the public record, Judge Coxe censored information from Ann Hinson. Leslie Patrick notes that Hinson revealed information to Coxe before she left prison, but in his testimony, Coxe deemed the words "too indecent to repeat." For whatever reason, Coxe "chose not to make the point that the institution and its employees did nothing on behalf of the female inmates" and it is clear "that there was more to her story than officials disclosed or cared to recognize."[35] Rogers and Hinson, in telling Coxe about events in the prison, regardless of whether their information made it into the public record, demonstrated an awareness of the control they still had over their lives, even if they were inmates. They had the potential to influence the testimony, and knew that what they were experiencing was a violation at some level of their rights and worth as individuals. While their testimony might not have changed their incarceration experience drastically, their words ultimately had more long-term implications concerning reforms in prison protocol for the institution after the investigation was completed.

William Parker, the sole inmate to testify at the investigation, declared that Ann Hinson was out of her cell often, telling a story about her going to get a light from him for Mrs. Blundin. He stated, "I asked her how she dared to come there, knowing it to be contrary to the rules of the institution—she said Mrs. Blundin sent her to get a light. I gave her a light and told her if she ever came back again, I would inform Mr. Wood of it. I saw her repeatedly after that—on Mr. Wood's side—could not help seeing her without shutting my eyes."[36] This event indicates yet another instance of the employees not caring to uphold the protocols of the institution, and that a female inmate was used in running errands for the employees.

Parker continued his testimony, noting that he had seen "convict females with other than prison clothes on standing at Mr. Wood's gate." He testified, "I have seen three or four female prisoners—one dancing and swearing at Mr. Wood's gate. She was a dreadful wicked woman—saw her repeatedly—both morning and afternoon—I heard her swearing . . . I cannot say whether she was drunk or sober—saw her more than three times three, and three times that. I don't really think I should know her again—the dress makes a great difference."[37] Not only were female inmates out of their cells, but they were not forced to wear prison clothing. This is a substantial privilege considering that prison clothing was part of the rehabilitative process that removed the individuality of the inmate to evoke personal reform and protect anonymity.

The effect of being out of the cells, interacting with prison officials in a casual, social manner, and being permitted to have liquor, different clothing, and extra provisions does not disconnect them from the outside world or evoke penitence. These inmates were not forced, as dictated by prison protocol, to stay in their cells and be in constant silent reflection. Prison officials actively ignored their duty to help these inmates rehabilitate, and the female inmates complied with what they were told or allowed to do during their incarceration. Did the minimal female population cause employees not to care about upholding prison rules? Did their race have anything to do with their differential treatment? It seems that the answer to these questions is yes to some extent. The small population probably made it easier for employees to treat them differently than the male inmates, yet similarly to one another in the fact that the entire female population was out of their cells performing duties for prison employees. Like Maria Penrose in Western State Penitentiary, the four women incarcerated at Eastern State during its early years experienced special treatment, presumably because of their sex. That they completed domestic tasks indicates that employees considered female inmates suited for this work and regularly asked them to perform these duties.

That all four were black women suggests it might have been easier for employees to use these women essentially as servants, especially in the years before the Civil War when many of the city's black population worked in menial positions. In 1820, the black population of Philadelphia made up only 11.88 percent of the total city population. In 1840, it fell to 11.21 percent; and by 1850, it had dropped again to 8.8 percent. Nearly one-third of the black population worked as servants. This number suggests that prison officials may have assumed these four female inmates were suited to domestic work and may have used their race as a reason to justify such exploitation, in addition to the expectation that women were suited for domestic tasks.[38]

Even with these suggestions, one must not forget that all four women were convicted of manslaughter, suggesting that the criminal justice system viewed them as dangerous at some level.[39] Since prison employees gave these women special privileges, it appears that the employees rather viewed these women as unthreatening, or at the very least less dangerous than a male inmate who had committed a similar crime, illustrating the double standard which so frustrated McElwee and which impeded efforts to reform female inmates. Yet, it is natural that these female inmates would take advantage of the freedoms and liberties the employees afforded them in the prison—it offered them an easy way to challenge prison protocol, without necessarily rebelling against it actively. They understood their place in prison society and took advantage of opportunities when they presented themselves.

Ironically, it was not until after the 1835 investigation that a female matron was officially hired to take care of female inmates. Although the Board of Inspectors approved adding a matron in 1831, no one was hired to fill the job. Instead, Mrs. Blundin informally acted in that capacity.[40] The experiences of the women inmates under Mrs. Blundin's supervision and their testimony given to Judge Coxe changed the manner in which the prison would deal with female inmates moving forward. Mrs. Harriet Hall was hired in 1835 as the first official matron, and all the female inmates were moved to the same section of a cell block. Employing a female matron would, hopefully, remove any discomfort male prison employees might have felt about housing women in the penitentiary. The Board of Inspectors' annual report for 1835 stated, "In consequence of the increase of female prisoners during the last year, the board directed the appointment by the warden of a female overseer. In the improvement already manifested among this class of prisoners, and from the christian [sic] character and discipline of Mrs. H. Hall, who has been appointed to this office, we feel confident that many of these unhappy females will be reclaimed from vice and wretchedness, and restored to the paths of virtue and true happiness." A few years after this investigation, a select committee of Pennsylvania's House of Representatives was sent to examine the management of Eastern State Penitentiary and noted that they "were much pleased with the peculiar neatness of the female ward. The appearance of both the cells and inmates, clearly indicate the good qualities of the lady who has the care and superintendence of them, and strongly exemplifies the propriety of having a female overseer over female prisoners."[41] Much had changed in the government of female convicts at Eastern State after the 1835 investigation exposed the institution's severe disciplinary flaws when it came to dealing with female inmates and treating them according to the penitentiary's disciplinary program.

Even with Mrs. Hall entrenched as matron, prison officials' perceptions of female inmates failed to improve and remained rather indifferent to their plight. Brief notations gave glimpses of the females' experiences in Eastern State after the investigation, and these sources seem to indicate the ongoing issue of officials not knowing how to handle these women. In August of 1837, minutes of the Board of Inspectors records that warden Samuel Wood was at a loss about what to do with Ann Steel. Steel was sent to Eastern State a year earlier and, after a month of incarceration, gave birth to a baby. She kept the child in the cell with her. This went on for almost a year when Wood determined, "I have thought best to bring the matter to the notice of the Board."[42] If this was so problematic, why leave the matter alone for the better part of a year? There is no indication of what the matron thought of the matter, or how it was resolved, but the excerpt indicates that female prisoners continued to present issues to prison staff with which men were rather ill equipped to deal.

Inmate 647, Margaret Beard, a young African American, died at Eastern State after an incarceration of just over two years. While she was admitted in "imperfect health," she experienced ongoing maladies including catarrh, diarrhea, and rheumatism. Upon her death it was noted in prison records, rather coldly, that "she died after an imprisonment of 2 yrs, 1 mo [sic], 11 days during the whole of which she was more or less indisposed & mostly on the sick list."[43] In both this example and that of Ann Steel, it seems as though the women were almost viewed as burdensome on the prison, whether it was having an infant in the cell or needing extended medical care. There is no indication of the possibility that these women needed special or different attention than the other prisoners, suggesting a lack of awareness or care for the differentiated treatment for inmates.

Western State Penitentiary took even longer to appoint a matron for female inmates, even though the initial problems with Maria Penrose occurred almost immediately after the institution opened its doors. Amazingly, even though there were women at Western State from its inception, there was no matron employed until 1865. Over that span of almost forty years, over one hundred women had been incarcerated at the institution. Until September 1865, "no matron had ever been employed to take charge of the female convicts." These women had been cared for by an "overseer who was obliged to perform duties altogether unsuitable for men towards women." The "advantages and even necessity of having a matron to take charge of the female prisoners are so obvious that it is matter of surprise that there never has been one before. It is altogether impossible for a man to exercise that surveillance over females which is essentially necessary to prevent improprieties among themselves and reprehensible familiarities with others." The first matron was Mary McPike. The board noted with happiness "her fidelity and good management. Much better order has prevailed, and a considerable amount of work in making garments and kitting socks for the prisoners has in a measure been cheerfully performed, without loss of material as was formerly the case." The board also reported that they "hoped that the Christian example and instruction of Miss McPike has exerted a wholesome restraint upon the conduct of those under her care. Not the least favourable effect has been the avoidance of all access to their cells by men."[44]

These excerpts, while brief in length, suggest the rampant problems Western State Penitentiary faced by the 1860s, and presumably even before then, with having female inmates in their care. Why the prison did not work to employ a matron for the female inmates earlier is unknown, particularly when its counterpart in Philadelphia appointed one in 1835. Once Miss McPike was hired, the existence of the female inmates probably improved in some ways—especially with regard to protection from male inmates or guards. While there was apparently now order and routine in the women's department, as exemplified by inmates being employed at sewing and knitting projects that would provide skills for a life outside of prison, the matron's presence among the female inmates ultimately provided social control over the inmates. Although board meeting minutes suggested that Miss McPike offered lessons in good conduct and a Christian example to the inmates, there are no records that detail how the inmates reacted to her authority. Officials and reformers paint an idyllic picture of the women's experiences under the eye of Miss McPike, but it would be surprising if all prisoner resistance ceased after she was hired. Perhaps most telling of all the changes made is the implied sexual activity that was occurring in the women's cells before the matron arrived. The suggestion that there were "improprieties" and "reprehensible familiarities" occurring in the prison while the women were under male supervision leads to more questions regarding the apparent sexual activity, as does the notation that once a matron was employed, men could not access the women's cells. Were male guards exploiting the female inmates? Were male inmates allowed to have sex with the female inmates? To what extent were the women possibly complicit in these activities? To what extent were the women seeking ways to exert control over their incarceration, using their bodies as leverage?

Without more information from the sources, it is difficult to know the extent to which sexual exploitation may have been occurring among the female inmates at Western State Penitentiary.

The lack of attention paid to the female inmates in the state's penitentiaries did not cause the women simply to accept their situation. At Eastern State Penitentiary, many found ways to resist the institution's attempts to ignore their existence. Although the four women who played so central a role in the 1835 investigation in their own way resisted the prison's isolation by taking advantage of certain opportunities that allowed them to be out of their cells and communicate with others, most inmates had to employ other ways of resisting their neglect and the institution's overwhelming isolation. Because female inmates often went unmentioned in the Board of Inspectors' annual reports, records must be gleaned carefully for evidence concerning their experiences inside the penitentiary. The results show how these women found ways to resist their incarceration.[45]

Women often broke the rules of the prison as a form of resistance. Women made noise, vandalized work equipment, and broke furniture. Hester Luff, who had been arrested for larceny, was a nuisance during her stay at Eastern State. She was punished for "shouting and disturbing the other prisoners" and, upon her release, when she complained that the matron had treated her badly, the warden responded, "The error in the matron in this case *was too much kindness* to the prisoner who was unruly and profane." Other women broke furniture in their cell, pretended to be ill to get out of work, and destroyed working equipment as a means to resist the prison's protocols. Marian Wilson, convicted of murder, intentionally spilled "dirty water" under her cell door, which kept the hallway stone floor, and likely her cell floor, "constantly wet & dirty."[46] These women used whatever means they could to not fall victim to the authoritarian institution insistent upon controlling their charges. Although the intention was to reform, the inmates who resisted reveal through their actions that reform was difficult to complete and that the prison's regulations often led to resistance.

Prison writings, such as letters and poems, like the letter mentioned at the beginning of the chapter, provided another way that female inmates resisted the anonymity of the prison system. Inmate writings, albeit incredibly rare, show an attempt to hold onto their personalities and maintain a connection with the outside world, something that prison officials, at least initially, wanted to avoid in order to carry out a thorough reformation project. Julia Wilt represents one such woman who appeared to write to a benevolent female visitor who befriended her. Her letter, recounting her thankfulness for such a friendship, was published as a pamphlet, *An Account of Julia Moore*, by the Female Prison Association after her death in 1844.[47]

Although one might question the authenticity of this letter, since there are so few documents regarding female inmates or coming from the inmates' perspectives, one has to think about this letter as being, to some extent, genuine. Prison policies dictated that "none but the official visitors can have any communication with the convicts, nor shall any visitor whatever be permitted to deliver to or receive from any of the convicts, any letter or message whatever" as enacted by Article VII of "Rules for the Government of the Penitentiary," passed on April 23, 1829.[48] In the 1844 annual report for Eastern State, however, there is an indication that letter writing in some instances was allowed. The warden wrote, "I have frequently witnessed with pleasure the pride and exultation a convict has evinced on handing out his first letter, written to his parents or relations, as a proof of having attained that art [writing] in prison." This is the first annual report to note that inmates sent out letters, indicating that the early rule of prohibiting communication with the outside world was at some point not enforced by prison officials. Four years later, in the 1848 annual report of Western State, the moral instructor writes, "The privilege of corresponding by letter with absent friends once in three months, has been granted to the prisoners during the year. This favor was forfeited by any violation of the rules of the prison. Whilst then it contributed to make better the heart of the outcast convict, by the softening and humanizing intercourse with beloved objects, it also aided in the preservation of order and good conduct within the prison."[49]

Letter writing created a connection to those who were free and thus could undo the strict isolation and anonymity that made the Pennsylvania system unique. The excerpts from the annual reports indicate that officials were shifting their attitude toward connecting with the outside world. Some officials now viewed letter writing as aiding in the reformation process as opposed to hindering it. A more cynical suggestion is that letters were allowed to be produced because officials needed to promote their prison system, and that letters of inmates extolling the virtues of the penitentiary might help toward that end. Because so few letters from inmates in these early days survived, or ever existed, the appearance of letter writing may be a combination of these possibilities. In any case, women who could write letters for some reason refused to disappear into the anonymity of the penitentiary system. Letter writing allowed them a sense of control and a sense of freedom, even though they were locked in a prison.

One set of letters and poems from a female inmate at Eastern State illustrates how writing provided a creative outlet for prisoners to help them weather their incarceration and resist the anonymous environment of the penitentiary. This set of writings appears to have avoided interference from reformers. In early 1862, a female inmate, Elizabeth Velora Elwell, sentenced to eighteen months for larceny, wrote a series of letters to another prisoner, Albert Green Jackson. These are valuable sources regarding prison life in the mid-nineteenth century and indicate again that Eastern State struggled with prisoner separation and discipline. Writing created another way for inmates to express their feelings about life and incarceration and to resist the isolating effects of prison. On April 18, 1862, Elwell wrote, "It is with in my lonseome sell that I take my pen in hand to inform you that my heart was very sad after leaving you to night but hope to see you every day but my dear Albert there is a time coming when we will not have to run when any one is coming [sic]." She warns him not to "let them hear you speak of me my dear. There is but one thing that you must be carfull not to let them catch you standing at the gate for they will mistrust us."[50] Not only is Elwell able to send and receive letters from another inmate at the penitentiary, these two appear to have conducted a love affair, hidden from prison officials. It is almost impossible to know the extent of this affair. While it is possible that it was a mutual affection, with perhaps a physical component, it could also be that Elwell saw Jackson from a distance and developed this infatuation, creating a one-sided "relationship." Without more context for the letters, we will likely never know, but what these sources demonstrate is Elwell's concerted effort to remain autonomous, to some extent, while incarcerated. She held on to feelings, emotions, and allowed herself this relationship, in whatever form, to give her a sense of control over her imprisonment.

By the 1860s, some of the stricter rules of the penitentiary had been alleviated, as excerpts in these letters indicate that Elwell worked during the day out of her cell. It is likely that prison officials made changes in the style of prison labor to be more profitable than the original plan of individual artisanal work in the cells. Furthermore, the strict rules of silence, isolation, and anonymity were increasingly difficult to maintain, thus resulting as early as the late 1840s in a relaxation in prison protocols. Even with these changes to prison discipline, interactions between male and female inmates were still strictly forbidden.[51]

In addition to these letters, Elwell penned poems in her cell, such as the following verse:

> It is very sad to be so lonely
> And far from friends or home
> But may my love proove to be true
> To cheer my sad hart ever more [sic][52]

Although the letters from Elizabeth Elwell depict the desire to be free from prison, the poetry provides a different perspective on her emotions and the role of writing in her attempt to maintain a sense of self. This is a dark poem, one that illustrates her sadness at being incarcerated, as she mentioned several times the struggles she faced with loneliness and knowing that friends and family were far away from her. This poem provides an intimate glimpse at the impact of prison life on inmates: sadness, gloom, broken hearts, and despair. Poetry became a way to verbalize her feelings, and the writing of it also provided a distraction for a few moments from her incarceration. The poem is interesting also in that it shows, along with the letters, that she has found solace in her incarceration with her friend Albert. It appears that the relationship was a way for Elwell to have something to keep her emotionally connected not only to herself but someone else during her sentence, especially during periods of homesickness and loneliness. Through these writings and the relationship, Elwell maintained individual dignity and self-hood. In an institution determined to strip inmates of these characteristics, writings (whether sanctioned or not) allowed them some type of control over their thoughts and feelings. Inmates' writings demonstrated that they sought to maintain their identities in an institution that strove to break them down.

———

The small numbers of female inmates in these early penitentiaries resulted in the women being treated differently than the male inmates. The women's disciplinary and reformation needs were often ignored, resulting in what appears to be a warehousing effect in some instances. The lack of discussion regarding female inmates in the prison reports indicates that rehabilitation was limited to male prisoners and that employees were not comfortable having women in the same institution. Yet, "the neglect with which the unfortunate and sinning female is treated" provides only one perspective on the way women experienced Pennsylvania's prisons before the Civil War.[53] Although their treatment was often rife with inconsistency and lack of rehabilitation, the fact that the four original female inmates of Eastern State, all convicted of manslaughter, spent a great deal of time out of their cells, or that Maria Penrose had freedom to roam Western State, illustrates the struggle prison officials had with handling female prisoners, often resulting in more freedoms being given to this particular set of inmates, which women readily took advantage of to mold their incarceration experiences.

Yet, although prison officials made an active choice not to push for women's moral reform and often left female prisoners to their own devices or allowed them more freedom within the prison, the women were not necessarily treated worse than male inmates. The female inmates used the flexibility or leniency they had in their incarceration and worked against the prison system. The access to extra movement in the prison or additional privileges due to being a female inmate allowed women to experience a less harsh incarceration. Other women resisted the stripping effect of the prisons on their personal identities by refusing to become anonymous by writing and resisting prison protocol in various ways. They refused to succumb to a system insistent on making them powerless. When examining the experiences of female inmates, both the inmates' and the employees' actions undermined the Pennsylvania system's claim of utilizing the ideal form of punishment.

Francis Lieber suggested women ought to be treated in ways similar to male prisoners, without needing separate facilities. From the evidence of the prisons, it does not appear that employees tried very hard to test his theory and indicates a failure of the Pennsylvania system of discipline. Furthermore, prison inspectors simply did not want women in the same facilities, as their presence was "a disadvantage to the Men."[54] The small female population in the state penitentiary made it nearly impossible to treat women in the same manner as their male counterparts. This neglect toward their presence in the prison and disparate treatment suggested the need for separate facilities for female inmates if reformers hoped to rehabilitate female them. Furthermore, the evidence of resistance, thwarting prison protocol, and seizing a level of freedom or control through writing demonstrates that women were anything but passive victims in these penitentiary systems. Even with this resistance, while many states created female institutions in the late nineteenth century, Pennsylvania held out until 1913 to pass legislation to create a separate female institution.

CHAPTER 5

"No Kind Treatment Can Subdue the Prisoner"

Chaos and Female Resistance in the County Jails

In 1855, a murder case gripped communities in Sullivan County, Pennsylvania. John Kamm, a German immigrant, was convicted of killing John Veitengruber. Anna Maria Veitengruber, also an immigrant and Kamm's lover, was imprisoned for her part in the murder of her husband. Mrs. Veitengruber maintained her innocence and accused Kamm of being the sole killer. Claiming mental instability, she demanded a separate trial, only serving to delay her fate. She remained in the Sullivan County Jail, where the sheriff treated her kindly and "permitted her more liberties than he would have allowed another prisoner."[1] At some point during her incarceration, Mrs. Veitengruber took advantage of her privileges and escaped. She was never apprehended.

A reward advertisement was placed in the *Sullivan County Democrat* on November 23, 1858, providing twenty-five dollars for the person who returned Anna Maria Veitengruber to the authorities. According to the advertisement, she escaped on November 19, 1858. She was described as being "about thirty-seven years of age . . . with strongly marked features, and with light, thin short hair. She has a gray blue eye and a large mouth" and only spoke "the English language but very brokenly."[2] While we have very little information about Anna Maria's involvement in the murder, she must have felt that she would have been found guilty of involvement in the crime, whether it was because she felt like an outsider as an immigrant or because she was actually guilty. Instead of leaving her fate to a jury, she chose to take advantage of her lenient incarceration in the county jail and fled.

Veitengruber's experience in the Sullivan County prison offers just one example of the issues women incarcerated in county jails faced across Pennsylvania. Just like in the state prisons, women incarcerated in Pennsylvania's county prisons experienced neglect, and yet they often took advantage of this situation for their own benefit, just like their fellow inmates in the state penitentiaries. While the small number of women in the state penitentiaries accounted for their reformation being ignored by officials, in the county jails across the state female inmates experienced more visceral, physical forms of neglect but still found ways to resist. Women in the Philadelphia County Prison, for example, were subjected to a chaotic environment with large and fluctuating inmate populations prone to violence. Female inmates in smaller county prisons had to deal with poor, unhealthy conditions, perhaps due to lack of funding to support these inmates in the county jails. In many cases they were allowed to interact with male prisoners, with little regard for their health or moral well-being. In some cases, women endured violent punishments. Many found ways to exert power over their situations. In Veitengruber's case, she was allowed extra privileges by the sheriff, aligning all the factors for her to make her escape.

As in the penitentiaries, female inmates in the county prisons resisted becoming lost in the correctional system, often employing direct forms of opposition to their living conditions or taking advantage of the common attitude that female inmates were harmless or less troublesome in order to escape or to gain privileges. Some women violently resisted their incarceration, adding to the already endemic chaos found in county jails. Their intransigence took the form of vandalism, sassing employees, and sometimes committing self-harm. In these ways, women in county jails exhibited their identity and made their presence known, forcing officials to acknowledge the need for special treatment and reform programs for these women. Female inmates were anything but powerless. Although they were incarcerated and had limited freedom, they adapted their situation when they could to their advantage to improve or alleviate their imprisonment, to frustrate employees as a form of rebellion, and to avoid becoming a victim to the system. They insisted on being heard and seen. Even if they could not change their experience dramatically, their actions served to start conversations about reform and policy changes in the future, just as their counterparts in the state penitentiaries did.

County jails housed offenders of lesser crimes, those awaiting trial, and vagrants. These institutions exemplified the inconsistent treatment that female offenders experienced in Pennsylvania prisons. County prisons were described as buildings "in which are kept persons of every age, and of each sex and color; of every rank, fortune, education and character; some of whom are charged with no offence, but are held to secure their appearance as witnesses . . . others of whom are already convicted of trivial offences and are subjected to only a few weeks or months of detention." Compared to the large penitentiaries, which worked hard to maintain a rigid lifestyle for inmates in order to reform them, county jails failed to live up to this standard, making daily life in these institutions rather chaotic. Inspectors of the various prisons across the state realized "that the discipline and general efficiency of the large penitentiaries themselves, were to a serious extent neutralized by the influences operating upon the prisoners during their preliminary confinement in the county jails."[3] One can imagine that if penitentiary officials had a difficult time treating the small female population equitably, then county jails would struggle even more with their female offenders, and they often did.

PROBLEMS IN COUNTY JAILS

To understand the environment in which these women were incarcerated and resisted imprisonment, we need to look at the conditions they faced in these county-level facilities. During the 1830s and 1840s, numerous county jails in Pennsylvania were either built or rebuilt, in order to improve the situation of inmates and to promote efficient punishment, yet many counties could not afford such construction. William Parker Foulke, a notable Pennsylvania prison reformer, recounted the situation in numerous counties: "The sheriff himself feeds his prisoners well, often upon the same kind of food which his own family consumes. He lets them out of their rooms, and into the yard, reasonably often. . . . Besides, it is not his fault that the prisoners are together; he has only four or five rooms, and yet often there are twenty or thirty persons under commitment at one time—white and black, male and female, old and young." Foulke blamed the commissioners who built these prisons for the failure to provide enough space for the inmates, illustrating what desperate need there was for improved facilities. The Pennsylvania Prison Society asked the state to force counties to produce annual reports of these prison systems, so that they could be easily monitored. Unfortunately, very few counties complied, making it difficult to explore the daily workings of the various county prisons. It was not until 1851 when state legislation compelled county prisons to make solitary cells available for all inmates in an attempt to emulate the state penitentiaries' discipline.[4]

An 1839 report of Pennsylvania's Secretary of the Commonwealth regarding county prisons provides snippets of information on different institutions and illustrates the problems of inconsistency about which Foulke lamented. Bedford County Prison, for example, afforded inmates "straw beds, coverlets, and blankets" and meals that often consisted of "bread, meat, and coffee." The report indicated that no moral education was provided for the inmates. Chester County reported that "male and female prisoners are confined in separate apartments, having no communication whatever between them. The construction of the prison is such, that criminals and debtors—juvenile and old offenders—have to mingle together both day and night, all having the privilege of the yard from sunrise to sunset." This seems to indicate that although men and women were separated during the night, they could interact with one another during the day. Prisoners were given one pound of wheat bread per day. Erie County had a different form of discipline: "Males and females, criminals and debtors, are kept in separate apartments. Young and old offenders are kept separate when convenience permits. . . . Books furnished when requested, but are seldom asked for. Criminals generally allowed one hour in the yard each day. When criminals misbehave their shackles are generally increased, or they are committed for a short time to a dungeon connected with the prison." In Mifflin County, prisoners were given books if they desired, but "no particular means in use for the moral improvement of prisoners, other than that adopted at the discretion of the jailer" and inmates ate the same food as the jailer's family and were only given blankets for bedding.[5] The spectrum of conditions across the state in antebellum county prisons portrays the lack of consistency faced by inmates subjected to these jails. Like in the penitentiaries, men made up the majority of inmates in the country jails. When females were sent to the county jails, the failings of the facilities were often exacerbated, leading to some female inmates being treated differently than males, perhaps less like criminals, or being provided with enough liberty to vandalize, escape, or otherwise resist their incarceration. As was evident in the records of the state penitentiaries, women took advantage of these situations when they arose.

In Dorothea Dix's 1845 plea to the state legislature to create a state hospital for the insane, she recounted her visits to county prisons in search of insane prisoners and corroborates the inefficiency and inconsistency frowned on by Foulke and other reformers. In visiting Somerset County in southwestern Pennsylvania, she wrote, "In one apartment I found a man and woman; they had been tried for adultery, were found guilty, and sentenced to the county jail. . . . What moral benefit was derived by either the prisoners or the community by this, neither separate nor solitary confinement, I leave others to determine; but I think that a law prohibiting indiscriminate association of the male and female prisoners cannot be too soon promulgated and enforced."[6] There is no evidence that this jailer cared to enact punishment for the crime or push for reformation in behavior by separating these two.

In another instance, Elizabeth Harker, a woman convicted of murder and sentenced to hang in Huntingdon County, whose case was detailed in chapter 2, was also given special treatment, similar to Anna Maria Veitengruber's. Harker never hanged for her crime but remained incarcerated in the county jail. Sources indicate that as time went on and doubt arose as to her guilt, prison officials allowed her to walk about the town as she pleased, returning in the evening. This treatment, if true, suggests again the trouble officials had in dealing with female inmates—even those convicted of murder. It suggests that women, like Harker, were not necessarily viewed as security threats, which the women knew and used in their favor. The fact that an execution date for Harker was never set offers evidence that officials may not have intended to hang her at all, but rather sentenced her to death because the criminal code required it for first-degree murder.[7] In any case, Harker took advantage of the lax discipline and maintained a level of freedom and power over her life until she died in prison.

Due to the poor oversight and conditions of many of these prisons, escapes like Veitengruber's were common. Another example demonstrates not only the unsecure lodgings of prisoners but the ingenuity of female inmates. In 1860, in Warren County, Pennsylvania, all the current inmates in the county jail (two women and two men) made their escape. It was reported that "the women up stairs [sic] burnt the clasp out that fastened the door through a single pine board" and proceeded to open "the cells in which the men were confined, by means of false keys," and made their escape with a stolen wagon.[8] Once again, the inmates were not content with simply serving their sentence and figured a way out of confinement.

These instances of roaming convicts, escapes, cohabitation of male and female inmates, and varied jail conditions and punishments, illustrate just how inconsistent the county prison experience was for all inmates, not only women. After seeing the wide range of quality of food, bedding, and discipline, it is little wonder that Foulke grew frustrated with what he observed in his travels and desired consistency for the county prisons in order to emulate the discipline of the penitentiaries. Creating mini-penitentiaries in each county, however, was likely only going to occur in an ideal world. Most counties did not have the money to build facilities that would have met Foulke's standards. That sheriffs sometimes lived on the property where inmates were housed, perhaps even in rooms attached to the family home. It is likely that sheriffs dealt with inmates on a case-by-case basis, accounting for inconsistency across counties and across inmates. As chronicled here, this inconsistency sometimes led to inmate resistance.

Tracking the conditions of county jails in the nineteenth century is a difficult task at best. Newspaper articles detailing a crime or trial might provide insight on the conditions of a prison. More likely, the information we have is from reformers or state officials who wrote reports. Very few records at the local level seem to have survived. There are, then, inherent gaps in the sources regarding county prisons. Although there are breaks in the records, by the late decades of the nineteenth century and early decades of the twentieth, conditions had only slowly improved for these inmates in county prisons. For example, in the 1890s, a report on prison conditions noted that in Butler County Jail "women could talk to the men, the former being in a cage cell nearby; keeper said the language used was often vile, and there ought to be a change."[9] Problems segregating men and women abounded, even in these late decades of the nineteenth century and well into the twentieth.[10] Decades after some of the early reports of poor conditions of county jails, many places had barely improved. Reform of the inmates in the county prisons was not feasible considering that basic necessities and separation could not be provided. In many of these counties, prisoners remained idle, without even work to occupy their time. The idleness and lack of consistent discipline and security leads to the possibility for more inmate resistance—and women, with their lax oversight, may have had an easier time of enacting this resistance.

THE SPECIAL CASE OF PHILADELPHIA

Few county jails kept copious records. What we can learn about these small institutions comes from reports from visitors, and these sources often remain statistical in nature with only snippets of anecdotal evidence (as exemplified above). We glean little about the inmates themselves. Sources from the Philadelphia County Prison, however, provide us with details of the daily lives of female inmates in a large county jail setting and illustrate some significant differences between county prisons and the penitentiaries, as well as the distinctions between urban county jails and rural ones.[11] Philadelphia's need to house a much larger inmate population undoubtedly created a unique set of conditions. Yet, its records offer a glimpse into the daily life of women in county prisons. While female inmates in the penitentiaries and smaller county jails sometimes received special privileges and often took advantage of these chances to resist or escape, women in urban county prisons, like Philadelphia, were often subjected to a more chaotic atmosphere. They still, however, found ways to resist their incarceration. The records of county prisons both in rural areas and in Philadelphia indicate that although these women were treated poorly, the women inmates viewed themselves in a different light—one that gave them some level of control over their imprisonment as evidenced through behaviors that challenged prison protocol.[12]

The Philadelphia County Prison, located in the Moyamensing district in South Philadelphia and often referred to as Moyamensing, was the successor to Walnut Street Jail. Moyamensing was originally meant to house inmates who had been sentenced for a period not exceeding one year. They were to "suffer punishment . . . by separate confinement at labour for and during the term of their sentence, and shall be fed, clothed and treated nearly as may be practicable, in the same manner as is provided by law in relation to persons confined in the Eastern State Penitentiary, in solitary confinement at labour." The prison opened on October 19, 1835. By the 1850s, it was receiving fourteen to fifteen thousand inmates yearly. Its stable population, however, remained around five hundred.[13]

One inspector to the prison seemed appalled by the plight of certain inmates, especially females. He wrote, "As one instance in many, a decent sempstress [*sic*] who, when an advantage was attempted to be taken of her, endeavored to force her way out of a room, and in so doing broke a pane of glass, was committed to prison for malicious mischief, and when I first saw her she had been there two months without trial."[14] This particular account portrays the inmate as an innocent victim, someone who had been arrested for an offense stemming from self-defense. Such a case illustrates not only the sympathy directed at some female inmates, but also the high standards to which women of the time were held. The fact that the woman was held to await trial for breaking a pane of glass struck the inspector as gratuitous.

The same inspector also discussed female intemperance and imprisonment:

> Unchaste females who are intemperate, soon find their way to prison. They inhabit those worst quarters of the city and those worst dens of infamy. . . . They are swept into prison along with those who create disturbance or shed blood. When released, being without home or other place of retreat than those from which they were taken, they return only to be arrested and imprisoned again upon the next visit of the police. Thus they are continually suffering not only for their own faults, but for the faults of others. . . . There is no sadder spectacle than these girls, oscillating between a life of debauchery and a life of imprisonment. . . . The female who has fallen so low as to be committed to prison for intemperance, becomes soon an habitual visitor. Many of them are committed twenty or thirty times a year.[15]

The author suggests that these women are in some way innocent and really do not want to live this lifestyle. The blame clearly lies with the violent men who inhabit these neighborhoods and with the police for not being more discriminating. By considering both the intemperate and the woman in jail for breaking a pane of glass as victims, there is a sense that both officials and visitors sympathized with the plight of many of these women and did not see them as a threat to society. Such public reactions mirrored penitentiary employee responses to those female inmates who were left out of their cells and given special privileges. They, too, were seen either as nonthreatening or a group not worthy of reform. Yet, the women inmates demonstrated that they could be threatening, at least in terms of prison discipline.

The records of the Philadelphia County Prison indicate that in some respects, these female inmates were treated differently from the female inmates in the state penitentiaries, most likely because of their shorter incarcerations and lesser crimes. The provisions ledger for the female ward of the county prison suggests that inmates had to pay for such supplies during their stay. For example, in 1829 at Walnut Street Jail, Susan Cork purchased one linsey petticoat and short gown, two old caps, handkerchiefs, shifts, blankets, an apron, one pair of shoes, and one pair of stockings. Later in the year, she purchased two summer petticoats and two summer gowns. In addition, she paid for 181 days of provisions. During the year, she totaled up a bill of $48.24. Another inmate, Sarah Engles, purchased provisions first for ninety days and later twenty-six days at a cost of $22.52.[16]

These records exemplify the types of goods inmates bought. It is striking that certain inmates purchased extra goods for comfort, while others purchased only provisions. It is unknown what clothing was provided for the inmates upon their arrival, if any. While the penitentiaries describe the prison garb inmates wore, this provision ledger suggests that inmates may have worn their own clothing, and could purchase extra garments if funds allowed. While it may have been a struggle for some merely to purchase basic provisions, others could make their incarceration a bit more comfortable with additional clothing and extra blankets. It is also unknown what the purchase of provisions entailed—whether it was meant to provide basic rations or food above and beyond that provided by the prison, or if it consisted of something else entirely, including hygienic goods such as soap or a comb.

Unlike the state penitentiaries, which originally had no plans to house women in separate quarters, Moyamensing seemed to have known that women needed to be dealt with separately, or had learned from some of the early problems faced by the larger penitentiaries. In Moyamensing, female inmates were "confined in a building on the adjoining lot" near the main men's prison. To reach the women's quarters, one "entered by a gateway from the yard of the main prison." The building was two stories high and housed one hundred eight- by twelve-foot cells, a suite for an infirmary, and two rooms for the matron. The building was also equipped with "hydrants, water-closets, warming, and ventilation," as was standard in the main prison.[17] Even with these conscious efforts to separate women from men, intended to ensure the inmates' reform, this goal was not to be achieved. Chaos, neglect, and resistance prevailed in the county prison as the women actively sought ways to exert control over their incarceration.

In addition to sources like the provisions ledger for Walnut Street Jail, the prison diary for the female ward from 1850 to 1860 provides accounts of daily life inside the walls of Moyamensing Prison.[18] While many of the entries are mundane, simply noting which employees were on duty, which inspectors visited the prison, or which inmates were ill, some entries provide more details, uncovering the darker layers of female imprisonment in this jail. Mrs. McDaniel, the matron of the female ward, was tasked with the responsibility of enforcing "order and good government," yet the diary reveals that her job was not simple.[19]

In looking at various excerpts from the diary, several things are of interest. One noticeable theme is the level of disorder in the prison. Women were strapped (either a form of restraint or beating) and put in dark cells for offenses such as "indecent singing," "insolence and abuse," "loud talking to the Men," "talking down the pipes," and "mutilating their Bibles." Other women found themselves in the dark cell for "being Disorderly and breaking cell furniture" or more violent acts like "drawing a knife on the keeper." On April 19, 1850, it was recorded that Catharine Jordin, alias Sarah Smith, was "put in the dark cell for *striking at the keeper* and *abusing the matron and her assistant* and *threatening them*." Prison officials asked the visiting inspector to order Jordin "to be kept locked in her cell and not taken from thence as no kind treatment can subdue the prisoner."[20]

Some female prisoners continually troubled the prison employees. Margaret Johnson, convicted of larceny in July 1849, occupied much of the keepers' time with her refractory behavior. In late September 1850, the visiting inspectors were asked to deal with "the abusive conduct" of Johnson" because she "has defied all control by the Keepers." The next day, the diary entry noted that she was "still straped [sic]" for her bad behavior. A few months later, on December 4, 1850, the diary keeper wrote that Johnson was "chained" and "wishes to see visiting inspector [sic]." On January 22, 1851, Johnson found herself "put in the Dark Cell . . . for Insolence to the Keepers." The prison staff informed the visiting inspectors that "this prisoner Cannot be subdued unless by this means."[21] The various accounts of resistance by Johnson illustrate that the punishments of being strapped, chained, or placed in a dark cell did not deter some women. Resistance appears to be a daily occurrence.

Johnson was not the only habitual offender of prison rules. On March 5, 1851, Elizabeth Wagstaff was put in a dark cell for being insolent to the keepers. The staff deemed Wagstaff "a great anoyance [*sic*] to the Prison." In August of that year, the visiting inspectors were called to observe Wagstaff as "her conduct is so bad, she keeps the place in Continual Excitement." In early February 1852, the inspectors were called again to visit Wagstaff because "her conduct is so outrageous that the Keepers cannot do anything with her she [*sic*] has destroyed the discipline of the prison." One month later, Wagstaff spent several days in the dark cell for being unruly and refusing to eat. Throughout 1852, Wagstaff plagued the employees with her behavior and thwarted prison order. She was strapped several times for noise infractions and abusing the matron. Prison officials realized that "good treatment makes her worse" and that "she is so outrageous that she keeps the place in a continual uproar from Morning until night." In April 1853, she was strapped again for "breaking her door by hamering [*sic*]."[22] After such a record of resistance to prison discipline, it is doubtful that prison officials were upset at the expiration of her sentence on August 9, 1853.

These inmates (and these few are by no means the only examples of this type of behavior in the diary!) seemed out of control. They acted violently, threatened the keepers, broke furniture, or in some cases stole prison property. These refractory inmates concerned officials, prompting inspectors to make frequent visits to their cells. The actions taken by the female inmates in the county jail illustrate blatant resistance to their incarceration. Taking on a more desperate approach, these women fought directly against their imprisonment and refused to become silent victims of the system. They made their presence known to employees and inspectors alike through their struggles against the system. The chaotic atmosphere of these prisons appeared to breed a more frenzied resistance. In the penitentiaries where order was of the utmost importance, resistance seemed to be more restrained and subtle, whereas in county prisons where there was much less control, inmate resistance was often more widespread and violent. Furthermore, because female inmates were viewed in the nineteenth century to be incorrigible, some states refused to admit women to penitentiaries and relegated them to the county prison systems.[23] It is clear that the women were not content to fade away into the recesses of the prison; rather, they demonstrated individual power to defy the rules of their imprisonment and, in some cases, wore down authorities.

Women giving birth in prison also added to the disorder of the county jails. Childbirth necessitated special care for inmates and their infants, including separate facilities that catered to their needs. For instance, on August 5, 1854, Anna Cormis, "a coloured woman" who was committed in July for adultery, "gave birth to a female child at 2 oclock [*sic*] this morning." It is not clear from the records what became of the infants who were born in the prison. Most likely they were sent to an almshouse or perhaps even an orphanage.[24] Childbirth was likely a more frequent occurrence in county prisons than in state penitentiaries due to the shorter sentences imposed and the fluctuating inmate population.

Violence inflicted on the inmates by the keepers is another major theme apparent in the diary. Inmates were sometimes restrained by straps; other times they were chained in their cells; and even on some occasions they were doused with cold water. On March 28, 1850, inmate Julia Bower was removed to cell 17 "chained to keep her from injury (Mania)."[25] While the diary author noted that the chain was for the inmate's protection from herself due to her alleged symptoms of some type of insanity, the use of chains and strapping for bad behavior is problematic. These punishments were contrary to the goals of the larger penitentiaries, which prided themselves on not using physical violence because officials believed that physical pain did not encourage inmate rehabilitation. The use of physical punishments in the county prison suggests that rehabilitation was a less important priority even though the county jails ideally were to follow the Pennsylvania plan of discipline as Foulke wanted. The shorter sentences of the inmates at the county jail made rehabilitation difficult, maybe even impossible. Exactly why the violent punishments were used is unknown, yet harsh punishments could, in the eyes of employees, serve to maintain order in an unruly population. The use of violent punishments may have added to the desire of the inmates to resist rules and employees' control, creating an unending cycle of chaos and punishments. While this resistance likely did not improve the experience for current inmates, the continued struggles of inmates revealed an issue that reformers and prison officials worked to remedy later in the century.

Female inmates also utilized their physical bodies as weapons of resistance because it was something they could control. Their bodies represented one defense that was difficult to take away. Refusing to eat provided one way they rebelled against their imprisonment or punishments for breaking prison rules. On August 2, 1855, Mary Bates was put in a dark cell for "throwing out of the wicket her tins into the corridor maliciously." During her time in the dark cell, a period of a few days, Bates refused "to take her bread" and dashed "her water out of her pan." Others followed suit.[26]

Other women found more extreme ways to use their bodies as tools of resistance. During the night of October 28, 1851, Elizabeth Young made such a commotion in the prison that the next day's entry in the diary noted that she was "very outrageous last night & made an attempt to strangle herself." On November 20, 1851, prison employees found two convicts in a cell, one of whom had "attempted to hang herself." The inmate was saved, and the two women were put in separate cells. In another case, Caroline Erwin was discovered and cut down by the keepers after she tried to hang herself. For her suicide attempt, she was chained in her cell.[27]

While some entries on attempted suicides are brief, such as the ones above, other cases prompted the diary author to detail the event more closely. In early November 1854, an inmate named Mary Smith "attempted to hang herself" from the window grating by "tearing up her bed quilt into strips." Prison employees found her in time and cut her down. Prison officials deemed that a deep feeling of despondency caused her suicide attempt. A little over a month later, on December 12, 1854, the diary entry noted that Ann O'Conner had a fit, causing the matron and assistant "to relieve her." When they arrived at her cell, they "found her face Purple, they tried to resuscitate her, in so doing, they found two cords one on each arm tied very tight also one around her waist stopping the circulation of blood." As a result, O'Conner "was stripped, and she fought manfully to prevent it, but she was overcome and was ordered to a solitary cell." In late August 1856, inmate Kate Murray tried at least twice to commit suicide. She was chained for her attempt "to hang herself." She "got a good choke" and was cut down by the prison keeper. In a second diary entry, Murray had "amused herself by choking herself by wrapping strips of blanket around her throat." As punishment she "was put in the shower bath."[28]

These entries point to the pure desolation of prison life, and the need for more specialized treatment and care for these women. The excerpts suggest that the prisons may have caused depression, leading some to contemplate ending their lives. The cases of self-harm demonstrate an extreme form of inmate resistance, since the women attempted to take back control over their bodies and lives and demonstrated the wherewithal to use the weapons of resistance available to them. These women shaped their own stories of their experiences in prison and did not relinquish narrative-writing power to the authorities. In these cases, suicides were prevented and the women were promptly punished, indicating that employees viewed these actions as a threat to the prison system and their authority. The evidence of chaining, being put in a solitary cell, and being doused in a shower bath solidifies the fact that prison employees deemed these actions as resistance to the prison regime and not necessarily as a sign of deeper emotional or mental issues. In the cases of self-harm, such actions indicated a need for more individual and specialized care. Because the county jail did not promote inmate rehabilitation and dealt consistently with a large and transient population, the prison may have promoted a feeling of hopelessness in its inmates, causing them to resort to such measures. While the women had their own department and separate staff, disorder still ensued in Moyamensing. Based on the evidence presented above, it appears that discipline often failed to control the inmate population in the female department, which perhaps also explains why reform efforts could not be upheld either.

While the records indicate that in the 1850s violent punishments may have been used to correct inmates, this was not the case a decade earlier (1839–41). A punishment register from these years illustrates this trend. As the table below shows, punishments for female inmates consisted of either time in a dark cell, or something noted as "cell and allowance," likely a combination of being kept in their cells and a reduction of food rations for the duration of the punishment.[29] The infractions for which the inmates were punished ranged from talking offenses, which made up the majority of the cases, to impudent behavior, to breaking cell furniture, to refusing to work. These offenses and their punishments illustrate a more direct connection to the penitentiary ideal of punishment. The punishments were not nearly as violent as those mentioned in the prison diary from the 1850s, and most infractions were for noise violations, suggesting that the county prison tried to emulate the regime of penitentiary discipline for the more serious criminals of the state, at least in its early years. By looking at this ledger and the evidence found in the prison diary a decade later, there is a sense that the county jail did not approximate the penitentiary protocols and let certain regulations lapse as the years progressed. As a result, there seems to be a marked increase in physical punishment of the inmates, representing a regression from penitentiary ideals.

TABLE 6. Philadelphia County Jail punishments for female offenders, 1839–1841

Type of offense	# of offenses	Dark cell	Cell and allowance*	Not specified
Talking offenses	140	20	120	
Destroying prison property	7	2	5	
Impudence	12	9	3	
Not working	8	4	4	
Indecent language	3	2		1
Stealing	1	1		

* This punishment entailed being left in their cells and having their provisions reduced.

Why this shift in punishment methods occurred is unclear, but there are a few possible explanations worth considering. The move to more physical punishments as noted in the diary might reflect the attitude that the female inmates could not be reformed and thus were treated as more challenging inmates as the decades progressed, whereas the ones reflected in the table suggest a more hopeful approach that aligns with the penitentiary model that was more recently instituted. As larger numbers of women were incarcerated and more stories about prison experiences filtered out to the public, female inmates may have found it necessary to challenge prison protocol in order to work for improvements in their conditions, thus causing the officials to react with more violent punishments to reassert control. Another possibility is that during this period female prison reformers became more involved in the lives of the female inmates (this is chronicled in the next chapter in more detail). As the reformers got more involved in the rehabilitation and reform efforts of the female inmates between the 1830s and the 1850s, perhaps the prison officials shifted their attention to more disciplinary order and left the task of reform in the hands of benevolent associations, thus accounting for the shift in punishment methods. A final possibility is that violent punishments may have been used earlier and simply not recorded in official records. A concrete answer may never be known.

ATTEMPTS TO ALLEVIATE THE PROBLEMS OF THE PHILADELPHIA
COUNTY JAIL

Beyond the middle of the century, the female department of Moyamensing continued to struggle with order and care for their charges. By the
mid-1860s, it was estimated that over one thousand women spent time in
the prison each year for various crimes and vices. Because their sentences
remained short, often thirty days or less, there was not adequate time
to help reform these women. Furthermore, even if there was a length of
time long enough to achieve reform, often the inmates were not isolated,
which "renders almost hopeless" any attempt at changing criminal or sinful
behavior.[30]

Throughout the 1860s, reports described varied observations of the
female department's conditions. In 1864, observers noted that there were
fewer short-term committals and an increase of convicted felons in the
department due to the root cause of intoxication. To acquire alcohol,
women tended to turn toward larceny, shoplifting, and burglary, which
resulted in higher numbers of convicted women in the prison. Disease
spread through the department in 1864 as well. During the epidemic of
fever, "a beautiful exhibition of generous devotion and kindness by the
keepers and matrons" occurred, as did the aid of "the healthful prisoners
to their suffering sisters." Observers noted that these actions, in times of
trouble, "illustrated the loveliness of their sex's nature" even though these
women were inmates.[31]

Other reports painted a positive portrait of life in the female department. Cleanliness was paramount, and "the great amount of sunlight
admitted renders obvious and pleasing the result of the labors of cleanliness." On the point of cleanliness, observers prided themselves that the
health of the female inmates was good due to the circulation of air and
sunshine. Inspectors noted that "the superior neatness, purity, and sanitary
order" of the female department was due to the fact that the employees
were female. They reported that "almost any man can keep a clean floor,
but it takes women to ensure clean corners—and in the corners and out-
of-the-way places are concealed the means and elements of disease."[32]

In the building where women were held, the sentenced female convict
was given an individual cell, although from other reports, we know this was
not always the case. Women were given access to reading materials, and

for work, they "make up the clothing, the bedding, &c." Even discipline in this report seemed minimal. Female inmates who "will converse with each other out of their windows, learn that a small strip of leather is hung up at their door, and while that remains, they must submit to a diet of bread and water, unless they be sick. Twenty-four hours suffice for this."[33] Considering this report was only a decade removed from the records of the prison diary, one can doubt whether life in the female department was truly this picturesque. Likely, this excerpt reflects the ideal situation, while the prison diary presents a more accurate depiction. There seems to be an attempt to limit the public from knowing the level of chaos and prisoner resistance in the prisons. Public reports paint a controlled atmosphere, while internal documents lay bare the challenges female inmates posed in their quest for autonomy.

With the large prisoner population that made its way in and out of Moyamensing in a given year in the mid-nineteenth century, efforts were made to alleviate the problem of overcrowding and protecting those individuals who should not be subjected to prison. Agent William Mullen worked diligently to intercede on behalf of people who wrongfully became entangled in the criminal justice system—an advocate for those who would not likely be able to help themselves. He was part of the Pennsylvania Prison Society since 1849 and had volunteered his time helping discharged prisoners. In 1854, he was hired as the prison agent.[34] His reports demonstrated his work with the untried prisoners, trying, when possible, to whisk them away from the prison system before they were incarcerated and had to fend for themselves inside. A case from 1872 is illustrative. A woman had been imprisoned with her infant child on the charge of threatening another person. She had been beaten by her husband for spending two dollars on a cradle for her ill baby. When her cries drew the police to her home, the family was arrested. Mullen interfered on behalf of the woman when it was learned her child was dying. He worked to have her immediately released. He noted that she was "a responsible, temperate woman, of good character, but had been badly misused by her drunken husband."[35] Mullen took very seriously his work to protect and aid the helpless.[36]

Perhaps the most striking element about these cases of women saved from incarceration at Moyamensing are the descriptions of their character. Phrases like "worthy woman," "the woman had the babe in her arms when she was tried," "respectable woman," "a woman, who had been wrongfully accused," "an industrious, worthy colored woman," and "peaceful woman of good character" portray sympathetic individuals.[37] The outcome for female convicts, or in these cases, the accused females, rested heavily on their character. In many cases, as mentioned in earlier chapters, the way women comported themselves in court or were described in character witness testimony could sway the court's decision on conviction. These cases from Mullen's reports throughout the nineteenth century are no different. Not only do they evoke sympathy from the readers, but his work and intercessions must have pulled at the heartstrings of court officials as well. While the women incarcerated in prison had to demonstrate their own worth and power through resistance against the disciplinary system, Mullen advocated to show women's worth before they saw the inside of a cell. His work demonstrates that not all women brought before the criminal justice system were beyond hope of reform; moreover, he used the nineteenth-century ideals of womanhood to aid these women, just as some women did for themselves in the courtroom.

––––––––

While women in the state penitentiaries were often ignored or treated leniently by officials due to their small numbers, women in county jails often faced dismal conditions. In rural jails, sheriffs were often not well equipped to deal with the few women who were sentenced. Their reformation was utterly ignored, and it was rare that there was even a separate space in which they could be housed. Yet, even in these primitive conditions, women found ways to assert control over their seemingly helpless situation and resist the discipline, improve their incarceration, or escape it all together. The Philadelphia County Jail presented an entirely separate set of issues. Large populations, which moved through the system quickly, led to inconsistent treatment for inmates. Although they were housed in a separate building from men, the women still broke the rules, resisting the forces pressuring them to fade into the oblivion of anonymity. These women vandalized the prison, talked back to employees, or even engaged in self-harm, which in turn cemented their existence in the historical record. Efforts to alleviate the problems of the county prison were made by people like William Mullen, who worked tirelessly to rescue innocent people from being sucked into the system. Yet, the looming problem for both the penitentiaries and county prisons was how to reform the inmates—finding a way to redeem these criminals to lawful society. Female inmates posed special problems, as we have seen from these sketches of their experiences with incarceration in the penitentiaries and county jails. Male reformers attempted to find ways to help women, but such efforts were minimal, as the main prize was the reformation of the male inmate population.

Female philanthropic reformers realized the need for specifically targeted treatment for female offenders. During the early years of the prison systems' existence, official visitors from the Pennsylvania Prison Society and other organizations met with inmates to talk with them, teach them, and provide friendship in order to ease the traumas caused by isolation and silence in order to help push them to reform their lifestyles. It remained the job of female reformers working for change to continue to drive the movement to establish female reformatories after the Civil War. While female inmates were often ignored, these female reformers noted that the prison gave "prompt attention and considerate kindness . . . to the young thief in his prison cell. . . . Once again in the world, the way of return of employment and trust, and even virtue, is not closed against him. But it is closed for ever against the erring girl."[38] Reformers worked diligently to create prison conditions more suitable for reform and rehabilitation for female inmates, an effort to put women on a more sustainable path to rehabilitation and self-worth than having to resort to resistance to make their presence known or protect their individuality.

CHAPTER 6

"Restoration to the Path of Virtue"
The Difficult Task of Reform

Inmate 974, Harriet Lane, was sentenced to Eastern State Penitentiary in 1838 to serve a two-year sentence for larceny. When interviewed by Thomas Larcombe, a Baptist minister and Eastern State Penitentiary's first official moral instructor, he was not optimistic about her prospects for reform. He recorded in his journal, "A very interesting looking girl, who has given evidence of being old in crime. Seems subdued, wept plentifully during my visit & has seemed deeply concerned for her soul. Since has been addicted to falsehood & deceit. Continues to deal in falsehood so that no confidence can be placed in anything she says." Upon her release in 1840, he noted that she remained "hopeless."[1] Although the penitentiary was intended to punish, Pennsylvania penal reformers also wanted their institution to reform their charges, to allow them, upon release, to be positively contributing citizens. To that end, prison regulations focused on rehabilitation, which began inside the cells of each inmate. The moral instructor's job was to help these inmates on their paths of reformation. Yet, based on this example of Larcombe's work, he held little faith in many of the female inmates to reform.

This chapter examines female inmates and their relationship with the prison reform movement that swept the northeastern United States in the antebellum decades.[2] Analyzing the shifting approaches to reforming female inmates demonstrates that initially, female inmates presented a problem that male reformers were not prepared to handle perhaps due

to their small numbers, the prevailing social notions about female criminals, or even the agency that the women inmates showed. Female activists
pushed an agenda to involve themselves in the reform efforts, focusing
their attention on this neglected class of inmates. They played a pivotal
role in improving and tailoring the inmate rehabilitation program toward
female inmates' needs, and by becoming role models and friends to these
prisoners. The reformers' work, though viewed by some as a form of social
control, strove to empower the female inmates, and through this process
the reformers empowered themselves to become more public figures. Like
the female criminals and inmates who challenged authority and social standards to shape their experiences within the courts and prisons, these female
reformers also challenged society. They defied the prevailing notion that the
female inmates' reformation should be ignored because they were hopeless;
rather, they entered prisons with the goal of restoring female inmates to
free society. These reformers worked to show the inmates that they had
value and worth to themselves and to the outside world in ways other than
just resisting discipline. In addition to helping the inmates value their self-
worth, reformers themselves demonstrated their awareness of the power
they wielded as middle- and upper-class women to contribute to the uplift
of their city, state, and nation.

GENERAL SENTIMENTS ON INMATE REFORM

The world of prison reform into which the women were thrust in the nineteenth century revolved around restoring inmates in order to release them
back into society as positively contributing citizens. This emphasis on individual reform and moral improvement illustrated a significant difference
between punishments of the past, which were meant to physically harm
and humiliate the offender. Incarceration would punish the inmate for his
or her crime but would also nurture them through rehabilitation efforts to
restore their humanity, both through religious teaching and artisanal work.
Although most of the discussion seemed to focus on the idea of helping
the individual inmates, the conversations on reforming prisons ultimately
had the goal of perfecting penal institutions. Inmate reform would be a
manifestation of successful institutions.

Reform in morals, industry, and education would be the features of this
new style of punishment. "To reform criminals," medical doctor Charles

Caldwell wrote, "is to improve them in morality and industry *always*, and in knowledge *very generally*; for vice and ignorance are usually associated." Caldwell also suggested that labor and instruction should not be used as punishments. To penal reformers, work and education were seen as privileges and a means to moral rehabilitation. George Washington Smith, a defender of the Pennsylvania system of isolation, argued that labor "is considered as an alleviation, not an aggravation of his sentence."[3] By providing work to inmates, not only did reformers relieve the tedium of isolation, but they hoped that the inmate would find joy in work. Upon release, they calculated former inmates would be able to earn an honest living.

Acting with humanity in the treatment of offenders was paramount to proponents of the Pennsylvania system. Reformers argued that while physical punishments degraded offenders, the penitentiary's design allowed inmates to keep their personal dignity by treating them with what was considered the humane punishment of isolation and reflection. Reformers strongly desired a system of punishment in which moral reform played a critical role. William Roscoe, an English prison reformer, lamented that "a Penitentiary, where *penitence* is of no avail, is a solecism; and these establishments . . . would no longer be places of *reformation*, but places of *punishment* subject to most of the objects of the ancient system."[4] To reformers, the penitentiary needed to be more than a site for punishment; it must act as a place where individuals could be helped and rebuilt.

The importance of penitence and moral reform echoed throughout discussions among reformers defending the Pennsylvania system of silent isolation. Quaker Roberts Vaux, a jurist and one of the original penitentiary advocates in Pennsylvania, argued that solitary confinement furnished inmates "with every opportunity which christian [*sic*] duty enjoins, for promoting his restoration to the path of virtue, because seclusion is believed to be an essential ingredient in moral treatment, and with religious instruction and advice superadded, is calculated to achieve more than has ever been done." To Francis Lieber, "solitude is the weightiest moral agent to make the thoughtless thoughtful" and has the capability of enabling "an elevating character."[5]

Solitude, as discussed by Vaux and Lieber, pushed the inmate to reflect. Alexis de Tocqueville and Gustave de Beaumont, in examining the Pennsylvania system of discipline, remarked, "Placed alone, in view of his crime, he learns to hate it . . . it is in solitude, where remorse will come to assail him."[6]

This passage exemplifies the first step in reforming inmates. By placing them in isolation, inmates were left only with their own thoughts and reflections on how they ended up in prison. Victory for reformers was achieved when inmates recognized the errors of their ways and could then be put on the path to rehabilitation by learning a trade, and being provided with education and religious instruction. The rhetoric of reform is geared toward males; as with the prison buildings themselves, reform for women was an afterthought. Women inmates, in their resistance and seeming intransigence, acted as the catalyst to get female reformers involved.

The ideals developed for the penitentiary system emerged from the wave of social reforms that swept the United States in the decades before the Civil War. The religious fervor spawned by the Second Great Awakening in the early nineteenth century in which people sought to promote salvation and improve morals as a means to improve society, was critical to the development of secular social reforms. For these reformers, however, enacting change in secular society was still strongly linked to religion. Scholar C. S. Griffin contends that religion and humanitarian reform could not be separated because doing "the work of God, the reformers said, was to make men happier on earth; to make men happier on earth was to do the work of God."[7] Religion and the individual's spirituality were closely tied to the antebellum reform movements, as is evident in the prison reformers' actions in pushing for individual moral reform through religious education while spreading their ideas through pamphlets, broadsides, and annual reports.

Not only was the upswing in religious fervor influential to the reformation of numerous social ills, but major changes in American society also propelled the development of antebellum social reforms. The rapidly expanding nation in the early nineteenth century—with its burgeoning cities, influx of immigrants, developing market economy, and westward expansion—broke down the small, tight-knit communities that were the norm during the colonial and Early Republic periods. Anxiety about these changes was compounded by the rise of crime and vice in cities as well as the lack of control over individuals' behavior. Such worry over social ills fostered a desire in some citizens, mainly those from the middle and upper classes, to fix, or at least alleviate, society's problems through a variety of reform organizations.[8] Although reformers feared for their society, they also clung to the hope that reforms could improve or even erase the social ills that concerned them. Fear of social disorder and vice, coupled with the religious ideal that humans could be improved and even perfected (a feature of the Second Great Awakening), created an environment in which individuals sought to improve society by throwing themselves into myriad reform causes.

While some activists may have had altruistic, purely benevolent motivations for becoming involved in such efforts, the specter of social control and class domination looms over the broad umbrella of antebellum reform—but to varying degrees, depending on the type of movement and the reformers' methods.[9] Political action to change laws to enact social reform was one means of coercion; however, such reform movements could be restrictive in other ways. The development of asylums, poorhouses, and prisons, all inventions of reform movements, are by their very nature coercive, as they are meant to shape human behavior into a form that is socially acceptable and necessarily dealt with discipline and punishment. The reformers, while they may have been inspired to help improve the lives of those less fortunate than themselves, may have unwittingly been coercing individuals into images of themselves (i.e., proper, virtuous citizens) by trying to persuade them that their habits were wrong or sinful. This tack assumes that reformers believed they were exemplars of the virtues they were trying to instill in others.

Prison reform and the interaction between female inmates and reformers in Pennsylvania can be viewed as a microcosm of this larger trend of social reforms as it embodied the emphasis on religious teaching and salvation, evident in the isolation, silent reflection, and religious instruction that was central to the penitentiary's reform procedures. The reformers who worked within the penitentiary system and interacted with the inmates wanted to improve the inmates' morality by instilling in them the virtues of religion, industry, and education so that they could return to society rehabilitated. Not only were reformers helping inmates improve themselves, they also strove to improve society as a whole through this reformation process. The more inmates that reformers could help transform into virtuous, hardworking citizens like themselves, the better off the entire nation would be.

Although the prison reform movement demonstrates a more distinct example of how reform could be viewed as a form of social control, some reformers, particularly female activists who worked with women prisoners, could be seen as providing a counter-narrative. Rachel Perijo, matron of the Maryland State Penitentiary in Baltimore, hired in 1822, improved the conditions of female prisoners. After introducing a work program, educational classes, and religious teachings, marked improvements in the female inmates' experiences were noted, such as decreases in sickness and recidivism.[10] In New York, the work of Eliza Farnham provides another example. Hired as a matron for Mount Pleasant Female Prison (associated with Sing Sing) in 1844, Farnham provided new ways of approaching female inmate reform. She did away with some of the strict rules of the prison, allowing the inmates to converse, read novels, and hear music. She supported the study of phrenology and believed that providing her inmates with positive influences would reduce their innate criminal tendencies.[11] Ultimately, the work of individuals like Farnham and Perijo, showed that when reformers became involved, the attention to female prisoners improved.[12] The female prison reformers in this chapter followed in this trend. Jen Manion notes that female reformers "seemed to be less self-serving than their male counterparts" and those involved with prison reform "sought connection, friendship, and intimacy with those they visited."[13] These women in Pennsylvania and elsewhere challenged the idea that the care of women inmates was limited; they worked to aid these incarcerated women by acting as role models and providing companionship, education, and material items, and putting pressure on prison officials to improve the prisoners' situation. They built relationships with female inmates and advocated on their behalf.

THE PROCESS OF INMATE REFORM

The road to reform began in the inmates' cells. As mentioned in chapter 4, penitentiary inmates were stripped of their identity, given a number, and led, hooded, to their cells to begin their sentences and embark on the path of reform. Artisan labor, completed in their solitary cells, was part of this process to become industrious, but so was the effort to reform inmates' minds and souls by providing them with education and religious teachings. Religious historian Andrew Skotnicki noted that many antebellum evangelicals believed that the "conversion of the individual heart was the prelude to social action, and without a heart renewed in Christ, no amount of reform could restrain the dissolute from falling into error."[14]

With this idea that religious salvation was paramount to developing personal reform, it is no wonder that religion was critical to the goal of inmate reform in American penitentiaries, particularly in Pennsylvania. Even the name "penitentiary" had religious connotations and explained its purpose as an institution. The inmates were supposed to learn to be penitent while alone in their cells. The daily routine of the inmates at institutions like Eastern or Western State revolved around the inmate having ample time to reflect on his or her crimes and seek religious salvation. Silent reflection, isolation, access to Bibles or other religious tracts, visits with the moral instructor, and weekly sermons all helped to facilitate inmate reform. Dorothea Dix, who visited numerous prisons around the United States, remarked that "the moral, religious and mental instruction" of Eastern State was "more thorough and complete than is supplied to the convicts of any prison in the United States."[15]

Pennsylvania's rival in penitentiaries, New York, which developed the "silent system" of communal work during the day and isolation at night, also had religious roots, namely, Presbyterian and Calvinist influences. Early attempts in the late eighteenth century at inmate religious education at Newgate Prison in New York City under the direction of Quaker merchant Thomas Eddy failed quickly due to overcrowding and inmate interaction (which defeated attempts at reformation). Eddy's Quaker ideals did not mesh well in a society steeped in the Calvinist "belief in the natural depravity of men and women" and "values of order and financial stability." So, while both penal systems used religious and moral ideals in their rhetoric, New York prisons attempted to create more obedient and disciplined citizens, while those in Pennsylvania wished to evoke more honest, moral ones.[16]

Religious conversion of the inmates was not a controversial part of prison discipline in Pennsylvania; in New York, however, it was a highly contested issue. Jennifer Graber argues that in nineteenth-century New York, Protestant prison reformers increasingly found themselves marginalized from their work as state officials exerted more control over prison operations. While reformers believed in the values of religion in rehabilitation, state officials disliked their work and preferred that inmates be shaped into obedient citizens under secular authorities and focused on creating profitable and orderly institutions. In Pennsylvania, the Philadelphia Society for Alleviating the Miseries of Public Prisons had more direct involvement in the daily workings of the prison and could install a more complete reform program, allowing religious reform to remain a high priority in the state. In New York, initially, Thomas Eddy wished prisons to be "gardens" where incarceration "provided an escape" from the bad influences of society. By the early decades of the nineteenth century, New York prisons were no longer seen as gardens of reform; rather, they had become a "furnace of affliction." Inmates were supposed to suffer for their sins, and physical punishment became part of this. It was not until the middle of the century, when the prison "had become a living hell," that reformers and ministers returned to focus on the inmates' spiritual well-being.[17]

While New York activists struggled to meet the individual needs of inmates to facilitate their reform, Pennsylvania's reformers and inspectors played an invaluable role in controlling how the state's prisons were run and constantly promoted its main goal of inmate reformation. Richard Vaux, son of Roberts Vaux, and later mayor of Philadelphia and member of the U.S. House of Representatives, recorded in the *Brief Sketch of the History of Eastern State* the expectations of prison officials to educate the inmates in religious matters. The inspectors' role in this proved to be quite simple as they were to find a suitable instructor. Vaux also described the duties of the religious instructor who would "attend to the moral and religious instruction of the convicts . . . so that when restored to liberty, they may prove honest, industrious and useful members of society" without disrupting the rules of the penitentiary.[18] One can see that these duties aimed to aid inmates on their path to recovery. Furthermore, the employment of a religious instructor speaks to the relationship that the reformers felt was there between inmate rehabilitation and religious education.

Interestingly, no one took the official role of moral instructor in Eastern State Penitentiary for the first few years of the prison's existence. Rather, volunteers helped in this position until the first chaplain was appointed. Reasons for this may be twofold. First, the reformers of the Prison Society acted almost like chaplains in their role. Second, Quakers feared sectarianism. Those acting as moral instructors, however, rarely seemed to be of Quaker heritage, thus potentially appeasing the institutions' critics. Volunteer moral instructors included Rev. Charles Demmé, who was German Lutheran, and Rev. Samuel Crawford and Rev. James Wilson, both of whom were Reformed Presbyterian ministers.[19]

Several letters from the religious instructors to the penitentiary were published in the *Register of Pennsylvania* in 1831 providing firsthand accounts of the moral instructors' opinions of the institution. Demmé was skeptical about separate confinement as an improved method of punishment, initially seeing it as cruel. Through observation of the institution in practice, however, he came to the realization that it was a benevolent process that could protect and help the inmates. With this change of opinion, Demmé became more active in aiding the prisoners in their rehabilitation. He wrote:

> The time is too short, to say with absolute confidence, that an improvement has taken place in the character of any one of the prisoners. The cure, which is to be affected in those diseased minds, must be slow and gradual. First impressions, indeed, of religious truth, if once it finds and entrance into their heart, may be very strong ... but whether these first impressions will have permanency, whether they will overcome the obstinacy of habitual errors, and subdue inveterate passions; whether they will produce a change of sentiment, and of principle, and of taste, so that the prisoner, after the expiration of his term, will despise his former enjoyments, and triumphs of guilt; will prefer honest labor to unlawful gains, will resist the temptation of vice and prosperous villainy, and shun the contaminating circle of his old associates.[20]

Demmé noted here that it would be a long, slow process to rehabilitation, if a full reform could take place at all. There is a sense of hope, too, however, in this observation, that with enough time, change could take place. Demmé fully believed that religious training could have positive effects on the inmates' rehabilitation. His observations and suggestions illustrated his desire to see this accomplished in Eastern State in the most efficacious way possible. In the midst of the Second Great Awakening and the subsequent explosion of reform movements in the secular arena of American society, this attitude makes sense. What the reformers met inside the prison walls with inmate resistance to their efforts, however, demonstrates that religious teaching was not going to be the only means to prisoner reform.

Interestingly, even with volunteers such as Demmé, the board of inspectors and officials continually noted in their reports the need for religion and consistent leadership in that area of inmate reform. In a letter to the Pennsylvania State Legislature, Prison Society president Charles Coxe discussed the importance of religion to the process of Eastern State. He pleaded with the state to consider the importance of and the need for consistent moral and religious instruction. Coxe praised the early volunteers for their efforts. Of Demmé, Coxe wrote that he "has found leisure to imitate the example of Him, who 'came not to call the righteous but sinners to repentance' by visiting the prisoners in their solitary cells, and affording them the aid, and comfort, of moral and religious instruction."[21] The direct correlation between Jesus's and Demmé's work is telling. This description with the allusion to Jesus is striking because it illustrates the idea that the moral or religious instructor was a type of savior of the lost souls of the inmates, and that such figures had the power to change the inmates' attitudes and to help them to the path of a Christian lifestyle.[22]

After years of effort to hire a full-time moral instructor, in 1839, Baptist minister Thomas Larcombe assumed the new role at Eastern State Penitentiary. He recorded notes about the individual inmates with whom he met. From these volumes, one learns about inmates' crimes, and Larcombe's personal opinions about the inmates' potential reform. Clearly, Larcombe was not hopeful. While Larcombe worked with all inmates, his entries regarding female inmates provide a glimpse into the ways female inmates reacted to initial reform efforts. Regarding inmate 1162, Mary Jenkins, serving a three-year sentence for larceny, Larcombe stated that he "endeavored to spread before her all the prospects of her crime and the truth of scriptures in relation to her character & state" in their meeting. Upon release, Larcombe noted that she "gives some evidence of sorrow for sin but not of faith. I fear that a sensuality of feeling will lead to a speedy fall." Charlotte Henry, inmate 1163, convicted of larceny, was "a very hardened girl" and had a bad temper. Larcombe stated that she "did not relish my plain talk assumed [sic] a dogged silence, has no proper sense of her criminality." Henry, "by laughing & contempt of court had her sentence doubled," and upon release, Larcombe determined that she was "incurably vicious." Marian Wilson, convicted of murder, presented a prevalent "spirit of anger and resentment" and was deemed hopeless.[23] These women seemed resistant to reform efforts and demonstrate a power to challenge Larcombe's teachings, even if that means he shapes the perception of female criminals as hardened and incorrigible—the worst of the worst. Even in their resistance to these reformation efforts, women established their personal agency over their incarceration.

Other female inmates feigned interest in reformation, perhaps in an attempt to garner privileges in the prison or even a reduced sentence—or they simply did not care to be reformed. Inmate 507, Hannah Brown, presented one such case early in Larcombe's tenure. He wrote in his journal that she was "lured from virtue in early life. Seems very sensible of her past guilt & shame, professes to be penitent & resolved with the [illegible] of God to walk circumspectfully in future. Serious & prayerful apparently. Subsequently, confesses she has no proper feeling in regard to her soul. Discharged & went to Magdalen Asylum." He later found out that she traveled to New York and returned to a life of licentiousness. Over time, Larcombe became skilled in seeing through the false professions of sincerity and piety—characteristics of a soul slowly being reformed under the prison's system. Mary Ann Rogers, inmate 1973, spent a year in Eastern State for robbery. Larcombe wrote in his book that she "feels deeply & bitterly her lost name & liberty and will promise anything to any person who would get her out," and that she "is certain that a complete & perfect reform should take place." When she was released, Larcombe noted that he had "not much hope" in her reformation.[24] Rogers's behavior indicates that she knew that the goals of the prison revolved around reform and tried to use her knowledge of the system for her benefit, although not in the way that officials had planned. Larcombe sensed the lack of sincerity of some inmates and failed to give in to their manipulation. Yet, the fact that women like Rogers tried to manipulate the system demonstrates the worth and power that they believed they possessed as individuals, driving them to attempt to improve their situation.

While the majority of female inmates were listed as having a bleak chance of reformation following their discharge, Larcombe noted several women he believed had benefited from being incarcerated under the Pennsylvania system. Eliza Smith, inmate 600, for example, was convicted of larceny and sentenced to three years. She told Larcombe "she is glad of being in prison, is satisfied, has no wish to leave it, it has snatched her from the vortex of ruin, will never enter such associations as formerly." He noted that she reads and prays. Letitia Kennard, inmate 1209, under a four-year sentence for larceny, listened to Larcombe's words "with some interest." When she received a pardon, she "wept . . . & was unwilling to go." Kennard worked in the warden's kitchen for nine days after her pardon. Susan Lyas, inmate 1039, died in prison. While we do not know if she truly left her sinful life behind, Larcombe seemed hopeful of her potential. On Lyas, he reported that she "seems to be very much affected and very tender; weeps, and affords some hopeful appearances, says she is sensible of her sins and prays to God but feels afraid there is no mercy for her. Never had religious instruction, until now."[25]

While the entries for each inmate are short, they provide details about the reasons for which the women were sent to prison. Larcombe's comments indicate that reform for certain inmates worked well. For other women, reformation was beyond their capabilities due to what he described as the hardness of their character. Determining whether that hardness was accurate or just a perception of Larcombe will remain unclear. The resistance could be a manifestation of women shaping their experience in prison, making a conscious effort not to submit to Larcombe's teachings as a way to demonstrate control over their situation. These volumes indicate the importance placed on tracking the inmates' moral and religious reform progress. These journals on the inmates show that the experimental reform protocol in the penitentiary was only partially successful, which could stem either from inmate stubbornness or Larcombe's obstinacy in his views.[26]

While Larcombe was the only moral instructor at Eastern State Penitentiary between 1839 and 1860 when he died, three different men held that post at Western State Penitentiary after 1842. While no papers or notes from these men have been found, their comments in the annual inspectors reports to Western State, although given in general terms, indicate they responded to the prisoners in ways similar to Larcombe. A. W. Black, in his report for 1844, states that in his efforts to reform inmates, he had "derived much assistance from the library belonging to the prison." While it only consisted of approximately two hundred volumes, Black argued that the books, having been "freely circulated amongst the prisoners, and together with the Bible and the Book of Common Prayer found in each cell, have contributed considerably to their moral and intellectual improvement."[27]

Like Larcombe, Black realized that many inmates would simply profess repentance of their sins in order to possibly receive extra privileges or perhaps an early release. In 1845, Black wrote in his report, "I take their professions [of religious conversion or repentance] ... with great caution, and watch with scrutinizing care the developments of christian [sic] character, before I rest satisfied in the reality of their change." In the following year, he reported that "imposition in some cases, may be practised by cunning convicts, though imposture in almost all instances betrays itself."[28]

Thomas Crumpton, moral instructor at Western State beginning in 1854, echoed the frustrations of Larcombe and Black in dealing with inmates who feigned reform. He doubted that even those convicts who expressed remorse were forever reformed. In 1858, he observed, "And even in those cases where there is a sincerity of purpose, there is often not that strength of principle, and that cultivation of grace, that will enable them to bear up against the seductions of old associates, and the repulses of the world, when they regain their liberty."[29] The reports of the moral instructors of Western State Penitentiary, along with the notes of Larcombe, indicate that reforming convicts was often trying. Very few inmates convinced the moral instructors that they were truly reformed. Even with these early efforts to aid inmates, female reformers remained unsatisfied in the way that the rehabilitation of female inmates was managed.

THE PIVOTAL IMPACT OF FEMALE PRISON REFORMERS

Prison reformers questioned how they should approach the rehabilitation of female inmates, particularly after women were admitted to the penitentiaries when they opened in the 1820s, yet it took years for a specific program to be put in place. This was apparent in the delayed hiring of matrons for the women prisoners. Some reformers observed a double standard when comparing male and female inmates and their abilities to reform. They believed that released male inmates could more easily move back into free society, and that the public would view such men with less abhorrence for being inmates than they would formerly incarcerated women. Society viewed men's crimes as "follies" rather than vices; after release, "his blood cools; he steadies down, wonders at his former self, and lives in usefulness and repute."[30]

Incarcerated women and released female inmates were not given the same latitude in their social standing. Reformers asked if the criminal woman should "suffer *without hope*, without a chance of repentance, without the means of escape, whether she is *to lose all and forever*?" Her reputation was forever damaged following a stint in the prison. One unnamed prison inspector stated that no one could understand "the depth of [the] misery, wretchedness and degradation" female inmates faced. They "feel that the door to heaven, to society and to respectability is forever barred against them."[31] Although many incarcerated women were already members of the lower classes and were often ethnic and racial minorities, any reputable social standing and chance at respectability evaporated once they were condemned to prison.

The opinions painted a bleak picture for incarcerated women, and they echo the comments of Thomas Larcombe. Benevolent female reformers wanted to challenge this unpromising prospect that many female inmates faced by meeting with female inmates and providing them with moral instruction and domestic education—abilities they would need to lead successful, crime-free lives after their release. The female reformers became advocates, voices for these women, because inmates were often left with resistance as their only means of expression once incarcerated. While resistance helped to keep the inmates actively involved in their imprisonment and kept them in the sights of the prison employees, the women were often voiceless when it came to seeking improvements in conditions, reform, or education. Reformers offered a more powerful, political avenue of empowerment.

The work of these reformers and the skills they taught offered hope, they believed, for female inmates that they could once again become respectable women within their social class outside of prison. These women fostered this hope of character reformation through a process of companionship, education, and domestication. Without their efforts, female inmates may have continued to experience the neglect they faced in prison and rely on resistance as a tool for change, without much hope for a good life after their release. The reformers' work illustrated the need for specific treatment for female inmates and helped to further the arguments for the necessity of separate prisons. These female reformers challenged what was expected of them by society by taking on public roles as prison reformers and putting themselves into environments where they interacted with inmates, who mirrored them in challenging the prison's status quo. Scholars such as Estelle Freedman and Lori Ginzberg suggest that the common bond that the female reformers shared with their counterparts behind bars as women was more important than the class differences that may have separated the two groups.[32] The idea that the two groups of women shared a common experience as females provided the reformers with a level of empathy and connection that male reformers simply did not have. Many reformers, according to Ginzberg, believed "that they had a special mandate *as women* to exert a virtuous influence in the world."[33] Through their work with the female inmates, reformers demonstrated to the inmates that they were valued and that they could contribute to society after their release. The reformers taught them religious and domestic virtues expected of women at the time. By befriending and domesticating female inmates, female reformers acted as embodiments of proper antebellum women and desired to sought the behavior and prospects of those less fortunate than themselves. The term "domestication" as part of the female inmates' reform process is useful because many prison reformers looked at the women as broken, beyond acceptable characters. The female prison reformers worked to readmit the female inmates to an appropriate level of respectable womanhood for the inmates' life situation through training for domestic tasks, better hygiene habits, reading and writing, and moral or religious education.

Reforming female inmates posed a special set of problems, and benevolent women felt they were best suited to promote this cause. Female reformers created their own niche in the larger prison reform movement and forged close bonds with the female inmates. These women not only tried to improve the female inmates' morals but also worked to rehabilitate their reputations into a form that would enable them to be seen by the public as virtuous, gentle, domestic women: characteristics that were valued by bourgeois antebellum culture, even if the reformed women were not part of this class. The goal was to be respectable in their own right. Male reformers very likely could not have accomplished these tasks, especially due to the widespread tendency of men blaming the incarcerated women for their circumstances and therefore treating them with hostility.[34] Furthermore, the female reformers focused less on improving the overall institution of the penitentiary and more on individual women living successful, respectable lives outside of prison. The female reformers showed a high level of compassion for the inmates; they empathized with the plight of the incarcerated women, seeing them as victims of legal and social limitations. Although the female reformers would not have expected the former inmates to become peers in the middle or upper classes, they would have expected the women to try to emulate behavior that would be respectable within their own social class. These reformers, even if they did not always understand the economic and social plight that their charges faced, played a pivotal role in increasing the efforts to work with the female inmate population and by challenging the hostility that male reformers and prison officials had for these women.

While most of the official visitors during the early years of Eastern State Penitentiary's existence were men, one of the more prominent visitors was not a member of the Prison Society at all—reformer Dorothea Lynde Dix.[35] Although well-known for her advocacy for humane treatment of the insane, Dix also spent a great deal of time visiting and commenting on the prison systems. Her written works, which recount her visits to the prisons and interactions with the inmates, stress prisoner reform and promote a sense of hope for their future. In an address she offered to the prisoners of Eastern State Penitentiary, Dix stated, "I am not willing to leave this prison without proving my interest in your temporal and eternal welfare; without trying to aid your own efforts, and to co-operate with your teachers in advancing the all-important work of reformation." Dix stressed that her visits were meant to help inmates, because she believed in reform. "My very soul has sickened at these aspects of desolation made by sin," she told inmates, but she was sustained by "hope" and "the desire of making a fellow being *better and happier.*" She was rewarded in her work by the inmates' efforts at individual reform. At another prison where she met with both men and women convicts, she provided the men with books and slates for education and the women with books and sewing materials. In her meeting with the females, she said "nothing about their wrong-doing . . . it was enough to have awakened some feeling of interest,—some willingness to be employed." She continued in her plea to the Eastern State inmates, "here is *some good* left in those who are most debased,—I am *sure* of that." Dix urged the prisoners to seek salvation so that God will provide forgiveness.[36]

Dix expressed much of the same sentiments in an address to inmates incarcerated at Western State Penitentiary. She told them that the important first step in reformation was admitting "that *they* are in the wrong; that they have sinned." Admitting wrongs, according to Dix, led to full repentance of sins. She implored inmates to "cultivate the powers of your memory" by learning scripture, hymns, or other pieces of instructional literature, which would put them on a path to a better life. Dix emphasized, "I believe that even in prison you may possess serenity of soul; peaceful thoughts; encouraging hopes."[37]

Although Dix mentioned the importance of education and employment on the path to reform, her primary aim was to promote true repentance for their sins and to show them that they were not beyond being reformed. She stressed the good inherent in all people, even those who have committed serious, sometimes violent crimes. Through her efforts, Dix ultimately provided inmates, both male and female, with hope for the future. It is through Dix's work that one can observe how benevolent women often felt about the inmates. Female reformers exhibited a sense of deeper compassion toward inmates as individuals than is evident from many male reformers.

The sufferings of prisoners, particularly female inmates, seemed to tug at the heartstrings of many female reformers, including Dix, and led them to want to make changes in the inmates' lives to help them after their release.

Dorothea Dix was not the only female visitor who met with inmates, but she might be one of the few female reformers who interacted with both males and females. Most female reformers dealt solely with female inmates. In 1823, an Orthodox Quaker, Mary Waln Wistar, organized the Female Prison Association of Friends in Philadelphia after being inspired by Elizabeth Fry's work in England at Newgate Prison in London. She and her husband, Thomas Wistar, along with a few other benevolent ladies, visited the local prisons, particularly Arch Street Prison, and dealt more directly with female inmates and juvenile offenders. From their visits, they saw the need for separate facilities for female inmates. Wistar, along with other like-minded women, continued to visit the prisons of Philadelphia to read from the Bible to the female inmates, and petitioned the boards of inspectors of public prisons in the city to allow them consistent access.[38] These female reformers exemplified ideal feminine characteristics: virtue, piety, gentleness, and compassion. They believed that through their visits, they could help wayward female inmates reset their lives in a way suited for law-abiding society.

Once permission was granted, members of the Female Prison Association visited the Arch Street Prison for two hours each Monday. Throughout 1823, they increased their number of visitors. During these visits, the women read to the inmates, usually from a religious text. The visitors offered "counsel and admonition . . . as ability was afforded," and ministers often accompanied them. Because the prisoners at this facility were not classified and separated according to crime or some other characteristic, the women found it difficult to teach the inmates to read. As a compromise, they distributed tracts "among those who could read, and short texts of Scripture, printed in large characters and pasted on boards, were hung on the walls in the prisoners' apartment." Although some inmates cared not for the reformers' attentions, "tears fell freely from the eyes of others. Their general condition was truly pitiable and affecting." Because Arch Street Prison held untried offenders, the inmate population fluctuated. The female visitors rarely dealt with the same inmates during visits and thus found it difficult to gauge the long-term effectiveness of their work.[39]

On other days, the women visited the sick inmates in the infirmary as well as those confined to their cells. Based on the descriptions of their visits to Arch Street, the inmates were not kept in isolation as was the protocol at Walnut Street, and later Eastern State Penitentiary. Thus, the women were able to reach a larger population of inmates all at once. In addition to providing religious and educational instruction, the women furnished the impoverished inmates "with needful apparel" and distributed "combs, needles, cotton, &c., among them to promote habits of neatness."[40]

While the Society for Alleviating the Miseries of Public Prisons aided Wistar and her fellow reformers with goods to supply the female prisoners, it appears that some of the male reformers in the Society were skeptical of her work. In an undated letter from Roberts Vaux to his mother-in-law, Mary Waln Wistar, Vaux voiced some of his concerns. Responding to Wistar's request for clothing for female inmates, Vaux noted that the Society would provide some "short-gowns" for the women, but that the Society rarely provided clothing to inmates "excepting in extreme cases during the winter season." Although she had succeeded in obtaining some clothing from Vaux, he spent the remainder of his letter warning her against the hardened characters of the female inmates. He wrote that the women with whom Wistar visited formed "a circulating medium of poverty & vice" and that their bad "habits have become chronic" and in "most instances beyond restoration." Vaux believed that if the women were given good garments to wear, within a few hours of their release from prison such items "would be surrendered as the price of some sensual appetite, the indulgence of which in a few more hours, would insure their return to Prison." He admonished Wistar to be wary of making the incarceration of habitual offenders easier with material goods, but rather hoped she would persist in her visiting and "make impressions of good which may yeild [sic] to you, & to them, a recompense more precious" than material items. While Vaux urged Wistar to continue her work, he remained skeptical about the women and their ability to be reformed.[41]

The skepticism voiced by Vaux is interesting considering that other male reformers in Philadelphia had created the city's Magdalen Society in 1800 to help wayward and fallen women, namely prostitutes, reform their lives. The Magdalen Society provided women with a place to stay, and the women received instruction in religion and domestic tasks, which was very similar to what Mary Waln Wistar wanted to provide to female prisoners.[42] If Vaux's opinions in this letter were general sentiments of the Philadelphia Society of Alleviating the Miseries of Public Prisons, it could be that they felt little need to help female offenders who, to some reformers, seemed incapable of changing their lives for the better. It appears that there is a hierarchy of female sins at work in nineteenth-century society, with female prisoners occupying the lowest position. This attitude represents the challenge that the female reformers faced time and again from male reformers and prison officials as they strove to improve the prospects of women in prison.

Such skepticism did not stop Wistar and the other members of the Female Prison Association. In 1824, they "urged the propriety of employing a conscientious matron to preside over the female prisoners, as it would be within her sphere to enforce cleanliness and industry, and to contribute essentially to the right conducting of the whole department on the women's side of the prison."[43] Most of the work done by the Female Prison Association was aimed, at least implicitly, at domesticating these women. By educating them, providing religious teachings, and sharing articles to promote personal hygiene, the visitors worked to break bad habits and to give female inmates the means to reform themselves into respectable women. This call for a matron suggests that the women felt it was within their "sphere" to help female inmates to be hygienic and industrious. Ideally, the matron would embody the traits of a respectable woman, who could teach the inmates, in a motherly manner, the proper ways to maintain themselves as well as teach them skills that respectable women should have. The matron's role exemplified the growing role of sentimentalism in American society during the antebellum decades. Karen Halttunen argues that sentimentalism led to new ways of thinking about child-rearing. Instead of using corporal punishment to make children obey, mothers used "the powers of persuasion and parental example."[44] In a similar way, the matron would mother these wayward female inmates and prepare them for life after prison.

From their early visits to Arch Street, the women became increasingly concerned about the "quite young girls, who were committed sometimes for trivial offences, and who were thus exposed . . . to the company of women who were hardened in crime." They worked to see a House of Refuge established for juvenile offenders to alleviate the problem of young minds being polluted by exposure to serious criminals. By 1833, there still was no matron employed in Arch Street. The visitors felt that there was "great loss sustained for want of the influence of a matron, to reprove and restrain the improper conversation and habits of the prisoners." They redoubled their efforts to place matrons in the county prisons when they learned that the new county prison in Moyamensing was to be established in 1835. The female activists lobbied the Prison Society to request that the state legislature hire a matron in the new prison because "little expectation could be entertained of raising female convicts above their deplorable situation, until they should be placed under the superintendence of officers of their own sex."[45]

In 1835, the Female Prison Association was finally invited to Eastern State Penitentiary. The female visitors quickly ascertained "the benefit the prisoners were deriving from their entire separation from each other, and the softening influence of the uniform kindness with which they were treated by the *Matron* and the other officers of the establishment." The women visited "weekly," during which time they "read to the women and [taught] them to read; and by their religious labors" exerted "a favorable influence upon those coming under their care." The reformers were pleased to see that Eastern State exhibited "those Christian principles which had so wonderfully ameliorated the condition of the prisoner" and did not destroy "the sensibility of the woman by chains and stripes, unkindness and reproach."[46] At Eastern State, they saw the value of separation and silence, because it enabled inmates to reflect and work on individual reform, whereas at Arch Street, the individuals were lost in the mass of chaos that joint living and no inmate classification promoted. The women visitors at Eastern State could more likely work with individuals and teach them to read and write, something they chose to forego at Arch Street because of the lack of classification. With the ability to pay attention to specific inmates, it is no wonder that the Female Prison Association members were pleased with what they saw in their work at Eastern State Penitentiary.

That the Female Prison Association was not granted access to Eastern State Penitentiary until 1835 is intriguing. The women of this reform group had been hard at work for almost a decade before they could meet with penitentiary inmates. Although Eastern State opened in 1829, it did not have a female inmate until 1831, as noted in chapter 4. Once women started being sentenced to Eastern State, however, it would have made sense to involve members of the Female Prison Association. The change of heart in 1835 may have been a direct result of the legislative investigation that the Commonwealth of Pennsylvania initiated into the management and treatment of prisoners in 1834. Women played a central role in the inquiry, and it was made painfully clear from the testimony that there was little discipline and no reform happening among the female inmates.[47] Inviting the Female Prison Association to begin visiting in 1835 could be seen as an effort to respond to the charges and problems that the state exposed, thanks in part to the testimony of the women inmates. Pennsylvania's penitential program, as vociferously touted by reformers in Philadelphia, had cracks at its foundation. Female prison reformers worked to fix the issues. These women took up the task of giving the women inmates a voice in ways that the inmates themselves could not.

The Female Prison Association's positive attitude toward the work done at Eastern State progressed into the 1840s. On November 21, 1842, Mary Anna Longstreth, in a letter to Rebecca Collins, her aunt and a leader in the Association, wrote joyfully that "Rosanna Lecounte and Maria Jones will be out in a few days, & then there will be but 14 female prisoners at Cherry Hill. An encouraging decrease from 32 to 14, since the visits of the Committee."[48] The visits, according to insiders at least, made positive inroads to the convicts, as evidenced through the dropping number of female inmates.

Longstreth continued reporting good news from the Penitentiary into 1843. On January 22, 1843, she wrote that for the past two months she has "been at the Penitentiary almost invariably every other week—our visits continue to be very interesting, though circumstances often occur, calculated to discourage & depress us." She recounted a story of two little African American boys who were imprisoned because there was not a House of Refuge in the city for African American juveniles, but stated that they "are improving nicely."[49] This suggests that the Female Prison Association was involved not only with female convicts at Eastern State, but with the younger inmates of both sexes as well. She continued in her praise for the penitentiary:

> The Warden is very kind & humane in his treatment of the prisoners, and attends in the most polite manner to the suggestions of the committee. Surely when Dickens visited our penitentiary, he must have had glasses, black, blue, or of some dismal colour, over his eyes, to see the gloomy pictures he described in his "notes on America." The female convicts are certainly contented & most of them happy, by their oft repeated acknowledgment—and with the frequent visits of the Matron & her assistant, the Moral Instructor, the Ladies' Committee, the ministers who out to read & preach to them, they are not too lonely.[50]

It is worth being a bit skeptical of the positive portrayal from Long-streth. She would want to see the work of her organization positively affect the inmates as well as promote the humanity of the warden and the prison system at large. In these personal, private letters, Longstreth could have very easily erased the veneer of positivity concerning what she observed in the prison. Yet, she did not do so, suggesting that she truly did see positive effects from the reformers' work. She mentioned at one point that circumstances had the ability to discourage and depress. It was not pleasant work seeing the inmates suffer or observing the two young African American boys who likely should not have been in the penitentiary at all. Through her words, we glimpse the varied reality of prison reform work: discouragement at times, though retaining an optimistic overall outlook.

The reformers' work continued throughout the nineteenth century at Eastern State. By the mid-1860s, reports commented on their success. In fact, their work was being deemed so important that more women visitors were needed! The Prison Society sought "the co-operation of females, in their labors in the prisons" to visit female inmates because their past work "has been realized by the faithful labors of women, when and where woman's peculiar adaptability to the work could be most successful." The report's author continued that women visitors were matched with female inmates who had the same religious upbringing, creating an instant connection. By 1868, the Prison Society solicited more visitors for the female inmates, stating that "we know that these visits are welcome to the inmates" and "cannot doubt that they are extensively useful." They hoped to increase the number of visitors because they believed that "a field so promising will be tilled to a rich harvest."[51]

Much of the Female Prison Association's work took place in the county jail in Philadelphia, Moyamensing. In the county prison, one can observe the progress the Female Prison Association made in their reform efforts. Moyamensing provided the female inmates with a matron who continued the reform activities of the Female Prison Association when visitors were not around. Inmates were housed in a clean, neat prison, which indicated a desire to promote such traits in the female inmates. Furthermore, the female inmates completed work that was domestic in nature. The women were tasked with "spooling or sewing," and the matron "who appears really interested for their good, often visits them, and attends to their lessons during the recess of the visiters."[52] In addition, a library was made available for the inmates, stocked with religious tracts and other educational literature. Assigned chores that were feminine in nature and provided appropriate reading material, the inmates essentially became trained in domestic, feminine behavior during their incarceration, with an eye to a domestic life beyond their term of imprisonment. These actions gave the female inmates another way to demonstrate their worth and presence in prison beyond resistance. It also showed that female reformers believed in the women's capabilities to improve their lives, a marked change from the attitudes most male prison reformers and officials.

In addition to their work of providing practical domestic education to the imprisoned women, the Female Prison Association also promoted religious goals. The visitors wanted to "set before" the prisoners "their sinful condition in the sight of a just and holy God, and to exhort them to flee from the wrath to come by repentance and faith in the Lord Jesus Christ." Even though at times their reform efforts failed to change the behavior of some of the imprisoned women, the Female Prison Association felt "that [they] dare not retreat from this field of labour," because they continued to hope that the women would be redeemed.[53]

One encouraging story of a black female inmate at Moyamensing exemplifies the purpose of the Female Prison Association:

> She had been several times committed for theft; and possessing naturally a weak mind, was easily overpowered by temptation, the sin of intemperance giving strength to her other evil propensities. The labours of the visiters for a while appeared ineffectual; but during her last commitment she was, through divine grace, enabled to see herself in a new light, assuring the committee that she felt more concerned for her soul than she had ever done before, and was determined to seek earnestly for salvation. ... Upon being reminded that the blessed Saviour came into the world "not to call the righteous, but sinners, to repentance," and her visiter [sic] pointing her to Him, as *the sinner's only hope*, she received it as glad tidings, and it seemed that the conviction, for the first time, darted into her soul, that SHE could be an object of redeeming mercy.[54]

Other examples from the late nineteenth century corroborate the influence these female visitors had on the inmates. Mrs. P. W. Lawrence told the Prison Society that she received a letter from a former prisoner "for whom she obtained a good situation in a neighboring State, and has no doubt of her thorough reformation; she knew she was a woman of more than ordinary ability." An elderly woman who was incarcerated in Moyamensing spent much time learning Christian doctrine from a female visitor, was reported as being a saved woman upon release. Another woman, who had served two sentences, owed much to the female visitors. They "united her with her family, and she went to live in one of the suburban towns, where she began church work, and was a most influential member of the church, starting many new societies and doing good work." When her criminal past was found out, she was driven from the congregation. Her prison visitors aided her in establishing another new life, although "this terrible sorrow in no wise shook her perfect faith and confidence in God. She took up her life and fought it out bravely and womanly."[55] Although the stigma of being a former prisoner sometimes haunted these women, these success stories point to the efforts of the female visitors to evoke lasting character change in their charges. These women proved their worth to themselves and to society and sought opportunities to right their path and reenter society.

As the stories above indicate, the Female Prison Association desired to promote individual salvation in the inmates they visited. The organization's work exemplifies the antebellum reform movement and the influence of the Second Great Awakening on American society. Reform groups provided women with an approved place to become involved in society, outside the home. In some ways, this was political action, because they could influence social change by working to improve public virtue.[56] Similar to women who committed crimes to effect social change as demonstrated in chapter 3, the work of female reformers took on a political tone. As the women reformers questioned the authority of male prison reformers and worked in the public sphere, they were ultimately challenging male authority of American political and social life and demonstrating their awareness of their place and worth in such a system.[57] Furthermore, Lori Ginzberg contends that these female reformers defined their mandate for benevolent work as "uniquely female." To that end, they saw it as their duty as morally upstanding women to work to improve society.[58] This belief in the moral superiority of women allowed them to work outside the home while remaining respectable women. The Female Prison Association was, therefore, not atypical of female reform work.

In their reform efforts, these women demonstrated their own worth to society by aiding those women less fortunate than themselves and helped the incarcerated women to prove their own value. They took an active, and implicitly political, role to effect change. Naturally, female reformers would be interested in reforming female inmates because they themselves embodied the characteristics of virtuous women, and thus would be the best role models for the erring women. Like the matrons in the prisons, female reformers could mother and shape the inmates with their visits by emphasizing virtuous conduct and domesticity. While the female reformers might not actually verbalize that they were acting as role models for female offenders, their actions and the types of education they provided inmates suggests that they sought to rehabilitate this group of offenders by domesticating them. Some may view this approach as coercive; however, because the reformers had the interest of the inmates at heart, these women probably did not view their own work in this way, but rather as a means to allow female inmates to reenter respectable society as skillful and empowered women.

The stories of individual female inmates recorded by the Female Prison Association provide historians with a view into the lives of incarcerated women who interacted with these reformers. The Association published "deeply interesting cases . . . in the form of tracts" in the hope that "they may be instrumental in encouraging other poor wanderers to accept the offers of redeeming love."[59] Not only do these published accounts depict female incarceration, they also illustrate the work of female reformers.

An Account of Julia Moore, a Penitent Female, Who Died in the Eastern Penitentiary of Philadelphia, in the Year 1843, published in 1844 by the Female Prison Association, offers one example.[60] Through its description of Moore's incarceration, one gets a sense of not only her pitiable situation in prison, but also of the female visitors' goals in meeting with these female inmates. The pamphlet chronicled Moore's religious conversion in prison before her death. The case demonstrated the broad antebellum desire to reduce crime in cities and the belief in the inherent good and redeemable nature of criminals in the penitentiary system. This pamphlet also acted as a pedagogical tool to illustrate to readers what befalls people, particularly women, when they turn to a life of crime.

Julia Moore was an alias for a real prisoner named Julia Wilt. Based on the prison records, it can be estimated that she was born around 1802, and she hailed from Easton, Pennsylvania, in the eastern part of the state. She was listed as being a servant, suggesting her position in the working class of society. She entered the criminal record in 1839, at the age of thirty-seven, but this was likely not the first time she broke the law. The May 19, 1839, issue of Philadelphia's *Public Ledger* reported Julia's case. She, along with two African American men (Julia herself was identified as white), were charged with mutilating a man's arm "with a penknife to such a degree that it afterwards required amputation." The victim testified in the case that he asked Julia where he could buy oysters and that she told him to follow her to the place. He stated that after he followed her into a house, "two colored men seized him, commenced robbing him, and with a knife nearly severed his wrist from his arm; that the men and woman then took from him $35, a pair of woolen mittens and a handkerchief, and that his arm was amputated at the Pennsylvania Hospital." Julia and one of her accomplices were sentenced to seven years at Eastern State Penitentiary for robbery. We learn even more about Julia once she enters the prison records: she had a light complexion with blue-gray eyes and black hair. She could read but not write, got intoxicated occasionally, and had left her husband.[61] We know little else about her life before her crime, but the registers of Eastern State imply a relatively tough existence.

The pamphlet recounting her experience took on a didactic tone from the outset. The anonymous author wrote that Julia "was in early life exposed to the temptations and snares of 'a world that lieth in wickedness.'" At a young age, Julia "forsook the paths of virtue, plunged into a vortex of iniquity, and involved herself in ignominious guilt." The pamphlet's author proposed that her early entry into the criminal world caused her demise. After suggesting that Julia tried to reform her habits, the author noted her failure to leave the life of crime. Julia's case demonstrated the nineteenth-century fear that one crime or vice led inevitably to more heinous crimes. Julia was painted as a person of weak morals. She "joined hands with the workers of iniquity" and, as a result of her participation in the robbery, was sentenced to seven years' imprisonment. The author of the pamphlet deemed Julia "a wreck of human nature."[62] The description of Julia as a depraved creature demonstrated her lack of femininity but also that she had only herself to blame for her actions.

The pamphlet discussed her experience in Eastern State Penitentiary, not from Julia's point of view, but from those of the penitentiary officials and reformers who hoped she would change. The reformers viewed her as a depraved inmate who needed to understand "the enormity of her sins, and her need of sincere repentance." The chaplain called Julia an "undone creature." She accepted his "unwelcome tidings," causing her "to behold her vileness" and subsequently to desire mercy. The author noted that God's mercy helped Julia, "for scarcely had a year registered her imprisonment, before the mists of doubt and darkness began to vanish from her benighted soul, and she seemed to enjoy a perpetual sunshine."[63] Julia was righting her own life of sin. But it also expressed the belief that a commitment to a Christian lifestyle will lift the burdens from one's soul. The emphasis on her religious conversion illustrated the great necessity for her to take God into her life to prepare her for eternity, as death was seemingly close due to a lingering illness.

Julia was portrayed as a model prisoner—penitent, quiet, thoughtful, and truly thankful for her incarceration. According to the author, "She spoke of herself with much humility, and great abhorrence of the wickedness of her former life; participating in almost every kind of sin, till in mercy she was arrested and thrown into prison." This type of portrayal of prison life was exactly what early reformers wanted outsiders to hear about their penitentiary: it promoted the superiority of the Pennsylvania system of solitude and reflection. It recorded that, although her illness sometimes occasioned the necessity of having another inmate in the cell to care for her, she "preferred being alone . . . that a companion diverted her mind from a train of useful meditation and communion."[64] By describing an inmate who preferred solitude so she could meditate and reflect, this pamphlet argued against people who believed that Eastern State's system actually promoted insanity and was cruel in its solitary confinement. Julia's desire for solitude helped to demonstrate the system's alleged success.

Although most of the pamphlet was written anonymously and extolled the values of the Pennsylvania penitentiary through the experience of Julia Moore, it did claim to copy a letter "precisely in her own language," from Julia to a female visitor of the penitentiary.[65] This letter, dated April 27, 1843, is the closest we get to retrieving her own voice:

> I improve this opportunity to inform my sincere friend that I am very feeble at present. . . . I long to hear your instructions once more. I feel thankful that I have been spared to express the sense of

gratitude I feel for those benefits you have all been pleased to confer upon me. I thank Almighty God for all his kind mercies to me . . . I have reason to bless the day I entered this Prison. I feel that I am a great sinner. Oh that I may feel more humble and lowly in heart. In the night when all is asleep, I think I sometimes hear a voice saying, "Be of good cheer; your sorrows shall be turned to joy." How sweet to my mind is this, "There is room for the chief of sinners." Here is my hope; Jesus is my refuge. He has heard me in a time accepted, and in the hour of great trouble *He* removed my burden. Blessed be God! I hope what few days I have here below, that the Lord will give me courage, strength and faith, that my soul may be saved, and his name be glorified. "Almighty God! Unto whom all hearts are open, all desires are known, and from whom no secrets are hid, cleanse the thoughts of my heart by the inspiration of thy Holy Spirit, that I may perfectly love thee, and worthily magnify thy Holy name, through Jesus Christ our Lord."

I sincerely thank you for the present you gave me, "The Sinner's Friend."

I remain your truly afflicted scholar,

Julia Moore[66]

While the legitimacy of this letter as Julia's might be questioned, one must also consider that it might be authentic. The Eastern State records for Julia, noted above, reported that she could only read, so even if this letter is of Julia's creation, it clearly was dictated to a third party (unless the prison records were inaccurate). Due to this possibility, it is difficult to know whether these were truly Julia's words or if the scribe converted her sentiments to read more eloquently. In addition, policies were in place since the penitentiary's inception that prohibited letter writing, indicating that unless Julia received special treatment in her ailing condition, this text may have been fabricated to some extent. Around the time of Julia's demise, however, the rules at Eastern State regarding letter writing relaxed somewhat, so there remains a possibility that this letter represents one of the first from an inmate.[67]

From this letter, and the pamphlet in general, one can see the virtues of the Female Prison Association's actions, at least according to the reformers' point of view. In the case of Julia Moore, according to the pamphlet, the female visitors had a positive impact on her during her last days on earth. They helped her to see the errors of her past life, provided companionship throughout her illness, and provided gifts such as the publication "The Sinner's Friend." Finally, the letter showed a strong bond had developed between Julia and her anonymous female visitor who had been so kind to her and befriended her during her incarceration and sickness.

The pamphlet closed with the death of Julia on May 10, 1843. When considering the overall motivations for the pamphlet, several themes become apparent. The goal of finding religious salvation is central to the document. It can be viewed as a propaganda piece for the penitentiary itself and for the work of the Female Prison Association. Julia was a model prisoner brought to salvation by the discipline of the Pennsylvania system and the efforts of female reformers. Julia, in this pamphlet, provided an antithesis to the belief that women inmates could not be reformed. Had Julia survived her sentence, she may have turned from her life of sin. Unfortunately, there is no way to know if she had truly repented, and it is difficult to ascertain the extent to which this pamphlet exaggerated her claims of success. The reform group had an agenda to promote, and Julia suited their cause. Yet, other evidence from the group's work suggests they really did seek to provide long-lasting reform and improvement in the lives of these women, demonstrating a level of altruistic motivation.

It is likely that the friend of Julia Wilt's referred to in the pamphlet was Mary Anna Longstreth, who wrote about Julia in a letter to her aunt, Rebecca Collins, a respected member of the Female Prison Association. Longstreth wrote:

> On the 10th of this month, poor Julia (at the Eastern Penitentiary) was released from her complicated sufferings. I saw her on the 8th, (in paying my accustomed visits,) and found her extremely ill with Erysipelas in the head, entirely blind, and her face swollen to such a degree that I should not have recognized her. On being informed that I was in the cell, she expressed pleasure and I addressed a few sentences to her, but she was too ill for conversation, and after that time, was insensible. We have, however, good ground for believing that she is among that innumerable company whose robes have been washed & made white in the blood of the Lamb, whose sins have been blotted out.[68]

While one might think the Association inflated its success to prove a point regarding the virtues of the penitentiary system, Longstreth's letter and the moral instructor's report on Julia corroborated the pamphlet's claims. Larcombe noted that Julia "hopes for happiness not here but in heaven because God is all sufficient." Before being sent to Eastern State she had "sunk into debased and brutal vice & hardness." Larcombe noted her long road to salvation, stating that she "has been subsequently the Subject of some very deep mental anguish on acct of her sins & now possesses a hope in the merits of Christ." After her death, Larcombe rounded out his entry, stating that she "presented entirely satisfactory evidence of preparation."[69]

Finally, the pamphlet is most simply a warning to both the public and future criminals of the damages that living a life of sin and crime can have on a person. The pamphlet at first portrayed Julia as a horrible wretch, who had totally succumbed to crime and cavorted with other felonious associates. Later, Julia turned her life around, albeit in the prison, and wanted to forsake her life of crime—an indication that the reform process worked for some inmates. The pamphlet is a morality tale, one that spoke directly both to the public's fear of individuals degenerating into a life of crime and to their reliance on a strong relationship with religion to save wayward souls.

Other examples of successful reform exist as well. Francis Lieber described a meeting with a female inmate of Eastern State who told him that the female reformers had educated her.[70] The female visitors helped this inmate to read and write, and offered her religious training. Because of this education, she was able to ask her mother to forgive her for living a life of crime. A prison visitor named Mrs. Nicholson received a letter from a former inmate in which the writer expressed gratitude for the good work these women did for the inmates. The anonymous former prisoner wrote, "Here I am to-night a happy girl and good home. . . . You have raised me from leading a bad life, which I would have continued only for your good, sweet advice you gave me the second year that you came to unlock that terrible door for me, poor sinner." She sent Mrs. Nicholson a small gift as a token of appreciation, stating, "I know that I ought to do ten thousand times as much, and yet I would not be doing enough for you. I never can repay you for what you have done for me."[71]

From these examples of the positive work the female reformers accomplished, one can see that bonds formed between some inmates and reformers. Estelle Freedman argues that when reformers talked about their work, they used a rhetoric of "sisterhood." Reformers saw these women as peers, ignoring class and racial differences to emphasize "the common bond of an innate womanly spirit."[72] The reformers felt a kinship with these women, and used that feeling to propel their benevolent work. While the female visitors might not be able to make such progress with all the women they visited, even a few success stories of providing hope to the female inmates—like this young woman and Julia Moore—probably fortified them in their work and demonstrated that some inmates were receptive to the efforts of the female reformers.

The work of these female reformers did not go unnoticed by contributors to the *Journal of Prison Discipline and Society*. Their work was a "pleasing and interesting spectacle" due to their "untiring efforts and laudable zeal." The language used by the journal describing these women and their work is truly positive and worth quoting at length: "During all weathers, and at all seasons, amid sunshine or storm, they are constant and regular in their attendance, and unremitting in their labors. Their mild and benevolent demeanor towards the prisons, the moral instruction they impart, and their words of encouragement and consolation, act in many instances, like a charm upon the unfortunate female inmate; and it is needless to say, that these visits are always attended with the most flattering results."[73] Reports from the post–Civil War period confirm the ongoing positive work of these reformers, demonstrating that these women saw a continuing need to work with this special population of prisoners.[74] These visitors had the ability to be models of expected female behavior, women for the female inmates to attempt to emulate in character and comportment. Female reformers realized that this role was important to fill for these women who obviously had lacked such mentorship to be pulled into a life of crime in the first place.

FEMALE REFORM EFFORTS OUTSIDE THE PRISON

The weekly visits with inmates constituted only part of the duties the Female Prison Association undertook. In the early days of their organization, the women of this association also worked to aid discharged female prisoners. They provided some of the discharged inmates with "situations at service, in respectable families, generally in the country," made possible by "the exertions of the visiters" for those women who "appeared to be sincerely penitent and anxious to 'cease to do evil and learn to do well.'"

Some of these prisoners sent the organization reports on their progress outside of prison. One such former prisoner had "been several years in a public institution in the neighbourhood of this city, where she continues to conduct in a becoming manner."[75] These testimonials reported on the success at rehabilitating at least some of these women and providing them with suitable service positions after their release. The women visitors, however, were at the mercy of the inmates' sincerity; there was no foolproof way of knowing if prisoners were truly reformed.

These female reformers feared what would happen to these former inmates if left to their own devices in the outside world. The "virtue of a discharged female convict is in imminent danger as soon as she leaves the walls of the prison." While they left "the Prison full of promise" with "a strong resolution to do wrong no more," in most cases these women had "no means to avoid the place, or the companions of early associations." These sentiments from throughout the nineteenth century suggest the continuing need to help discharged female prisoners in their transition to free society. Formerly incarcerated women needed the "evidence of hope in the visitor" and a place to continue their reformation. As advocates suggested, "we must plant before we can hope to harvest, we must trust before we can be assured of improvement, we must compel the convict to earn all she gets before she gets it."[76]

These fears, and the resulting desire for such an institution, were voiced by members of the Female Prison Association as early as the mid-nineteenth century. They lamented "the want of an asylum, in which, as a temporary home, we could place the liberated convict and test her resolutions, before venturing to obtain a situation for her in a private family." To this end, the Association worked diligently throughout the antebellum decades to establish such an asylum, particularly as the numbers of female inmates increased. The Acting Committee minutes on October 12, 1852, for the Pennsylvania Prison Society indicate that the Association wanted a "*refuge* in which the penitent female might find both occupation and moral training calculated to discipline them for future usefulness." The women saw this refuge as "a stepping stone between the Prison, and the wide world." They argued that their work in the prison "sustained a loss without such an auxiliary; and we believe the time has come for us to make a vigorous effort, in aid of these *miserable females* many of whom now young in vice, may be permitted to grow old in sin, for the want of efficient helpers." In the plea, the organization noted that "we tell them to shun the haunts of wickedness; to engage in some honorable employment; but we point them to no safe retreat; we afford them no means of procuring an honest living."[77] Without a place for the discharged inmates, the Association feared that their hard work in the prison would be forgotten and the freed women would eventually lapse back into a life of crime. The reformers sought long-term, permanent rehabilitation.

Four months later, the women found themselves still pleading with the Pennsylvania Prison Society about their desire for a home. On February 26, 1853, Susan Lloyd, stated before the Prison Society meeting that they wanted an institution designed to "protect such females as are exposed to temptation and crime; and where they may be trained in habits of neatness and industry." The women in the home would be "instructed in useful knowledge to qualify them for eligible situations" and would be given "the advantage of a religious influence and be strengthened in their resolutions of amendment."[78] From this statement, one can see that the proposed institution might not only cater to discharged female inmates, but also to women who were suspected of eventually becoming criminals. At the same time, the institution would act preemptively as well as aiding in the continued redemption of freed inmates.

The Association soon got its way. The Howard Institution, named after British prison reformer John Howard, opened its doors on September 1, 1853, first on Spring Garden Street before moving to a larger location on Poplar Street. The home would "board and clothe" women for three to six months. The Committee believed that six months was adequate in helping women "sincerely desirous of amending their lives, and by endeavoring to surround them with right influences" to help them lead a virtuous life.[79]

The Institution, like the prisons themselves, published annual reports. While some have been lost throughout the years, the extant reports provide a glimpse into the workings of the home, the female managers of the society, and its influence on its inhabitants. Yet again, we are limited to the reformers' perspectives themselves. Out of the thirty-one different women who served as managers of the Institution during the years 1858–60, five had husbands who were part of the Howard Institution's Board of Advisers. Many of the women who were part of the Howard Institution were Quaker and married men with middle- and upper-class occupations, such as attorneys, merchants, tea dealers, and presidents of coal and railroad companies.[80]

By belonging to the middle and upper classes of society, these women had time to spend in running the organization, helping with the upkeep of the home, and working with its inhabitants.

Initial reports suggest the need to continue promoting the rationale for the Howard Institution and their methods of reform. These benevolent women had lobbied for decades to establish a place for released female prisoners who "really wished to reform their lives, but who, being destitute of respectable relatives or friends, were induced to return to their former evil haunts and wicked companions," which resulted in further incarceration. They hired Mary Murray as matron and Catherine Horn as assistant matron to help the women learn tasks like sewing. Catherine Horn also devoted "a portion of the evenings to instructing them in reading and writing." In the first three years of the Institution's existence, fifty women spent time in the home. The managers reported that they were "at times cheered and encouraged to hope, by the industry and general good conduct of the inmates" and hoped "that the care and labour bestowed upon them, will not be wholly in vain." By 1856, the managers still mentioned the necessity of their work, stating that the home provided a refuge for former prisoners where "their feeble resolves may be strengthened, and where, surrounded by hopeful and religious influences . . . be encouraged to give up the practice of vice" and have a fresh start in life. The work the inhabitants engaged in was to "qualify them for filling useful and respectable stations in life."[81]

The report for 1857 observed that the women were "instructed in a knowledge of household duties by the matron and her valuable assistant, who also evidence a conscientious regard for the moral and religious welfare of those under their care." The emphasis in the institution continued to be on domesticating these women and molding them into suitable domestic workers. By providing former inmates with a place to be educated and reformed, the Howard Institution sought to create women like themselves: gentle, educated, and domestically industrious. While the inmates would likely never reach the upper echelons of society, they could become proper, hardworking women of their station—respectable in their own right and thus of value to society. The managers also reported that some inmates who had left the home "have purchased useful articles and presented them to the Institution."[82] From these instances of returned kindness from former inhabitants, one can see that this institution made an impact on the lives of these women by continuing the work that was begun inside the prison walls.

Later reports and documents provide further insights into the reasons why the Association wanted a home for discharged female inmates. The report for 1858 noted that the Institution aided approximately fifty women, most of whom came straight from prison. It suggested that the public had little idea of "the trials and disabilities, to which the discharged female prisoner is subjected." Whatever her offense, however insignificant, "the *name* and *stigma* of *convict*, is upon her. . . . She is pointed at with scorn." No matter how well the former inmate behaved while incarcerated, there remained "a moral atmosphere about her, which repels even the charitable, and which makes the unthinking and the selfish turn from her with abhorrence."[83] The public still viewed these women as broken, even after their release: they had transgressed societal rules and as such had revoked their womanly nature. Because of the moral standard to which women were held, criminal women were often viewed as beyond hope. The Howard Institution reformers sought to change this attitude and once again be voices and advocates for the aid and improvement of these women.

In contrast to the public sentiment, the Association believed that young criminal women still retained "a remnant of womanly feeling, and a hope of redeeming the past."[84] The managers of the Howard Institution reported that "it is this '*helping hand*' in the '*needful time*,' that we have endeavored to extend to those, who have been the objects of our care." Upon arrival, "[a] kind matron welcomes her . . . searches for what germs of goodness may yet be remaining; and if there be but a smouldering spark of virtuous hope, sedulously preserves it from extinction." Each inhabitant was treated "as a woman and sister." They argued that "the Institution has been a blessing to those who have been the subjects of its discipline. Many have given evidence of *radical* improvement."[85] The Female Prison Association and the Howard Institution were bent on providing hope to this class of females and treating them as women, not as wretched creatures. With this persistent belief in the redeemable nature of the criminal women, the reformers again exhibited their sisterhood with the erring women. By treating them as peers, the reformers were able to regard them with respect and aid them in reentering society as acceptable, self-sufficient women who could ultimately seek to advocate for themselves.

Some women were grateful for the hope and support the Howard Institution provided. The annual reports often included letters from former residents. One resident, identified only as M. L. F., wrote, "If it had not been for Mrs. W. and Miss H. where would I have been at this time? perhaps in eternity, for I was tempted by Satan on every side, but the Lord heard my prayers and delivered me out of all my troubles, by raising up friends for me who I never thought existed a few days before." On December 13, 1858, a woman referred to as R. G. wrote to the institution, "How indebted to you for the kindness bestowed, and the very comfortable home, I with the rest of my erring sisters have found through your charity. I frequently think of the pleasant days I have spent in the sewing-room with Miss M., she was always so very kind to us."[86] These letters from women who received direct help from the Institution illustrate the importance of the Association's efforts at establishing the Howard Institution and helping female inmates beyond the prison walls.

The work of the Howard Institution continued into the postwar years, although perhaps with less zeal than in the 1850s. By the late 1860s, managers admitted that their work was not foolproof, yet still clung to the hope that their work had a positive effect on inhabitants: "In many cases there may be a relapse, but we trust the good seed sown would not be wholly lost." They took pride, however, in the small numbers of women they reached. "Although we may not be able to point to hundreds, who we can say are reformed under the care of 'The Howard Institution,'" the report observed for 1869, "there are many happy homes to which mothers and daughters have been restored, 'clothed, and in their right mind,' after a year spent at 'The Home.'" Others who spent time in the home are also improved due to diligent religious instruction and domestic work. The activists' aim continued to be character reform and to "perfect each in some trade" so that the inmate can make an honest living after leaving the Institution. Yet, by this period, the Howard Institution was not solely focused on released prisoners—it was "truly a home for fallen women, discharged female prisoners, and outcasts."[87]

———

Reformation of Pennsylvania's inmates was a multilayered process that utilized a top-down approach. While some inmates may have desired reform efforts, this process was driven largely the reformers themselves. These activists mused over the best means to achieve this change in the inmates.

The process itself began in the prison cells with volunteer chaplains and later the prison moral instructor, men who were employed by the institution to promote the penitentiary's goals of individual reformation and repentance. For some reformers, women in particular, the question remained whether the current means of reform actually helped female inmates. While Thomas Larcombe visited with both men and women in prison, could he really understand the plight of female inmates? Was he best suited to help these erring women improve themselves? Were the official visitors paying close enough attention to how the female inmates were treated in comparison to males? Could they distinguish neglect or mistreatment? Female reformers thought not. They realized quickly once they began visiting the county prison that the women in Eastern State languished under bad conditions and needed the reformers' advocacy. Thus, female prison reformers had a new goal: to become voices of compassion and support for the small population of female inmates in Pennsylvania's prisons in order to help them transform into advocates for themselves.

Members of the Female Prison Association believed that the female inmates might respond more positively to reform efforts and be more successful if they were guided by women themselves. These female visitors provided the inmates companionship, gentle and sympathetic encouragement, domestic education, and moral instruction. The female visitors embodied the ideal characteristics of nineteenth-century women and could thus provide the inmates with figures and traits to emulate during their rehabilitation and after their release from prison. The female reformers, despite their altruistic motivations, can be seen as somewhat controlling. By offering their white, middle-to-upper-class behavior and morality as the ideal for female inmates, the female reformers worked to mold these inmates into respectable citizens. While the inmates would likely never rise out of the lower strata of society, they were taught skills and traits by the reformers that could help them live respectable lives among their peers. Although oftentimes the success stories are the only ones preserved for posterity, in many instances the inmates did not change, perhaps owing to the differences in class, race, and ethnicity between the reformers and the prisoners. Such different life experiences naturally impeded these two groups seeing eye to eye. However, the reformers continued their work, and success stories and receptive inmates allowed them to maintain their efforts.

The female reformers also realized the failure of the penitentiary system to help inmates after their release. Without a program to help women after prison, there was little reformers could do to ensure that ex-prisoners would stay away from vice and crime. The Female Prison Association, in their conception of the Howard Institution in Philadelphia, provided released female inmates with a place to continue their individual reform efforts. The Institution allowed former inmates to continue to be molded into respectable women; they were, in effect, being domesticated by learning household duties and womanly skills so that they could provide for themselves—legally—in the future. The members of the Female Prison Association believed that female inmates needed to be treated differently than did their male counterparts and thus created opportunities for benevolent women to aid female inmates in their moral and domestic rehabilitation. The efforts of the visitors from the Female Prison Association and those who worked with the Howard Institution provided female inmates with skills and hope so that they, by becoming virtuous and industrious, could be active, valuable members of society—women of worth and voice.

Conclusion

In 1897, inmate A6583, Josephine Smith, testified at a legislative investigation undertaken by the state to consider troublesome practices at Eastern State. While not as extensive as the investigation in 1835, it dealt with a very important issue—the fact that the state believed the number of insane inmates was being underreported. Josephine Smith was twenty-six at the time her twelve-year sentence for second-degree murder began in December 1891. She was one of only two women who spoke up about the mistreatment endured at the hands of prison officials. Her willingness to testify about her experiences demonstrates the continued challenge to prison discipline that many women participated in during their incarcerations in the nineteenth century. By voicing her complaints, Josephine acted in accordance with a long line of former inmates who openly resisted and challenged prison protocol and treatment of female inmates—problems that had not been previously rectified. She testified:

> Well, gentlemen, when I was down there . . . and they rang the bell, there were two young men outside of my gate and they began to talk to me. I answered them back, and she . . . said it wasn't just right and that the few things I said weren't altogether right. It was in the corridor. I began to pound and knock down [illegible] I wanted to know why she couldn't give me a good report to the Warden. So they took me down to the Insane ward and kept me for nine months. Then she came and I went back. She said I called her out of her name because she called me out of my name. I thought it was out of my

name because it was through her ignorance and I didn't think she was right. Then they kept me without food for going on seven days. I didn't take any food because I didn't want it.

Q: You had some food?

A: No, I had bread and water for seven days. So then she gave me back my food. Well, now, I am down there now.

Q: Is the Matron, or whoever is in charge of you, kind to you?

A: They are kind enough now. I find them all right enough now.[1]

As is evident from the transcription, Josephine's testimony is sometimes difficult to follow and leaves readers wondering where she was located and with whom she was conversing. It can be supposed that she may have been placed in a punishment cell when she mentions that she was "down there" and on a bread and water diet, which were designated punishments in the earlier days of the institution. Perhaps some of those practices continued into the latter half of the century. She may have also been referring to the matron as the "she" who would not give a good report to the warden. These suggestions, however, remain only suppositions. Considering Eastern State's history of punishing problematic inmates with dark cells and reduced diets, Josephine was likely recounting her experience in one of these cells. She may have even resisted the bread and water until her regular diet was restored—a hunger strike of sorts. If she was mentally unstable, it is possible that prison employees punished her for her behavior rather than seeking out medical help for her condition.[2]

Josephine Smith's testimony, while valuable in providing a window into how one woman's incarceration played out at Eastern State, remains problematic for historians. For one, she exhibits signs of incoherence and confusion, which limits just how much we can treat her words as fact. If she did initiate a form of resistance by refusing even the bread and water provided to her, Josephine Smith may be exerting more prisoner agency than one might expect considering her alleged mental instability, calling into question her true state of mind. Was she less unstable and more manipulative than initially thought? Another factor to consider when analyzing her testimony is the fact that her sentence was not over. She was released on June 25, 1900, according to the prison's population records. Her testimony indicates that her food was returned and that the mistreatment had stopped before she took the witness stand. Was this done to limit how much she complained about conditions during the testimony? Did she limit what she said to protect herself from other inmates or prison employees when she returned to prison? With these possibilities, the inmate testimony poses more questions than it answers. In any case, the 1897 investigation exposes continuing problems with inmates' treatment at Eastern State. Furthermore, it demonstrates the continuing power that individual inmates had in resisting the oppressive nature of the institution. With her public testimony, Josephine Smith marshaled her personal agency to potentially shape the investigation's findings and perhaps change prison protocols moving forward.

The same year as the investigation, warden Michael J. Cassidy published *Warden Cassidy on Prisons and Convicts*. Meant to be of interest to organizations dealing in prison management, it can be read as a way for Cassidy and Eastern State to promote their ideals and do some damage control after the investigation. He noted that there were no firearms on the property, that guards were not trained in deadly force, and that much of the unruly behavior stemmed from prisoner disagreements among themselves. Furthermore, in response to the charge that Eastern State's isolation program caused insanity, Cassidy was careful to call their system "individual treatment" in that prisoners were treated as their needs dictated and noted that inmates interacted with many people, including visits from family once every three months. In Cassidy's determination, Eastern State did not practice solitary confinement because inmates were not fully isolated. An excerpt from the testimony demonstrates Cassidy's stance on the matter:

> Q: Are there cases here of what is commonly known as solitary confinement, where a prisoner is kept entirely to himself?
>
> A: o, sir; there never was such a thing here.
>
> Q: What is the least number you put in a cell?
>
> A: One. That is not solitary confinement. An occupant of a cell has communication with the people who come to the prison, except the convicts.
>
> Q: Are you ever compelled to put them in irons, or to place them in dark cells or dungeons?
>
> A: We have no mechanical appliances for punishment of any sort.
>
> Q: You have none of any kind?
>
> A: We have none of any kind; nothing but what you see. We have no dark cells.[3]

This exchange paints a positive picture of the inmate treatment at Eastern State. Yet, Josephine Smith's testimony suggests that inmates faced mistreatment and perhaps they distrusted employees. It is possible that Smith was in a type of punishment cell, something that Cassidy denied existed at Eastern State. Discrepancies between what inmates and Cassidy reported in terms of the daily procedures at Eastern State are evident throughout the records.

Furthermore, there is obvious distrust of inmates from the employee perspective. Cassidy recounted examples of the deception inmates used to appear insane, perhaps in hopes of better treatment. In part of his testimony, Cassidy stated, "Yes, most of the mentally-affected or feeble-minded people exhibit great ingenuity. One woman who was here,—had been several times before,—had a trouble called 'galvanic rheumatism.' She couldn't walk, but had to go on crutches. She fooled her three years' sentence in that way. She then complained at another time of some internal trouble, and called the doctor for treatment. When leaving the institution, as soon as she reached the outside, she flung the crutches aside."[4] Cassidy's testimony demonstrates that he believed many of the "insane" convicts were actually playacting in some capacity. While Cassidy discussed so positively the system of which he was in charge, his evident skepticism regarding inmates' mental capacity and capability for rehabilitation makes one question whether the policies he touted were truly the ones used on a daily basis.

The investigations open the door for outsiders to view daily life inside the prison, albeit at times of extreme stress in the institution's history. Once the investigations concluded, the daily goings-on at Eastern State were closed off from public knowledge. Yearly reports from the officials paint optimistic portraits of prison life, yet the fact that investigations occurred at all suggests that there was often a different story than that told by officials. What really happened behind the walls of the prison was prisoner resistance and struggles by those in authority to keep order and discipline in place. The inmates, including women, as exemplified above, proved time and again that they were unwilling to become victimized by the oppressive nature of the penitentiary. By using their voices, resisting food, feigning illness or physical incapacitation, these women challenged the prison employees and the system itself on a daily basis. These actions in the late decades of the nineteenth century follow in a long line of women criminals and inmates in Pennsylvania who understood their place in society as women—oftentimes members of ethnic and racial minorities and members of lower social classes—yet felt empowered to challenge the legal and prisons systems, as well as society at large, that remained determined to limit female power and liberty.

Women caught up in the legal system remained active participants in the process at every step. These individuals did not play the role of passive women or appear victimized. Instead, they took control of their situations and worked to shape their own stories. They realized they had some level of agency and used that in various ways to put themselves in a more active position to mold or improve their experience. This study has looked at the ways that women interacted with, dealt with oppression by, and influenced the criminal justice system of the antebellum period. The wide range of approaches that women took in navigating criminal acts, court trials, prison sentences, and reform efforts demonstrates the flexibility and mobility that women had in society and how they worked to challenge the expectations that they would adhere to certain norms of idealized womanhood, or that because they were not part of the white middle class that they could not strive to be respectable in their own right. At all phases of their criminal lives, these women pushed against societal norms and leveraged their knowledge of them to their advantage when they could, strategizing and acting to place themselves in the best possible situation. Because of the court records, newspapers, pamphlets, prison records, and reformers' papers that have survived, we are able to gain insight into the dynamic world of these women and the various ways they understood their place in Pennsylvania's communities and the criminal justice system and used that knowledge to their benefit.

While many women in this book never would have naturally fallen into the idealized notions of womanhood that prevailed in the antebellum decades due to their race, ethnicity, or class, these women who committed crimes and ended up entangled in the court and prison systems were very much aware of these norms and found ways to manipulate them for their own purposes. To these women, their choice to turn to crime to solve economic, marital, or other personal problems may have been the last feasible option in a society that limited other opportunities for them. These women showed an understanding that their current place in society may pose some limitations but they did not necessarily need to be bound by them. In fact, some women harnessed the characteristics of the white, middle-class gender ideology and used that knowledge to shape their experience in the antebellum legal system. There was power in their awareness. Female swindlers and shoplifters often used the guise of respectable femininity to enact their cons or avoid arrest. Others stole items in order to appear respectable, to raise their social status, or to provide their families with needed items such as food or clothing as a good mother or wife should. In court, some women used expectations of womanhood to sway the judge and jury into a lighter sentence or an acquittal. By appearing to be a sympathetic individual, sometimes making an emotional plea or telling a sad story, some women played on the sympathies of the court officials and avoided prison. Other women portrayed themselves as respectable in court—either in physical appearance, in character witness testimony, or by maligning a victim's character to appear more trustworthy in contrast. These women who employed these strategies demonstrated awareness of what society in general expected of women. Considering that judges and jury members likely shared this mind-set, the women's tactics sometimes worked in their favor—especially if the crime was a first offense, of a minor severity, or if there were extenuating circumstances, like the defendant's age.

Other women who committed crimes eschewed social conventions by perpetrating infanticide and murder. They directly challenged these social conceptions of proper womanhood by venturing into the realm of typically male actions of aggression and violence. Yet, looking beyond the simple fact that these women committed violent acts tells us more about the women's experiences in society at this time. Severe social and economic restrictions limited the power of the women arrested for these types of crimes. For example, women who committed infanticide were sometimes driven to the act because of financial hardship or fear of losing employment. Many of these women were of the working classes, and many were recent immigrants—populations with little recourse for other options or improved economic situations. These women may likely have felt that committing the crime may have been the only way to protect what little stability they had in in terms of employment or finances. Many of the female murderers in this study poisoned their husbands. Although the motives of these women varied from abusive relationships to simply wanting to marry a different lover, these women's actions reflected the difficult legal situation they were in as married women. The trouble of acquiring a divorce, for these women, was too much due to laws and the standards by which divorces were granted; so they chose the route of poisoning, which they believed would hide their crime. Not only were these women aware of their legal status, but they selected a method of murder that might allow them to get away with the crime, a seemingly feminine method, particularly if they appeared as caregivers during the process while their spouse was dying or showed visible grief at the passing of their husband. These women, at the same time that they challenged society's limitations on their legal rights and freedom as married women, still adhered to and played the role of domestic caregivers to cover their crimes. This dynamic ability to challenge societal expectations and adhere to them at the same time is remarkable and demonstrates their keen cognizance of their place in society but also their power to manipulate that to achieve certain goals—even if the method to do so was murder. These women must have believed they had no other alternative.

Some women took the idea of challenging societal expectations further by participating in political riots regarding labor conditions, fugitive slaves, and nativism. While the world of traditional politics was a male domain, women found ways to have a voice and to challenge the expectations that they could not be political actors. Female participants in riots, which often turned violent, demonstrated that their actions could be a mechanism through which they could work for economic, social, and political change. Rioting provided a way that women could stand up for and protect their families and their communities. Their willingness to be involved in these politically charged crimes, and possibly go to prison for them, demonstrates that they had a desire to be heard and to act as active agents for change, believing that public, direct action gave them their best chance for success.

Women sentenced to prison for their crimes continued this pattern of resistance inside their cells. They continually demonstrated their worth as individuals and strove to maintain distinctiveness while incarcerated. Simply being female was an initial challenge to the prison system. Prison employees had a difficult time dealing with female inmates, whether it was due to their own preconceived notions about them or because the women prisoners defied their authority. The female inmates were sometimes given special privileges because prison officials believed women were not really capable of committing crimes. Other women took a more active, overt role in challenging the oppressive nature of penitentiary life. Some wrote letters and poetry, others willfully broke prison rules and property, and still others resisted reformation efforts. Many women's rehabilitation in prison was often neglected because they were viewed as being beyond the bounds of acceptable womanhood and therefore unable to be reformed. Even the moral instructor, whose task it was to help in the reformation efforts, viewed most of the female inmates as hopeless cases. Perhaps these women were simply demonstrating their power to shape their time as prisoners and to control their experiences by resisting rehabilitation to help the inmates know their worth to society.

Yet, members of the Female Prison Association believed that the female inmates might respond more positively to reform efforts if they were guided by women themselves—there would be some level of shared experiences, and the interaction between reformers and inmates might serve as an act of empowerment for both the reformers as public figures and the inmates in their quest for rehabilitation. These activist women saw the neglect the female inmates were exposed to in the prisons, wished to improve that situation, and saw themselves as the means by which such improvement could be attained. Although the female visitors embodied the characteristics expected of proper nineteenth-century women—they were white and middle-to-upper-class—they believed they were better suited than men to work with these women, in that they could act as motherly figures and provide the inmates with feminine traits to emulate during their rehabilitation.

From the moment she embarked on her path of crime, a female criminal was often at the mercy of how others in power perceived her, yet she herself had power to manipulate these expectations to benefit her own situation, thus co-opting and challenging the expectations of antebellum women when it suited. By others, Elizabeth Harker was considered depraved, and Julia Moore, an undone creature. These two women met their fate in prison, yet their legacies illustrate that they refused to be passive victims of Pennsylvania's criminal justice system. Their challenge to the antebellum standards of womanhood and their resistance to becoming silent sufferers in prison demonstrates the power that women criminals had to shape their own story. The challenges that many of these women posed to their communities' mores, to public expectations, to prison officials' disciplinary efforts, and to reformation endeavors throughout the phases of their criminal careers shows that they found ways to empower themselves in a time when societal institutions were set on limiting their role and importance in society. The very systems implemented to restrict the power or influence of women in the nineteenth century were often thwarted by women committing crimes or their insistence on being seen and heard while incarcerated. Without their willingness to challenge and resist expectations and oppressive policies, these women very well could have been lost to history. Their defiance and social awareness allowed their lived experiences to survive in the archival record.

———

Women's continued challenges to prison discipline and reform efforts once convicted in the period following the Civil War caused reformers to look once again at how women criminals were being punished. States returned their attention to looking for a better way to deal with female criminals. The reformatory movement became that next approach. New York, which blazed the trail in developing solely female penal institutions, saw the inherent problems of housing women in the same institutions as men in the early years of the state's penitentiaries. The prison at Auburn, however, experienced problems similar to Eastern State when it came to dealing with female inmates. Sing Sing's officials wanted nothing to do with female inmates. They attempted to get all the state's female inmates sent to Auburn. When that plan was rejected, women were housed at Bellevue Hospital in New York City. This solution did not last long. As early as the late 1820s, plans were put in place for a women's prison on the grounds of Sing Sing. After years of discussion regarding the best arrangement for a women's prison, New York planned to build two women's prisons, one close to Auburn, the other near Sing Sing. By 1839, however, due to financial difficulty, Auburn's women's facility would send most of its inmates to Sing Sing, thus making the women's institution at Sing Sing the sole facility for females.[5]

Even with this separate institution for women, disciplinary problems remained. The new facility was located close to the men's quarters, making it possible for interaction between the sexes. The women's building was not equipped with a kitchen, requiring male inmates to bring food over to the women's prison. Furthermore, the women's prison's construction allowed for communication between the inmates. Overcrowding also became an issue. While officials thought women would be better behaved in their own facility, this was not to be the case. Women "carried knives, fought with one another, and made the air ring with ribald songs and lusty yells." Under the guidance of Eliza Farnham, in 1844 the women's prison at Sing Sing became more organized with educational programs and rehabilitation efforts, but state officials viewed these programs as too lenient and thus ended Farnham's tenure. By the 1870s, the state had reverted back to the plan of shipping female inmates to New York City. During the next two decades, three reformatories for women opened at Hudson, Albion, and Bedford Hills, ushering in a new era of discipline for women offenders, something started by Farnham almost a half century before.[6]

Pennsylvania lagged behind New York in moving to the reformatory model. New York built Elmira Reformatory for men in 1870 and the three women's institutions at Hudson, Albion, and Bedford Hills soon after. Pennsylvania did not open its first reformatory until 1889. This institution, known as the Huntingdon Industrial Reformatory, was opened to provide a correctional institution for young men guilty of less serious crimes.[7] Unlike the state penitentiaries which focused on the anonymity of the inmates, these reformatories dealt with inmates as individuals. Inmates were classified according to crime, health, age, and other determining factors. In addition, these institutions provided inmates with skills and education that would benefit them after release and offered a promotional system with rewards for good behavior.

A female institution, similar to the one at Huntingdon was approved by the Pennsylvania legislature in 1913. The State Industrial Home for Women was built in Muncy in 1920. Initially, women and girls from ages sixteen to twenty-five could be sent there for no more than three years. By 1922, officials at Eastern State Penitentiary began removing inmates to the new facilities or to the Philadelphia County Prison at Moyamensing. Three years later, the state designated monies for a new department to be built at Muncy for older women, thus creating both an industrial reformatory and a penal institution on the same grounds. Two years later, in order to alleviate overcrowding at county jails, the state allowed women who were sentenced to county prisons for one year or less to be sent to the appropriate institution at Muncy.[8]

Almost a century earlier, in 1833, Francis Lieber in the introduction to Alexis de Tocqueville and Gustave de Beaumont's study of American prisons foresaw the problems that faced penal institutions if they did not quickly note that female inmates needed differential treatment. "Are separate penitentiaries for females required?" he asked. "I believe they are," he continued, "if the Pennsylvania system is not adopted, and with that system a matron at least will be necessary for the special superintendence of the female prisoners." Women were best suited for this job, in Lieber's opinion. Female inmates must be treated differently: "Besides, the moral management of female convicts must differ from that of male criminals, and even their labour requires a total separation. . . . If it should be found impossible to make the labour of female convicts as profitable as that of men, we must not allow ourselves to be retarded by a financial consideration in providing for them, since we have seen how important their proper treatment is."[9] Lieber was decades ahead of the times with his ideas. As this study has shown, women were not a criminal population to be cast aside. They challenged convention in committing their crimes and in the way they manipulated definitions of proper behavior to suit their needs. They rebelled against prison protocol time and again throughout the antebellum and postwar periods, demonstrating a willfulness in the face of poor conditions, strict discipline, and reform efforts. Even so, the state struggled to justify a separate style of penal institution for women. Perhaps the small female population allowed the state to delay its legislation for a female institution. The efforts of female reformers to visit female inmates and help them transition back to free society may have been viewed as a stopgap solution for the state; it allowed them to ignore the problem that this small population caused by committing crimes and being sent to predominately male institutions. Yet, the power that female criminals and inmates had to challenge the standing systems showed that they were not powerless, but rather possessed the influence to shape their lived experience within the legal and prison systems. Although many viewed this class of criminals as beyond hope of reform, this small population of women showed their awareness of how they were viewed and sought to challenge such conceptions through the way they navigated these societal institutions.

APPENDIX A: COUNTY CRIME STATISTICS

This table was constructed from the Court of Quarter Sessions dockets for the counties listed below. These counties represented my sample for this study, as explained in the introduction. Every county's records was searched from 1820 to 1860, where records existed, with the exception of Philadelphia County, where, due to the high volume of records, I used records from every five years: 1820, 1825, et cetera, up through 1860. The categories devised helped to illuminate a broader picture of the types of crimes committed in each county. The individual chapters of the book discuss the ramifications of this further.

TABLE A.1. Percentage breakdown of types of crime by county

County	Moral/petty	Property	Violent
Adams	66.13	12.90	20.97
Allegheny	43.39	23.55	33.06
Bedford	40.38	18.27	41.35
Berks	31.13	16.98	51.89
Chester	27.68	36.16	36.16
Cumberland	65.62	17.61	16.77
Dauphin	55.17	24.38	20.45
Erie	64.10	17.95	17.95
Huntingdon	32.35	15.69	51.96
Lancaster	49.15	20.92	29.93
Luzerne	42.61	24.35	33.04
Mifflin	48.55	12.32	39.13
Philadelphia	21.52	40.05	38.43
Washington	46.29	25.09	28.62
Westmoreland	40.74	11.11	48.15
York	61.89	11.01	27.10

APPENDIX B: EASTERN STATE PENITENTIARY
FEMALE DEMOGRAPHICS

Collated from convict reception records and "Descriptive Registers," ESP. Many of the prison records are simply line entries for each inmate. By focusing on various categories from these sources, the tables below provide a picture of the female population imprisoned at Eastern State Penitentiary. Without many sources on individual women, these statistics offer a glimpse into the lives of these women.

TABLE B.1. Admission age of female inmates at Eastern State Penitentiary

Age upon admission	Number of women admitted, 1829–1860	% of women admitted, 1829–1860	Number of women admitted, 1861–1900	% of women admitted, 1861–1900	% of all women admitted, 1829–1900
12–19	53	23.04	69	16.83	19.06
20–29	128	55.65	179	43.66	47.97
30–39	31	13.48	82	20.00	17.66
40–49	15	6.52	50	12.20	10.16
50–59	1	0.43	23	5.61	3.75
60+	2	0.87	7	1.71	1.41

TABLE B.2. Place of origin of females admitted to Eastern State Penitentiary

Place of origin	Number of women admitted, 1829–1860	% of women admitted, 1829–1860	Number of women admitted, 1861–1900	% of women admitted, 1861–1900	% of all women admitted, 1829–1900
Pennsylvania	90	39.13	189	46.10	43.59
Rest of the United States	82	35.65	121	29.51	31.72
International	58	25.22	100	24.39	24.69

TABLE B.3. Race of females admitted to Eastern State Penitentiary

Race	Number of women admitted, 1829–1860	% of women admitted, 1829–1860	Number of women admitted, 1861–1900	% of women admitted, 1861–1900	% of all women admitted, 1829–1900
White	98	42.61	176	43.35	43.08
Nonwhite	128	55.65	230	56.65	56.29
None listed	4	1.74	0	0	0.63

TABLE B.4. Occupation of females admitted to Eastern State Penitentiary

Occupation	Number of women admitted, 1829–1860	% of women admitted, 1829–1860	Number of women admitted, 1861–1900	% of women admitted, 1861–1900	% of all women admitted, 1829–1900
Cook	8	3.49	2	0.49	1.56
Factory work	1	0.43	3	0.73	0.63
Housewife	8	3.49	18	4.39	4.06
Housework	0	0	92	22.44	14.38
Keeping bawdy house	1	0.43	5	1.22	0.94
Laborer	0	0	3	0.73	0.47
Laundry	6	2.61	7	1.71	2.03
Making clothes	36	15.65	36	8.78	11.25
Medicine	4	1.74	4	0.98	1.25
None listed	49	21.30	33	8.05	12.81
Other	8	3.49	12	2.93	3.13
Servant	104	45.22	164	40	41.88
Textiles	5	2.17	1	0.24	0.94
Thief	0	0	30	7.32	4.69

TABLE B.5. Crime of females admitted to Eastern State Penitentiary

Crime	Number of women admitted, 1829–1860	% of women admitted, 1829–1860	Number of women admitted, 1861–1900	% of women admitted, 1861–1900	% of all women admitted, 1829–1900
Abortion	0	0	7	1.71	1.09
Accessory to murder	0	0	1	0.24	0.16

TABLE B.5. Crime of females admitted to Eastern State Penitentiary (continued)

Arson	7	3.04	18	4.39	3.91
Assault and battery	7	3.04	20	4.88	4.22
Assault and battery to kill	0	0	7	1.71	1.09
Bawdy house	12	5.22	14	3.41	4.06
Bigamy	2	0.87	2	0.49	0.63
Burglary	5	2.17	6	1.46	1.72
Concealing death of bastard child	3	1.30	6	1.46	1.41
Conspiracy	4	1.74	1	0.24	0.78
Embezzlement	0	0	1	0.24	0.16
False pretenses	0	0	5	1.22	0.78
Felony	0	0	1	0.24	0.16
Forgery	0	0	1	0.24	0.16
Kidnapping	1	0.43	2	0.49	0.47
Larceny	149	64.78	237	57.80	60.31
Manslaughter	9	3.91	9	2.20	2.81
Mayhem	2	0.87	0	0	0.31
Misdemeanor	1	0.43	0	0	0.16
Murder (first degree)	0	0	7	1.71	1.09
Murder (second degree)	5	2.17	19	4.63	3.75
None listed	1	0.43	2	0.49	0.47
Other	0	0	4	0.98	0.63
Passing counterfeit money	5	2.17	8	1.95	2.03
Perjury	1	0.43	11	2.68	1.88
Poisoning	0	0	2	0.49	0.31
Receiving stolen goods	5	2.17	14	3.41	2.97
Robbery	11	4.78	5	1.22	2.50

APPENDIX C: WESTERN STATE PENITENTIARY FEMALE DEMOGRAPHICS

Collated from the "Descriptive Registers," WSP. Many of the prison records are simply line entries for each inmate. By focusing on various categories from these sources, the tables below provide a picture of the female population imprisoned at Western State Penitentiary. Without many sources on individual women, these statistics offer a glimpse into the lives of these women. The records for Western State Penitentiary are not as extensive as those from Eastern State, hence the difference in end date for the statistics.

TABLE C.1. Admission age of female inmates at Western State Penitentiary

Age at time of incarceration	Number of women admitted, 1826–1860	% of women admitted, 1826–1860	Number of women admitted, 1861–1876	% of women admitted, 1861–1876	% of all women admitted, 1826–1876
14–19	27	31.76	19	21.11	26.29
20–29	44	51.76	45	50.00	50.86
30–39	5	5.88	16	17.78	12.00
40–49	7	8.24	4	4.44	6.29
50–59	1	1.18	2	2.22	1.71
60–69	0	0	0	0	0
70+	0	0	1	1.11	0.57
Unlisted	1	1.18	3	3.33	2.29

TABLE C.2. Place of origin of females admitted to Western State Penitentiary

Place of origin	Number of women admitted, 1826–1860	% of women admitted, 1826–1860	Number of women admitted, 1861–1876	% of women admitted, 1861–1876	% of all women admitted, 1826–1876
Pennsylvania	58	68.24	48	53.33	60.57
Rest of the United States	19	22.35	18	20.00	21.14
International	8	9.41	24	26.67	18.29

TABLE C.3. Race of females admitted to Western State Penitentiary

Race	Number of women admitted, 1826–1860	% of women admitted, 1826–1860	Number of women admitted, 1861–1876	% of women admitted, 1861–1876	% of all women admitted, 1826–1876
White	22	25.88	54	60	43.43
Nonwhite	61	71.76	36	40	55.43
None listed	2	2.35	0	0	1.14

TABLE C.4. Occupation of females admitted to Western State Penitentiary

Occupation	Number of women admitted, 1826–1860	% of women admitted, 1826–1860	Number of women admitted, 1861–1876	% of women admitted, 1861–1876	% of all women admitted, 1826–1876
Cook	2	2.35	0	0	1.14
Dressmaker	2	2.35	2	2.22	2.29
Farmer	0	0	1	1.11	0.57
Hired out	0	0	2	2.22	1.14
Laborer	1	1.18	16	17.78	9.71
None listed	29	34.12	1	1.11	17.14
Nurse	2	2.35	0	0	1.14
Seamstress	5	5.88	8	8.89	7.43
Servant	42	49.41	60	66.67	58.29
Washer-woman	2	2.35	0	0	1.14

TABLE C.5. Crime of females admitted to Western State Penitentiary

Crime	Number of women admitted, 1826–1860	% of women admitted, 1826–1860	Number of women admitted, 1861–1876	% of women admitted, 1861–1876	% of all women admitted, 1826–1876
Adultery	0	0	1	1.11	0.57
Arson	6	7.06	2	2.22	4.57
Assault and battery	0	0	5	5.56	2.86
Burglary	2	2.35	2	2.22	2.29
Concealing death of bastard child	3	3.53	3	3.33	3.43

TABLE C.5. Crime of females admitted to Western State Penitentiary (continued)

Forgery	0	0	1	1.11	0.57
Larceny	68	80.00	66	73.33	76.57
Murder	2	2.35	1	1.11	1.71
Passing counterfeit money	0	0	2	2.22	1.14
Perjury	2	2.35	3	3.33	2.86
Poisoning	0	0	2	2.22	1.14
Receiving stolen goods	2	2.35	2	2.22	2.29

APPENDIX D: GENDER AND RACE OF
MOYAMENSING ADMISSIONS

From Pennsylvania Abolition Society Papers, Historical Society of Pennsylvania, Series S.10, Volume—Miscellaneous Statistics on Black Crime in Philadelphia, 1859. This table provides a breakdown of inmate admissions to the Philadelphia County Prison at Moyamensing, the institution that replaced Walnut Street Jail, and depicts trends in incarceration patterns through gender and race.

TABLE D.1. Gender and race of Moyamensing admissions

Year	White males	White females	White total	Black males	Black females	Black total	Total admissions
1835	70	10	80	53	23	76	156
1836	150	22	172	92	41	133	305
1837	136	18	154	92	38	130	284
1838	120	8	128	84	36	120	248
1839	99	15	114	105	41	146	260
1840	75	11	86	76	40	116	202
1841	91	20	111	78	27	105	216
1842	91	15	106	77	38	115	221
1843	92	10	102	59	13	72	174
1844	79	9	88	52	12	64	152
1845	95	8	103	68	18	86	189
1846	95	9	104	56	18	74	178
1847	86	11	97	58	20	78	175
1848	83	13	96	46	18	64	160
1849	88	13	101	67	8	75	176
1850	99	10	109	35	10	45	154
1851	157	20	177	54	15	69	246
1852	212	21	233	71	13	84	317
1853	171	28	199	57	17	74	273
1854	181	25	206	49	11	60	266
1855	133	23	156	53	20	73	229
1856	146	29	175	44	9	53	228
1857	171	37	208	43	18	61	269
1858	230	33	263	61	19	80	343
Total	2,950	418	3,368	1,530	523	2,053	5,421

Abbreviations

JPDP   *Journal of Prison Discipline and Philanthropy*
PDD   *Pittsburgh Daily Dispatch*
PPL   *Philadelphia Public Ledger*

Introduction

1. *PPL*, April 16 and 22, 1839.
2. "Prison Punishment Docket," Philadelphia Prisons System Papers.
3. *PPL*, May 15, 1840; "Miscellaneous Descriptive Books, 1829–1842," Eastern State Penitentiary Papers (hereafter "Miscellaneous Descriptive Books," ESP). The ESP Discharge Records also say Mary was thirty-two at the time of her release. We can assume she was in her early to mid-thirties when she was first incarcerated. While unconfirmed, it is very possible that these two reports reference the same woman. It was not uncommon for the same individuals to show up often in criminal records. Furthermore, the timing between cases is such that both Mary Woodwards are likely one and the same.
4. This issue will be taken up more fully in chapter 1.
5. Rothman, *Discovery of the Asylum*; Foucault, *Discipline and Punish*, 82, 138, 235. Other important books on the rise of penitentiaries include Ignatieff, *Just Measure of Pain*; Hirsch, *Rise of the Penitentiary*; Hindus, *Prison and Plantation*; and Dumm, *Democracy and Punishment*. On the development of an organized police force in the nineteenth century, see Johnson, *Policing the Urban Underworld*; Liebman and Polen, "Perspectives on Policing in Nineteenth-Century America"; Lane, "Urban Police and Crime in Nineteenth-Century America"; Monkkonen, "History of Urban Police."
6. Meranze, *Laboratories of Virtue*; Kann, *Punishment, Prisons, and Patriarchy*.
7. Freedman, *Their Sisters' Keepers*; Rafter, *Partial Justice*. On women in prison, see also

Dodge, *Whores and Thieves of the Worst Kind*; Patrick, "Ann Hinson"; Branson, *Dangerous to Know*; Gross, *Colored Amazons*. Other notable works on early nineteenth-century inmates include Smith, *Prison and the American Imagination*; Nash, "Incarcerated Republic"; Tarter and Bell, *Buried Lives*; Hayden and Jach, *Incarcerated Women*; Manion, *Liberty's Prisoners*, 1, 5.
8. For further discussions on this issue of societal and institutional control in the nineteenth century, see Manion, *Liberty's Prisoners*; and Gross, *Colored Amazons*.
9. Rush, *Enquiry into the Effects of Public Punishments*, 10–11.
10. Preyer, "Penal Measures in the American Colonies," 336–37.
11. Meranze, *Laboratories of Virtue*, 21; Preyer, "Penal Measures," 343; Masur, *Rites of Execution*, 71. On infanticide, see Klepp, *Revolutionary Conceptions*, 226–29, but chapter 6 more broadly.
12. Kann, *Punishment, Prisons, and Patriarchy*, 5.
13. Welch, *Punishment in America*, 4.
14. Bacon, *Quiet Rebels*, 165. Emphasis in original.
15. Quoted in Teeters, *Cradle of the Penitentiary*, 29. For a continuation of how the Pennsylvania system worked, see Teeters and Shearer, *Prison at Philadelphia*.
16. Teeters, *Cradle of the Penitentiary*, 31; Pestritto, *Founding the Criminal Law*, 40.
17. Statistics and charts are located throughout the chapters as well as in a series of appendixes at the end of the study.
18. "Historical Census Browser." See also Miller, *Geography of Pennsylvania*, 87–89; and Meinig, *Shaping of America*, 131–44.

Chapter 1

1. *PPL*, April 16, 1836.
2. Papke, *Framing the Criminal*, 35.

3. See also Manion, *Liberty's Prisoners*, 79–83, for how women in the Early Republic used legal precedent regarding women's culpability (or lack thereof) in crimes to their advantage.

4. Dorsey, *Reforming Men and Women*, 88; Smith-Rosenberg and Rosenberg, "Female Animal," 334; Saxton, *Being Good*; Welter, "Cult of True Womanhood"; Cutter, *Domestic Devils, Battlefield Angels*, 21.

5. Zagarri, *Revolutionary Backlash*, 5. For more on Republican Motherhood, see Kerber, *Women of the Republic*. While Kerber focused on the Revolutionary era and the Early Republic, vestiges and new formations of the ideal of Republican Motherhood continued well into the nineteenth century. See also Cott, *Bonds of Womanhood*; Kerber, "Separate Spheres, Female Worlds, Woman's Place"; Harris, *Beyond Her Sphere*, particularly chapter 2, "The Cult of Domesticity"; Ryan, *Womanhood in America*, 106, 139, 145.

6. Kleinberg, *Women in the United States*, 42; Harris, *Beyond Her Sphere*, 33. Even contemporary nineteenth-century women who accepted their domestic role spoke out against the sexual double standard women faced or moved beyond that sphere to engage in social reforms. See Tonkovich, *Domesticity with a Difference*; Hewitt, *Women's Activism and Social Change*; Hoffert, *When Hens Crow*; Clinton, *Other Civil War*; Matthews, *Rise of Public Woman*; Smith-Rosenberg, *Disorderly Conduct*; and Haynes, *Riotous Flesh*, as some examples of studies of women who did not fit the definition the cult of domesticity.

7. Lasser and Robertson, *Antebellum Women*, xii.

8. Lyons, *Sex Among the Rabble*; Klepp, *Revolutionary Conceptions*; Manion, *Liberty's Prisoners*, 79.

9. *PPL*, August 8, 1836; January 11, 1837.

10. Newman, *Embodied History*, 20.

11. Welch, *Punishment in America*, 4.

12. I emphasize the importance of urban crime in this chapter simply because the source base is more prevalent in the urban centers of Philadelphia and Pittsburgh. While I have court data for other counties, the case descriptions in rural locales have either been lost or never existed.

13. Manion, *Liberty's Prisoners*, 3, 92–93.

14. Another case corroborates this point regarding a common prejudice against probable immigrants. On August 19, 1839, Bridget Early was arrested by the city police for vagrancy. Early was sentenced to thirty days in the county jail and the child who was with her in court was sent to the Guardians of the Poor. *PPL*, August 20, 1839.

15. Knobel, *Paddy and the Republic*, 56, 88.

16. *PPL*, November 5, 1839.

17. Kann, *Punishment, Prisons, and Patriarchy*, 16, 211. See also Manion, *Liberty's Prisoners*; and Gross, *Colored Amazons*, 32.

18. *PPL*, November 5, 1839.

19. Davis and Haller, *Peoples of Philadelphia*, 100, 128; Kann, *Punishment, Prisons, and Patriarchy*, 193.

20. Appendixes B and C provide demographic information on women prisoners, reflecting the correlation between race, ethnicity, and sentencing patterns.

21. *PPL*, December 16, 1841. It is safe to assume that most "commitments," unless otherwise noted, are to the county prison at Moyamensing. If the offenders were sent elsewhere, the newspaper tended to report that information.

22. For statistics on petty crime in the sampled counties, see appendix A. From 1820 to 1860, moral and public disturbance crimes ranged from 21.5 percent to 65.7 percent of all female crime in the counties sampled. Out of the entire sample, 2,335 (or 38.7 percent) of crimes fell into this category. In thirteen of the sixteen counties sampled, alcohol-related crimes and disorderly conduct charges ranged from 69 percent to 97 percent of the moral and petty crimes committed by women. See also Dorsey, *Reforming Men and Women*, 99.

23. *PPL*, July 29, 1836.

24. Manion, *Liberty's Prisoners*, 102.

25. Klepp, *Revolutionary Conceptions*, 242–43; Lyons, *Sex Among the Rabble*, 4–5. Newspaper reports where females were arrested for prostitution are not discussed in this chapter since the practice was not necessarily considered criminal, although it certainly fell into the category of social ills and vices that might lead to crime. Michael Meranze notes that many women who prostituted themselves

did so out of "financial necessity" and "were an accepted and understood part of working-class life. Rather than a rigid mark of social deviance and marginality, prostitution was a fluid social state for most of its practitioners." Meranze, *Laboratories of Virtue*, 279.

26. Rowe, "Women's Crime and Criminal Administration in Pennsylvania," 347. See also Marietta and Rowe, *Troubled Experiment*, 85. Fornication and bastardy carried a punishment of a fine of $100 to be given to the local guardians or overseers of the poor to help support the illegitimate child. See the *Report of the Commissioners on the Penal Code*, 109.

27. *Pittsburgh Gazette*, April 10, 1851. Bigamy carried a punishment of a $1,000 fine and up to two years of imprisonment at hard labor. The second marriage would be null and void. *Report of the Commissioners on the Penal Code*, 117.

28. *PPL*, July 11, 1844; "Descriptive Registers, 1829–1903," Eastern State Penitentiary Papers (hereafter "Descriptive Registers," ESP).

29. *Lancaster Intelligencer*, November 24, 1857. The Dutch referred to here are the Pennsylvania Dutch, or the Amish, many of whom settled in Lancaster County.

30. *Lancaster Intelligencer*, November 24, 1857.

31. Ibid. See also *Lancaster Examiner and Herald*, November 24, 1858. Physicians often believed that the female reproductive system—in addition to women's propensities for highly emotional responses to situations, and a generally weaker mind than that of males—caused women to be more susceptible to bouts of insanity, particularly during pregnancy or the postpartum period. Mary Jane Sebastian is a prime case for seeing how these beliefs played out in a criminal court in the nineteenth century. See Jarvis, *On the Comparative Liability of Males and Females to Insanity*; Combe, *Observations on Mental Derangement*; Spurzheim, *Observations on the Deranged Manifestations of the Mind*.

32. In 1850, Lancaster County's population was 98,944, although Marietta, the town where Sebastian's case took place, was very small. Compare this to the largest urban center in the state, Philadelphia, which at the county level

had 408,762 citizens in 1850. "Historical Census Browser."

33. For more on the racial tensions and makeup of the region, see chapter 3 of this book.

34. Manion, *Liberty's Prisoners*, 121; Gross, *Colored Amazons*, 14.

35. Cutter, *Domestic Devils, Battlefield Angels*, 67. This issue will be examined further in chapter 2 as well.

36. The trend of property crimes in urban centers in the antebellum decades is a natural progression from the location of eighteenth-century property crimes, which often occurred in well-established market towns such as York, Chester, Carlisle, and Lancaster, in addition to Philadelphia. In the antebellum decades, Philadelphia County's property crime accounted for 40 percent of female crime, and in nearby Chester County, 36.2 percent. Of Dauphin County's crimes, 24.4 percent were property offenses, Allegheny County, 23.6 percent, and Washington, 25.1 percent. The higher rates of property crime in the eastern urban center are likely due to the greater concentration of small businesses as well as the size of the population, which increased the probability for thefts to occur. Population lagged behind Philadelphia in Allegheny and Dauphin County, resulting in fewer opportunities to commit property crimes and smaller numbers of women committing them. See Rowe, "Women's Crime and Criminal Administration in Pennsylvania," 344; County Court of Quarter Sessions Dockets. In 1820, Philadelphia County had a total population of 137,097; Allegheny, 34,921; and Dauphin, 21,653. By 1860, Philadelphia totaled 565,529 people; Allegheny, 178,831; and Dauphin, 46,756. "Historical Census Browser."

37. Abelson, *When Ladies Go A-Thieving*, 4–7.

38. Gross, *Colored Amazons*, 33.

39. *PPL*, March 10, 1842, January 20, 1844, February 10 and 12, 1841.

40. Abelson, *When Ladies Go A-Thieving*, 7–8, 174.

41. Ibid., 174.

42. Johnson, *Policing the Urban Underworld*, 72. Because several of the case reports detailed above note that the crimes happened in South

Philadelphia, it is likely that these women were of a lower class.

43. See Lasser and Robertson, *Antebellum Women.*

44. Painter, *Sojourner Truth*, 198–99; Cutter, *Domestic Devils, Battlefield Angels*, 67–69. For more discussion on gender ideology and race, see Manion, *Liberty's Prisoners*; Haynes, *Riotous Flesh*; Gross, *Colored Amazons*, 62; Lasser and Robertson, *Antebellum Women*, 14–15; and Horton, "Freedom's Yoke."

45. *PPL*, August 24, 1839.

46. *PPL*, January 2, 1841, October 18, 1852; *Philadelphia Inquirer and Daily Courier*, July 12, 1837.

47. *Pittsburgh Daily Gazette*, June 15, 1850; *PDD*, June 15, 1850.

48. De Grave, *Swindler, Spy, Rebel*, 57–58.

49. According to the Pennsylvania criminal code, a first offense of larceny carried the maximum punishment of a $500 fine and up to four years of imprisonment at hard labor. A second offense carried a maximum penalty of ten years' imprisonment at hard labor. *Report of the Commissioners on the Penal Code*, 128.

50. *PPL*, September 2, 1837, March 10, 1838, February 7, 1839, March 11, 1839, February 17, 1840, October 6, 1840; *Pittsburgh Gazette*, December 25, 1855; *Pittsburgh Daily Morning Post*, March 25, 1847.

51. See also Gross, *Colored Amazons*, 41, which suggests that crime helped some African American women to improve their lives and that they might only steal sporadically.

52. *Huntingdon Globe*, February 20, 1851.

53. *PPL*, February 9, 1860.

54. *PDD*, January 11, 1855. In the U.S. Census Records for 1850, an Emeline Keating was found in Washington County, born in 1829 in Ireland. She was twenty-one at the time of the census; if this is the same Keating, she would have been twenty-five or twenty-six at the time of the crime. See U.S. Federal Census, 1850, Pennsylvania, Washington County.

55. *PDD*, January 12–13, 1855.

56. *PDD*, January 15, 1855; *Pittsburgh Gazette*, January 11–15, 1855.

57. *PPL*, June 6, 1839.

58. *PPL*, December 4, 1841.

59. "Descriptive Registers, Western State Penitentiary," Western State Penitentiary

Papers (hereafter "Descriptive Registers," WSP). See also "Descriptive Registers," ESP; and "Miscellaneous Descriptive Books," ESP.

60. *PPL*, November 4 and 6, 1840, January 6, 1841.

61. *PPL*, January 7, 9, and 13, 1841.

62. *PPL*, January 13, 1841.

63. *PPL*, January 12, 1841.

64. *PPL*, January 13, 1841.

65. *PPL*, January 14, 1841.

66. *PPL*, January 25, 1841.

67. *PPL*, May 18, 1841.

68. Ibid. I have not been able to track down whether she received a pardon from the state, nor could I find a record of her execution.

69. While not discussed in this book, a famous case from Pennsylvania falls into this category—that of Lucretia Chapman. She and her lover were accused of murdering her husband with poison yet was acquitted. Her case is well documented. See Brown, *The Forensic Speeches of David Paul Brown; The Trial of Lucretia Chapman*; Wolfe, *The Murder of Dr. Chapman.*

70. *PPL*, January 4 and 30, 1841, February 2, 1841.

71. Cutter, *Domestic Devils, Battlefield Angels*, 68–69.

72. Ibid., 26. See also the case of Hannah Mary Tabbs from the late nineteenth century in Philadelphia. While this was a complicated murder trial, Tabbs was able to sway the jury and frame herself as a fallen woman in order to elicit sympathy. See Gross, *Colored Amazons*, 94–99; and Gross, *Hannah Mary Tabbs and the Disembodied Torso.*

Chapter 2

1. Rung, *Rung's Chronicles of Pennsylvania*, vol. 1, 408; Rung, *Rung's Chronicles of Pennsylvania*, vol. 2, 184.

2. *Huntingdon Globe*, November 23, 1853. Census records for Huntingdon County in 1850 reveal a John Harker and Elizabeth Harker, aged sixty-one and sixty, respectively, living in Walker Township. The same census records a Samuel Harris and Margaret Harris, fifty and forty-nine, respectively, living in Penn Township. The two townships neighbor each other. See U.S. Federal Census, 1850,

Pennsylvania, Huntingdon County, Walker Township and Penn Township.

3. The law to make first-degree murder the state's sole capital crime was enacted in 1794. For specific wording of the law, see *Report of the Commissioners on the Penal Code*, 121. This is the 1828 revised Penal Code for Pennsylvania, but the genealogy of each section of the code is noted, allowing readers to see when the law was originally enacted.

4. *Huntingdon Globe*, November 30, 1853.

5. *Huntingdon Globe*, January 4, 1854; Rung, *Rung's Chronicles of Pennsylvania*, vol. 1, 408.

6. Lane, *Murder in America*, 202; Lombroso and Ferrero, *Criminal Woman*, 98.

7. The sample of Pennsylvania counties in this book yielded only a small number of women who committed violent crimes, particularly murders. Even fewer of these have any type of paper trail remaining. I queried all county historical societies in Pennsylvania (outside those counties that I included in my study since I already examined those court records) regarding female murderers. I sampled sixteen counties out of Pennsylvania's sixty-seven. Twenty-four other counties responded to my query stating that no cases of female murderers occurred from 1820 to 1860. Clearfield, Venango, and Montour Counties had cases, and these are included in this chapter. A Margaret Mabon, from Indiana County, was indicted in June 1845 for poisoning with an attempt to commit murder, but no other information about this case is available. See Indiana County Court of Quarter Sessions Docket Book 3.

8. For a discussion of historiography on women's roles in the antebellum United States, see chapter 1.

9. Out of the 6,035 indictments of female criminals gathered for this sample, 1,929 (or 31.9 percent of indictments) were violent crimes. Out of the entire sample, assaults and batteries made up about 30 percent of women's crime. For statistics by county, see appendix A.

10. *PPL*, February 16 and 18, 1837, August 7, 1837; *Huntingdon Globe*, May 22, 1851; Wheeler, "Infanticide in Nineteenth-Century Ohio," 407.

11. Daniels and Kennedy, *Over the Threshold*, 173; Rowe, "Infanticide, Its Judicial Resolution,

and Criminal Code Revision in Early Pennsylvania," 230; Klepp, *Revolutionary Conceptions*, 226–29; Lyons, *Sex Among the Rabble*, 95–100. As reflected in the table, courts were granted more leniency and flexibility when dealing with infanticide cases, with more options as to how to classify the offenses.

12. *PPL*, May 19, 1838; *Pennsylvania Inquirer and Daily Courier*, February 24, 1838. See also Lyons, *Sex Among the Rabble*, 95; and Klepp, *Revolutionary Conceptions*, 16, for discussion on servants and women in the lower classes facing unwanted pregnancies. In slave societies, some slave mothers resorted to infanticide to stop their children from having to experience slavery and to protect them from potential abuse. The crime itself was an act of protest against enslavement and in some cases, as is argued by Elizabeth Fox-Genovese, these mothers were "resisting from the center of their experience as women." She continues, suggesting that these women "were implicitly calling to account the slaveholders, who protected the sexuality and revered the motherhood of white ladies while denying black women both." These women challenged the assertion by slaveholders that womanhood was limited to white, upper-class women. See Fox-Genovese, *Within the Plantation Household*, 323–24; as well as Landers, *Black Society in Spanish Florida*, 185–91; King, "'Mad' Enough to Kill," 42; Genovese, *Roll, Jordan, Roll*, 496–97; Gross, *Colored Amazons*, chapter 1, for the case of Alice Clifton; and Taylor, *Driven toward Madness*, for more on the experience of Margaret Garner and her choices regarding murder and fear of returning to slavery.

13. *Pittsburgh Daily Morning Post*, December 4, 1846; *PPL*, August 5, 1852, January 21, 1853.

14. In the colonial and post-Revolutionary period, women used self-divorce as a way to end marriages in Pennsylvania, yet the economic burden of supporting oneself and dependents could pose problems. See Manion, *Liberty's Prisoners*, 78; Lyons, *Sex Among the Rabble*, chapter 1.

15. *Trial and Conviction of Mary Myers and John Parker*, 5–15.

16. Ibid., 16–18.

17. Ibid., 7, 9.

18. Ibid., 22.

19. Ibid., 9, 18–23, 31–35, 40, 48.

20. Ibid., 50, 54. There is no indication that these two were actually hanged. I have not been able to find anything about the aftermath of the trials or Myers's baby.

21. "Tale of Passion and Poison," 203–4; Brower, *Danville, Montour County, Pennsylvania*, 213.

22. *Danville Intelligencer*, February 19 and 26, 1858.

23. "Tale of Passion and Poison," 204; *Danville Intelligencer*, May 21 and 28, 1858.

24. *Danville Intelligencer*, October 1 and 29, 1858.

25. Smith, *Women's Roles in Eighteenth-Century America*, 35. A woman who received a divorce benefited a great deal from the end of the marriage because she "became a feme sole able to transact business as a single woman, or she could remarry." See Smith, *Breaking the Bonds*, 12. For specific wording of the laws, see "An Act Concerning Divorces and Alimony," 94–99; "Supplement to the Act, Entitled 'An Act Concerning Divorces and Alimony,'" 834–35.

26. McQuown, *History of Capital Crimes, Confessions, and Death Penalties*, 9, 11.

27. Ibid., 8–10. Census records indicate that in 1860, Lena was living with her husband, Peter, and three children, Mary, John, and Catharine, in Covington Township, Clearfield County. See U.S. Federal Census, 1860, Pennsylvania, Clearfield County, Covington Township.

28. Roger Lane argues that poisoning captured nineteenth-century society's imagination because of "the stealthiness of the method" and "its violation of the cozy sanctuary of the home and kitchen." See Lane, *Murder in America*, 202. Another poisoning case from Pennsylvania, similar to those discussed here, should be noted. In Pittsburgh in 1866, Martha Grinder was hanged for murdering two women by poison. Although she was only convicted for these two deaths, it was widely believed that she murdered many other people, earning her the moniker "the American Borgia." There seemed to be no apparent motive for the murders other than sheer opportunity and exhilaration, as well as a penchant for enjoying the study of chemistry. See the *New York Times*,

January 20, 1866; Segrave, *Women and Capital Punishment in America*, 49–56; and Shipman, "The Penalty Is Death," 127–32; *Life and Confessions of Martha Grinder*. The story of Pamela Lee Worms, a serial murderer convicted in Allegheny County in the early 1850s, while having the trappings of a real case, cannot be verified in court records or newspaper reports and might be a fictionalized morality tale. See Dimick, *Private History and Confession of Pamela Lee*.

29. Hull, *Female Felons*, 47.

30. The total population in Huntingdon County for 1850 was 24,786, and in Venango County the population was 18,310. Montour County's population was 13,239. In 1860, Clearfield County's population was 18,759. "Historical Census Browser."

31. *Huntingdon Globe*, November 30, 1853.

32. McQuown, *History of Capital Crimes, Confessions, and Death Penalties*, cover image, 12.

33. Smith-Rosenberg and Rosenberg, "Female Animal," 334; Zagarri, *Revolutionary Backlash*, 168. See also Corrigan, *Business of the Heart*, specifically chapter 6, "Men, Women, and Emotion."

34. The population for Allegheny County in 1850 was 138,290. Pittsburgh was a much smaller city than Philadelphia, as its western location slowed its growth rate. Because Philadelphia was the entry point for European settlers to Pennsylvania, the eastern section of the state was more highly populated than the middle and western sections of the state well into the nineteenth century. By 1860, the population in Allegheny County had grown to 178,831. Philadelphia by this time had reached over half a million in population. "Historical Census Browser." See also Meinig, *Shaping of America*, 138–40. Census records for 1850 show that George Wilson and Elizabeth McMasters were living in Elizabeth Township, aged fifty-eight and fifty-nine, respectively. See U.S. Federal Census, 1850, Pennsylvania, Allegheny County, Elizabeth Township.

35. *PDD*, May 5 and 8, 1857; July 2 and 3, 1857.

36. *PDD*, June 15, 1857. Emphasis in original.

37. *PDD*, July 2, 3, 6, and 7, 1857. See also Casey, *Pennsylvania State Reports*, 429–40.

38. *PDD*, July 11 and 13, 1857.

39. Casey, *Pennsylvania State Reports*, 430, 435–36; *PDD*, January 26, 1858, February 12, 1858.

40. *Confessions of Henry Fife and Charlotte Jones*, frontispiece, 9, 28, 30–31. Emphasis in original.

41. Ibid., 36–37, 39, 40.

42. *PDD*, January 26, 1858.

43. *PDD*, February 13, 1858.

44. The population in Philadelphia County in 1840 was 258,037. "Historical Census Browser." These two cases illustrate crimes that were not committed within the family. It is possible that more highly populated urban areas provided the opportunity more often for violence to be committed against mere acquaintances or even strangers.

45. *PPL*, August 1, 1840.

46. *PPL*, November 13, 14, and 16, 1840.

47. Ibid. Wilson, who was described in the records of Eastern State as illiterate, sober, and widowed, served her full sentence and was released on December 26, 1850. The discharge records also note that upon admission her mental health was good but upon discharge she was deemed insane. "Discharge Books, 1830–1858" and "Admission and Discharge Books, 1844–1850," Eastern State Penitentiary Papers.

48. See Lyons, *Sex Among the Rabble*, for extended discussions about how the lower classes in Philadelphia during the colonial, Revolutionary, and Early Republic periods challenged limitations about sexual behaviors and demonstrated a level of freedom with regard to sex that the elites of the city found concerning. While some women committed crimes that pushed boundaries and defied expectations, others achieved such effects in their personal lives.

49. *Pittsburgh Daily Morning Post*, October 14, 1847.

50. *PPL*, March 8, 1837.

51. *PPL*, August 12, 1841.

52. *Pittsburgh Gazette*, August 1, 1855.

53. For information on the antebellum temperance movement, see Walters, *American Reformers*; Abzug, *Cosmos Crumbling*; Dorsey, *Reforming Men and Women*; Parsons, *Manhood Lost*; Epstein, *Politics of Domesticity*; and Martin, *Devil of the Domestic Sphere*.

54. *PPL*, July 11, 1839. Emphasis in original. While it is difficult to know for sure if this is the same woman in each offense, the fact that the newspaper notes that she is recently released from prison illustrates that she is a common sight in front of courtrooms. See also *PPL*, May 14, 1840, August 8, 1840.

55. *PPL*, May 9, 1837, February 19, 1839, May 10, 1837, June 18, 1841, November 2, 1841, December 15, 1841.

56. See Manion, *Liberty's Prisoners*, 85, for a discussion of women in public life in the post-Revolutionary period.

Chapter 3

1. *Pittsburgh Daily Gazette and Advertiser*, March 2, 1850; Linaberger, "Rolling Mill Riots of 1850," 1–11; *Pittsburgh Daily Dispatch*, April 9 and 11, 1850. Details of the trial follow later in this chapter.

2. Fines could run as high as $500, and prison sentences could be up to two years in length. See *Report of the Commissioners on the Penal Code*, 120.

3. I draw on Paula Baker's definition of politics: "to include any action, formal or informal, taken to affect the course or behavior of government or the community." See Baker, "Domestication of Politics," 622. While her essay focuses on middle-class women, Baker's definition applies also to the lower-class women discussed in this chapter.

4. Rudé, *Crowd in History*, 8–9. See also Feldberg, "Crowd in Philadelphia History"; Hobsbawm, *Primitive Rebels*; Thompson, *Making of the English Working Class*.

5. Rudé, *Crowd in History*, 60; Graham and Gurr, *Violence in America*, 97.

6. Thompson, *Customs in Common*, 188–89, 265; See also Tilly, "Collective Violence in European Perspective," 109.

7. Riots in eighteenth-century America were often focused on British policies, and the middle-class rioters in the colonies saw their actions as quasi-legal. Furthermore, the colonial governments were virtually powerless in trying to resist mob action, which limited the overall damage done. See Maier, "Uprisings and Civil Authority in Eighteenth-Century America," 28. See also Smith, *Dominion of*

Voice, especially chapter 1; Bridenbaugh, *Cities in Revolt*; Wood, "Note on Mobs in the American Revolution"; Wood, *Creation of the American Republic*; and Wood, *Radicalism of the American Revolution*.

8. Feldberg, "Crowd in Philadelphia History," 332. See also Prince, "Great 'Riot Year'"; Geffen, "Violence in Philadelphia in the 1840s and 1850s"; Richards, *"Gentlemen of Property and Standing"*; Grimsted, "Rioting in It Jacksonian Setting"; Grimsted, *American Mobbing*. For a perspective on how nineteenth-century leaders tried to quell these riots through their rhetoric and creating alternatives to rioting as political action, see Smith, *Dominion of Voice*, particularly chapter 2.

9. Zagarri, *Revolutionary Backlash*, 2. See also Kerber, *Women of the Republic*; Norton, *Liberty's Daughters*. For information on women's politics in the Early Republic, see Allgor, *Parlor Politics*; Branson, *These Fiery Frenchified Dames*; Newman, *Parades and the Politics of the Street*; and Waldstreicher, *In the Midst of Perpetual Fetes*.

10. Zagarri, *Revolutionary Backlash*, 6, 8. See Theriot, *Mothers and Daughters in Nineteenth-Century America*, 32–33, 35. See Harris, *Beyond Her Sphere*, 33–34; and Kleinberg, *Women in the United States*, 37–38, for more on the characteristics of the ideal domestic woman. See also Clinton, *Other Civil War*, 55–58; and Baker, "Domestication of Politics," 625, 632–33.

11. Lasser and Robertson, *Antebellum Women*, xi–xii. Emphasis in original.

12. Kleinberg, *Women in the United States*, 28–29, 92–93; Harris, *Beyond Her Sphere*, 74–75. See also Ginzberg, *Untidy Origins*; Matthews, *Rise of Public Woman*; Varon, *We Mean to Be Counted*. For more on women and work, see Dublin, *Women at Work*; Dublin, *Transforming Women's Work*; Baron, *Work Engendered*, particularly chapter 1.

13. Tate, *Unknown Tongues*, 3. See also Lasser and Robertson, *Antebellum Women*, 69–71; Yellin and Van Horne, *Abolitionist Sisterhood*; Jeffrey, *Great Silent Army of Abolitionism*; and Cutter, *Domestic Devils, Battlefield Angels*, particularly chapter 3.

14. For a discussion of earlier anti-Irish sentiment, see Manion, *Liberty's Prisoners*, especially 135–37.

15. See Grimsted, "Rioting in Its Jacksonian Setting," 392; Feldberg, "Crowd in Philadelphia History," 326; *Full and Accurate Report of the Trial for Riot*; and Hoeber, "Drama in the Courtroom, Theater in the Streets." By 1840, Philadelphia County had a population of 258,037, a figure that rose dramatically to 408,762 ten years later. By 1850, 72,000 Irish called the county home, almost 18 percent of its total population. "Historical Census Browser." See also Clark, *Irish in Philadelphia*, 27, 86; and Lane, *Murder in America*, 104–5.

16. See Dorsey, *Reforming Men and Women*, 203–5.

17. Feldberg, *Turbulent Era*, 9–13, 17; Feldberg, *Philadelphia Riots of 1844*; Lannie and Diethorn, "For the Honor and Glory of God," 65–66; Dorsey, "Freedom of Religion," 12–17. See also the testimony of Bedford and other female teachers in *Olive Branch*, 30–33. Interestingly, some Catholic students complained that one teacher, Miss Jackson, told them "that if they heard the Bible read it would kill them" (33).

18. Feldberg, *Turbulent Era*, 18–19. See also *Pennsylvania Inquirer and National Gazette*, May 7, 1844; and *PPL*, May 7, 1844.

19. *PPL*, May 7, 1844; Lee, *Origin and Progress of the American Party in Politics*, 57. The original publication date of the latter source was 1855.

20. Belisle, *Arch-Bishop*, 226.

21. Feldberg, *Turbulent Era*, 20–23; *Pennsylvania Inquirer and National Gazette*, May 8–9, 1844; *PPL*, May 8–9, 1844.

22. Wainwright, *Philadelphia Perspective*, 167–68.

23. Feldberg, *Turbulent Era*, 24–26.

24. Beyer-Purvis, "Philadelphia Bible Riots of 1844," 371, 366.

25. Lannie and Diethorn suggest that "although Irish Catholics had initiated the disorder, they quickly were forced on the defensive and received a great deal of punishment. And whereas the nativists enjoyed strong support from a portion of the Protestant press and many ministers, Catholics never received any encouragement from Kenrick

[the local bishop] or his clergy." See Lannie and Diethorn "For the Honor and Glory of God," 76. It could be that the Catholic clergy believed that lending their support would simply prolong the violence or make matters worse for their parishioners when the chaos settled down. Feldberg, *Philadelphia Riots of 1844*, 121.

26. *PPL*, May 27, 1844.

27. See *PPL*, January 18, 1844, June 6, 7, and 10, 1844. Prison records indicate that Sweeney, inmate 1866 at Eastern State Penitentiary, was only twenty years of age when she was incarcerated. Although the newspaper noted that she was sentenced to five years, the descriptive registers for the prison state that she had a sentence of two years. See "Descriptive Registers," ESP. Looking at discharge records for the prison, Caroline Sweeney served her full sentence, being discharged on June 8, 1849, at the age of twenty-five. "Discharge Books, 1830–1858," Eastern State Penitentiary Papers. The Convict Reception Register also notes that Sweeney, at the time of her incarceration, was "enceinte. Apparently within 2 or 3 months of her confinement." Based on this information, it is possible that not only did she have an infant to be confined with her, but that she was pregnant with her second child as well. "Convict Reception Register, 1842–1929," Eastern State Penitentiary Papers.

28. In the Southwark district of Philadelphia in 1850, the Irish were the second-largest group living there, accounting for an average of 18 percent of the population in each of the area's six wards. Davis and Haller, *Peoples of Philadelphia*, 72. See also Feldberg, *Turbulent Era*, 29–30; and *PPL*, July 6, 1844.

29. Feldberg, *Turbulent Era*, 30–32; *PPL*, July 8–9, 1844.

30. *Full and Complete Account of the Late Awful Riots in Philadelphia*, 33; *PPL*, July 8, 1844.

31. *PPL*, July 15–27, 1844.

32. *PPL*, July 20, 1844.

33. See Dorsey, *Reforming Men and Women*, 213–19; *American Woman*, August 6, 1844.

34. *PPL*, September 4–24, 1844, October 15–21, 1844. Other murder trials associated with the riots ran in the newspapers on November 8–11 and 14–18, 1844. Trials for riots

in both Kensington and Southwark continued to occupy the courts' time well into 1845.

35. Carlisle, Pennsylvania, was only one such place. The community was described as "a quiet and orderly element of the population . . . neither beggars or vagabonds." Crooks, *Life and Letters of the Rev. John M'Clintock*, 144. Martha C. Slotten notes that the 1850 census for Cumberland County recorded 349 blacks among 4,581 residents in Carlisle, constituting a very high percentage of the county's black population. Furthermore, she suggests that many of these men and women probably arrived via the Underground Railroad, and then the black community helped others to set up lives in freedom. Slotten, "McClintock Slave Riot of 1847." See also Oblinger, "New Freedoms, Old Miseries."

36. Harrold, *Border War*, 152–153. For other works on the border tensions during these decades, particularly on the ways black individuals sought freedom and resisted the encroaching southern slave catchers, see Griffler, *Front Line of Freedom*; Pease and Pease, *They Who Would Be Free*; Horton and Horton, *In Hope of Liberty*; Smith, *On the Edge of Freedom*, 1.

37. Miller, *Geography of Pennsylvania*, 92, 97.

38. Smith, *On the Edge of Freedom*, 17.

39. Horton and Horton, *In Hope of Liberty*, xi.

40. Pease and Pease, *They Who Would Be Free*, 17.

41. Smith, *On the Edge of Freedom*, 95.

42. "Fugitive Slave Act of 1793"; Pease and Pease, *They Who Would be Free*, 212–13; Smith, *On the Edge of Freedom*, 92; Slotten, "McClintock Slave Riot of 1847"; *Carlisle Herald and Expositor*, June 16, 1847. This last article states the 1847 law in full.

43. Slotten, "McClintock Slave Riot of 1847."

44. In 1840, Cumberland County had a population of 30,953, 996 of whom were designated as "free colored" and 24 were still slaves. By 1850, the total population was 34,327, and 957 were designated as "free colored." "Historical Census Browser." Although specific numbers of those living in Carlisle are unclear, there most likely would have been a significant free black population in the town. See also Slotten, "McClintock Slave Riot of 1847."

45. *PPL*, June 5, 1847.

46. Slotten, "McClintock Riot of 1847."

47. Ibid.; Papers re: Carlisle Riot Trial, John McClintock Papers, MSS33, Box 7, Folders 6–10 (hereafter McClintock Papers); *PPL*, June 5, 1847. See also *Carlisle American Volunteer*, June 10, 1847. Reports of this riot reached beyond the borders of Pennsylvania, with articles printed throughout the northern part of the country. For an account of the incident focused on McClintock, see Smith, *On the Edge of Freedom*, 107–10. For an account of anti-abolition violence, see Richards, *"Gentlemen of Property and Standing."*

48. Crooks, *Life and Letters of the Rev. John M'Clintock*, 159. The numbers of those arrested and on trial range from the high twenties to mid-thirties. Furthermore, the names in various sources sometimes differ. In the Docket Books for the Cumberland County Quarter Sessions, records show that Elizabeth Cribbs and Hannah Decker were not arraigned. Furthermore, Rachel Cox, Ann Garver, Susan Hunter, Sophia Johnson, Clara Jones, and Elizabeth Procter (who was not mentioned by Slotten) were found not guilty. The docket books do not mention Elizabeth Boon or Amelia Butler. See Cumberland County Court of Quarter Sessions Dockets. Slotten notes the names of the defendants in addition to McClintock: Anthony Bell, Anthony Boon, Elizabeth Boon, Robert Brisseton, Amelia Butler, Eli Butler, John Clellans, Augustus Coates, John Cox, Rachel Cox, Elizabeth Cribbs, Hannah Decker, George Fisher, William Fisher, Jr., Ann Garver, Jacob Garver, John E. Grey, William Hanson, Hall Holmes, John Hunter, Susan Hunter, Richard Johnson, Sophia Johnston, Clara Jones, Moses Jones, James Jones, Charles Marshall, Henry Myers, Hiram Myers, George Norman, Valentine Thomas, Charles Turner, Achilles Vandegrift, and Nicholas Williams. Eli and Amelia Butler were also found in the docket book for assault and battery and not keeping the peace with each other at an earlier date, meaning the riot was not their first brush with the law. Slotten, "McClintock Riot of 1847."

49. Riot Trial 1847 I, Box 7 Folders 6, 8, and 9, McClintock Papers; Papers re: Carlisle Riot Trial, Box 7, Folder 6, McClintock Papers.

50. Riot Trial 1847 I, Box 7, Folder 9, McClintock Papers. Seeley Lawson does not appear in the indictment in the docket book, the newspaper reports, or other trial notes as being arrested or standing as a defendant.

51. Papers re: Carlisle Riot Trial, Box 7, Folder 6, McClintock Papers; Riot Trial 1847 III, Box 7, Folder 10, McClintock Papers; Riot Trial 1847 VI, Box 7, Folder 13, McClintock Papers.

52. Riot Trial 1847 V, Box 7, Folder 12, McClintock Papers. Emphasis in original. John Clellan, Jacob Garver, Moses Jones, Augustus Coates, Anthony Boon, John E. Gray, Achilles Vandegrift, Valentine Thomas, George Norman, Henry Myers, and Chris Turner were sentenced to three years each to Eastern State Penitentiary. James Jones was sentenced to six months in the county jail, and Eli Butler received a sentence of ten days in the county jail. *Carlisle Herald and Expositor*, September 8, 1847. Those sentenced to the state penitentiary were released almost a year later after it was found that the sentence was unusually harsh, given that rioting was only a misdemeanor. Slotten, "McClintock Riot of 1847."

53. Tate, *Unknown Tongues*, 206.

54. Other instances of race issues in Philadelphia resulting in major violence can be seen in Runcie, "'Hunting the Nigs' in Philadelphia"; and Lapsanksy, "Since They Got Those Separate Churches." A riot in Philadelphia in 1842 stemmed from a celebration of the anniversary of emancipation in the British West Indies. While the disturbance was started by boys, the crowd swelled as "men and women mingled with it—brickbats were thrown in showers, a number of persons were knocked down, and several of both colours were seriously if not fatally wounded." *Philadelphia Inquirer and National Gazette*, August 2, 1842. Perhaps the most prominent issue involved the burning of Pennsylvania Hall in 1838, newly opened to host interracial abolition meetings. For accounts on the events surrounding the attack, see Lovell, *Report of a Delegate to the Anti-Slavery Convention of American Women*; Brown, "Am I Not a Woman and a Sister?"; Brown, "Racism and Sexism," 127–28; *Philadelphia Inquirer and Daily Courier*, May 18, 1838; Tomek, *Pennsylvania Hall*.

55. Foner, *History of Black Americans*, 499; Boromé, "Vigilant Committee of Philadelphia," 323; Tate, *Unknown Tongues*, 210–13; Dunbar, *Fragile Freedom*, 89.

56. For examples of free black communities coming to the aid of alleged fugitives, see Eggert, "Two Steps Forward, a Step-and-a-Half Back"; Eggert, "Impact of the Fugitive Slave Law on Harrisburg"; Houts, "Black Harrisburg's Resistance to Slavery."

57. Katz, *Resistance at Christiana*, 4. Accounts were not limited to local (i.e., Maryland and Pennsylvania) newspapers. Periodicals in Vermont, New York, Massachusetts, and even Mississippi, to name only a few, covered the riot. See *Huntingdon Globe*, October 2, 1851; *Pennsylvania Freeman*, September 25, 1851; *PPL*, September 19, 1851. See also Hensel, *Christiana Riot and The Treason Trials of 1851*, 21–22. For other accounts of the riot and trial, see Smith, *On the Edge of Freedom*, 133–39; Pease and Pease, *They Who Would Be Free*, 225–27; Harrold, *Border War*, 153–55.

58. Between 1790 and 1810, the black population of city of Lancaster grew at a rate of 126 percent while the white population only grew by 43 percent. By 1820, the city's black population had grown by another 42 percent, to 308 black inhabitants of the 6,633 total residents. Although that works out to only about 5 percent of the population, the white citizens of Lancaster County were still concerned. See Slaughter, *Bloody Dawn*, 34, 36. For Lancaster County, the population in 1840 was 84,203, with 3,003 "free colored" and 2 slaves. By 1850, the county had 98,944 inhabitants, with 3,614 "free colored." "Historical Census Browser."

59. Hensel, *Christiana Riot*, 23. Census records for 1850 show that Parker; his wife, Eliza; and Hannah Pinckney and her husband were all living in the same household in Sadsbury, Lancaster County. See U.S. Federal Census, 1850, Pennsylvania, Lancaster County; Parker, "Freedman's Story, in Two Parts," 161.

60. *PPL*, September 13, 1851.

61. Parker, "Freedman's Story, in Two Parts," 284, 286; Katz, *Resistance at Christiana*, 93–94.

62. Hensel, *Christiana Riot*, 33; Parker, "Freedman's Story, in Two Parts," 288. Emphasis in original.

63. Parker, "Freedman's Story, in Two Parts," 288, 292; *PPL*, September 15, 1851; *Pennsylvania Freeman*, September 18, 1851; Hensel, *Christiana Riot*, 45; Slaughter, *Bloody Dawn*, 92.

64. Smith, *On the Edge of Freedom*, 137–38.

65. Horton and Horton, *In Hope of Liberty*, 176.

66. Yellin and Van Horne, *Abolitionist Sisterhood*, 120; Jeffrey, *Great Silent Army of Abolitionism*, 192, 206.

67. Hensel, *Christiana Riot*, 60, 64, 90, 92–93, 99; *National Era*, October 9, 1851. See also Harrold, *Border War*, 155.

68. Looking at the census data for Allegheny County in 1850, the total population was 138,290, comprising 3,431 "free colored" people, 68,986 free white men, and 65,873 free white women. Of the total population, there were 14,653 people, or approximately 10.6 percent, at work in manufacturing establishments. "Historical Census Browser"; *Pittsburgh Daily Gazette and Advertiser*, March 2, 1850; Linaberger, "Rolling Mill Riots of 1850," 12–14.

69. *Saturday Visiter*, March 9, 1850.

70. Ibid.

71. *Saturday Visiter*, March 16, 1850.

72. The editor of the *Saturday Visiter*, Jane Swisshelm, was a progressive woman, and these articles and their implicit frustration at the social environment for women and the working classes reflect these views. A frustrating marriage influenced her views of women's roles and marriage, leading her to assert that women had the right to get out of a marriage, either by divorce or running away. Swisshelm deserted her husband and spent years trying to get her rightful money and property back. Her newspaper venture was a way to provide for herself, allow other women to delve into the professional sphere of work, and create a forum for discussing politics and pertinent social issues. She was an ardent woman's rights supporter, although she never joined a formal organization. Ultimately, there is no way to know who penned the articles in the *Saturday Visiter* or what Swisshelm thought about the riot. See Hoffert, *Jane Grey Swisshelm*, 24–25, 49, 73, 191, 196.

73. Enstad, *Ladies of Labor, Girls of Adventure*, 93, 96–97.

74. Linaberger, "Rolling Mill Riots," 16; *PDD*, April 9, 1850.

75. *PDD*, April 11, 1850.

76. Ibid.

77. *PDD*, April 12, 1850; Linaberger, "Rolling Mills Riots," 16.

78. Parke, *Recollections of Seventy Years*, 78.

79. *Factory Riots in Allegheny City*, 3–6, 8. Emphasis in original. See also Parke, *Recollections of Seventy Years*, 78; and Wilson, *Standard History of Pittsburg, Pennsylvania*, 243.

80. Baron, *Work Engendered*, 16, 27.

81. *Factory Riots in Allegheny City*, 7, 6. See U.S. Federal Census, 1850, Pennsylvania, Allegheny County.

82. *Factory Riots in Allegheny City*, 13–15. There is no follow-up on what their sentences were or whether they were carried out. See also Parke, *Recollections of Seventy Years*, 81.

83. Baron, *Work Engendered*, 11.

Chapter 4

1. April 25, 1862, Elizabeth Velora Elwell Correspondence, Series III, Folder 1, State Penitentiary for the Eastern District Papers (hereafter Elwell Correspondence). For more on these letters, see Hayden and Jach, *Incarcerated Women*.

2. Kahan, *Eastern State Penitentiary*, 48. See also Teeters, *They Were in Prison*, 401.

3. Colvin, *Penitentiaries, Reformatories, and Chain Gangs*, 135.

4. Kann, *Punishment, Prisons, and Patriarchy*, 15, 194. See also Rafter, *Partial Justice*; Newman, *Embodied History*, 46–47; Freedman, *Their Sisters' Keepers*, particularly chapter 1; and Meranze, *Laboratories of Virtue*. In some respects, women in the Pennsylvania system had a better incarceration experience than did women in other contemporary state penitentiaries, but a general trend of focusing on the needs of male inmates over those of the women did exist. In New York's Auburn State Prison, for example, women were relegated to an attic room, "consigned to oblivion," where windows were kept shut even in the summer to prohibit communication with male inmates. Officials at the Sing Sing Correctional Facility did not even want women at the institution and tried to get them incarcerated

at other prisons in the state; by the early 1840s, however, a separate women's prison was constructed on the grounds at Sing Sing. Even so, the females incarcerated there still faced poor living conditions and neglect in their reformation. See Lewis, "Female Criminal and the Prisons of New York," 220–21, 222, 229, 231. In Illinois state prisons during the antebellum decades, women also faced ill-equipped facilities, no attempt at reformation, and prison employees who blamed the few female inmates housed at the institutions for all the prisons' problems. Employees could not fathom housing women alongside men and considered women to be more troublesome inmates than men. See Dodge, "One Female Prisoner Is of More Trouble Than Twenty Males," 909–12. The state penitentiary in Maryland attempted from the outset to treat female inmates more equitably. They were housed in a separate wing of the prison, worked "in a separate yard at spinning, knitting, and laundry," and were not allowed to interact with the male inmates. The women were not, however, subjected to silence and separation at night, as women slept up to ten to a room, and two to three to a bed. See Shugg, *Monument to Good Intentions*, 15, 18, 27.

5. Rafter, "Prisons for Women," 145.

6. See Manion, *Liberty's Prisoners*, particularly for discussions of how women in the Early Republic negotiated freedom, societal limitations, and elites' attempts to control them through the rise of the prisons; and Gross, *Colored Amazons*, for discussions of race and prison system in the late nineteenth century. See also Patrick, "Ann Hinson."

7. De Tocqueville and de Beaumont, *On the Penitentiary System*, xvii.

8. This view works against the social control theory of prisons set forth by Michel Foucault, Michael Ignatieff, and David Rothman in the 1970s. Prisons, according to Foucault, were to create "docile bodies" that were "subjected and practiced." Prisons were to be a total institution, an "exhaustive disciplinary apparatus" responsible "for all aspects of the individual," including labor, behavior, morality, and health. See Foucault, *Discipline and Punish*, 138, 235; Ignatieff, *Just Measure of Pain*; and Rothman, *Discovery of the Asylum*.

9. De Tocqueville and de Beaumont, *On the Penitentiary System*, 2; Colvin, *Penitentiaries, Reformatories, and Chain Gangs*, 135.

10. Foulke, *Remarks on the Penal System of Pennsylvania*, 6–7; McElwee, *Concise History of the Eastern Penitentiary*, 5. See also Manion, *Liberty's Prisoners*, for more context on Pennsylvania's penitentiaries.

11. De Tocqueville and de Beaumont, *On the Penitentiary System*, 5.

12. Doll, "Trial and Error at Allegheny," 8, 10.

13. Ibid., 12, 11.

14. De Tocqueville and de Beaumont, *On the Penitentiary System*, 8.

15. Doll, "Trial and Error at Allegheny," 18, 20; McCleane, *Report of the Committee to Visit the Western State Penitentiary*, 3.

16. Smith, *Defence of the System of Solitary Confinement*, 21.

17. McElwee, *Concise History of the Eastern Penitentiary*, 8; Tyson, *Essay on the Penal Law of Pennsylvania*, 58–59. For a detailed architectural plan of the penitentiary in Philadelphia, see Haviland, *Description of Haviland's Design for the New Penitentiary*.

18. "Governors' Papers," in Pennsylvania Secretary of the Commonwealth, *Pennsylvania Archives*, ser. 4, vol. 5, 728.

19. *Acts of the General Assembly Relating to the Eastern State Penitentiary*, 13, 15–16. Records regarding the procedures of Eastern State Penitentiary are much more copious than those for Western State, resulting in a more detailed description of daily life in the Philadelphia penitentiary.

20. McElwee, *Concise History of the Eastern Penitentiary*, 14.

21. Doll, "Trial and Error at Allegheny," 14; "Convict Docket, 1826–1859," Western State Penitentiary Papers (hereafter "Convict Docket," WSP); and "Descriptive Registers," WSP.

22. McElwee, *Concise History of the Eastern Penitentiary*, 107–8.

23. Ibid., 26.

24. Ibid., 26–27. See also Lieber, *Popular Essay on Subjects of Penal Law*, 39.

25. *Annual Reports of the Inspectors for Eastern State Penitentiary*, 1829–58.

26. It is unclear whether these women were convicted of voluntary or involuntary manslaughter, since the prison records only note manslaughter. The Pennsylvania penal code indicates that voluntary manslaughter carried the punishment of imprisonment at hard labor for no more than ten years, and involuntary manslaughter was punished by imprisonment at hard labor for no more than two years. It can be deduced, then, that Rogers and Johnson would have committed voluntary manslaughter, while Hinson and Anderson, with a sentence of two years, could have been convicted of either voluntary or involuntary manslaughter. *Report of the Commissioners on the Penal Code*, 122.

27. "Descriptive Registers," ESP.

28. McElwee, *Concise History of Eastern Penitentiary*, 145–46. For a more specific account of Ann Hinson, see Patrick, "Ann Hinson." Patrick notes that Ann Hinson, of all four female inmates, played a central role in the investigation, due to her close association with the warden and Mrs. Blundin, the wife of the prison's underkeeper.

29. Patrick, "Ann Hinson" 366. For another account of Mrs. Blundin's interactions with the female prisoners, see Manion, *Liberty's Prisoners*, 186–87.

30. McElwee, *Concise History of Eastern Penitentiary*, 150–51, 168.

31. Ibid., 172–73, 184.

32. Ibid., 190.

33. Ibid., 193–94.

34. *Acts of the General Assembly Relating to the Eastern State Penitentiary*, 12.

35. Patrick, "Ann Hinson," 370. The quote from Judge Coxe is in McElwee, *Concise History of Eastern Penitentiary*, 244.

36. McElwee, *Concise History of Eastern Penitentiary*, 205.

37. Ibid., 214

38. Du Bois, *Philadelphia Negro*, 47, 136.

39. Du Bois also looked at the issue of crime commission in the city in relation to race. He noted that "the problem of Negro crime in Philadelphia from 1830 to 1850 arose from the fact that less than one fourteenth of the population was responsible for nearly a third of the serious crimes committed." For lesser crimes, Du Bois looked at the statistics of black inmates at Moyamensing Prison, the county prison for Philadelphia. In 1850, he

notes that blacks made up only 5 percent of the population but accounted for 32 percent of the inmates received at Moyamensing because, before the Civil War, blacks were arrested for lesser crimes and received longer sentences, demonstrating an apparent racial bias. Ibid., 238–39. Kali Gross notes that the higher percentage of black women incarcerated at the penitentiary in the post–Civil War years represented societal views about black women and urban crime. See Gross, *Colored Amazons*, 111–12, 140.

40. "Board of Inspectors Minutes for Eastern State Penitentiary," December 3, 1831, Eastern State Penitentiary Papers (hereafter "Board of Inspectors Minutes," ESP).

41. *Seventh Annual Report of the Inspectors of the Eastern State Penitentiary*, 4. Hall was a widow with no children and a member of the Presbyterian Church. "Board of Inspectors Minutes," ESP, November 21, 1835; *Report of the Select Committee Relative to the Management of the Eastern Penitentiary*, 6.

42. "Eastern State Penitentiary Administration Records, Minute Books, 1829–1852," August 1, 1837, Eastern State Penitentiary Papers (hereafter "Administration Records, Minute Books," ESP).

43. "Administration Records, Minute Books," ESP, December 1, 1838.

44. "Minutes of the Board of Inspectors and Board of Trustees," Western State Penitentiary Papers (hereafter "Minutes of the Board of Inspectors," WSP).

45. With few extant records, finding examples of resistance at Western State Penitentiary beyond Maria Penrose's implications in an escape attempt is difficult.

46. Warden's daily journal, as quoted in Janofsky, "There Is No Hope for the Likes of Me," 166–67. Male inmates resisted in similar ways. Details of Marian Wilson's trial can be found in chapter 2.

47. A more detailed analysis of this pamphlet and letter can be found in chapter 6.

48. Vaux, *Brief Sketch of the Origin and History of the State Penitentiary*, 36, 50.

49. See *Sixteenth Annual Report of the Inspectors of the Eastern State Penitentiary Pennsylvania*, 22; *Annual Report of the Board of*

Inspectors of the Western Penitentiary of Pennsylvania, for the Year 1848, 20.

50. April 18, 1862, Elwell Correspondence. There is little context for these letters, yet they are invaluable because they represent some of the rarest sources, handwritten letters from a nineteenth-century female inmate. Elwell entered Eastern State on December 10, 1861, and was discharged on June 10, 1863. Folder 2, Series III, State Penitentiary for the Eastern District Papers, American Philosophical Society. See also Hayden and Jach, *Incarcerated Women*, 37–51.

51. Jennifer Janofsky notes that by the mid-1850s, officials at Eastern State were even experimenting with housing two inmates in the same cell. This was done in the cases of mentally ill patients in the hopes that human interaction would alleviate their symptoms. See Janofsky, "There Is No Hope for the Likes of Me," 248–49.

52. Elwell Correspondence, n.d.

53. "Female Penitentiaries," *JPDP*, October 1848, 190.

54. "Committee on the Eastern Penitentiary, Minutes, 1854–1862," February 21, 1860, Pennsylvania Prison Society Papers.

Chapter 5

1. *Williamsport Grit*, April 1931.

2. *Sullivan County Democrat*, November 23, 1858.

3. Foulke, *Remarks on the Penal System of Pennsylvania*, 12, 14.

4. Ibid., 15–16, 20, 21, 29.

5. *Report of the Secretary of the Commonwealth, Relative to the County Prisons of the State*, 7, 8, 11, 17, 28.

6. Dix, *Memorial Soliciting a State Hospital for the Insane*, 18.

7. Rung, *Rung's Chronicles of Pennsylvania History*, vol. 2, 184, 358. By 1794, only first-degree murder was punishable by death. Second-degree murder, on the other hand, was punished by solitary confinement for five to eighteen years. *Report of the Commissioners on the Penal Code*, 121.

8. "Brief Notices," *JPDP*, January 1860.

9. See "Report of John J. Lytle," *JPDP*, January 1897.

10. In Cumberland County, male and female inmates had "plenty of time to consider their sins," although they were not separated and engaged in "unhallowed conversations" and were able to "lounge about their inside corridor most of the day." In Juniata County, there was "absolutely no place for women" unless they were locked in a cell constantly. Conditions in Pike County were so bad that if a woman was arrested, "she must lodge in the part of the edifice reserved for the family of the sheriff." See "The County Prisons of Pennsylvania," *JPDP*, May 1920.

11. Due to what records remain about county prisons in Pennsylvania in the nineteenth century, this chapter necessarily focuses heavily on Philadelphia's county prison.

12. Kann, *Punishment, Prisons, and Patriarchy*, 15.

13. *Acts of the General Assembly Relating to the Eastern State Penitentiary*, 23; *First Annual Report of the Board of Inspectors of the Philadelphia County Prison*, 6; An inspector, "In and Out of the County Prison," *JPDP*, April 1857, 64. For demographic statistics of Moyamensing in the late nineteenth century, see Gross, *Colored Amazons*, 161–62; and appendix D of this book.

14. An inspector, "In and Out of the County Prison," 65.

15. Ibid., 72.

16. "Provisions Ledger, Female, 1829–1831," Philadelphia Prisons System Papers.

17. "Philadelphia County Prison," *JPDP*, July 1849.

18. Unfortunately, with these sources, the records only give glimpses into the life of the county prison for snippets of time, making chronological comparisons nearly impossible.

19. "Prison Diary, Female Department, 1850–1860," March 21, 1850, Philadelphia Prisons System Papers (hereafter "Prison Diary").

20. Ibid., April 2 and 11, 1850, May 20 and 30, 1851, February 15, 1855. Catharine Jordan was imprisoned for disturbing the peace and was sent to prison on July 23, 1849. For information on the inmates and their crimes, see "Commitment Docket, Female Department, July 1849 to November 1851," Philadelphia Prisons System Papers (hereafter "Commitment Docket").

21. "Commitment Docket," July 1849 to November 1851; "Prison Diary," September 24 and 25, 1850, December 4, 1850, January 22, 1851. Chaining was apparently a common practice to punish insubordinate offenders in the nineteenth-century penitentiaries. See Ignatieff, *Just Measure of Pain*, 198.

22. "Prison Diary," March 5, 1851. Wagstaff, a white woman, was imprisoned on June 13, 1850, for larceny. "Commitment Docket," July 1849 to November 1851. See also entries in the "Prison Diary" on August 29, 1851, February 3, 1852, March 13, 15, and 16, 1852, April 10, 1852, August 26, 1852, November 19, 1852, December 4, 1852, and April 8, 1853. For further sources on punishment in the Pennsylvania system, see Kashatus, "Punishment, Penitence, and Reform"; Thibaut, "To Pave the Way to Penitence."

23. Kann, *Punishment, Prisons, and Patriarchy*, 193; Dodge, "One Female Prisoner Is of More Trouble Than Twenty Males."

24. "Prison Diary," August 5, 1854.

25. "Prison Diary," December 2, 1854, August 26, 1856, March 28, 1850.

26. "Prison Diary," August 2–4, 1855, August 12, 1856.

27. "Prison Diary," October 29, 1851, November 29, 1851, August 12, 1856. Caroline Erwin was imprisoned for vagrancy on January 22, 1856. "Commitment Docket," August 1854 to December 1856.

28. "Prison Diary," November 6, 1854. It is difficult to identify this Mary Smith in the inmate registers. There are multiple Mary Smiths listed, many who were incarcerated multiple times in the 1850s for crimes such as disorderly conduct and breaking the peace. See also entries in the "Prison Diary" on December 12, 1854, and August 26 and 28, 1856. Like Mary Smith, Kate Murray is difficult to identify in the commitment dockets. Multiple Kate and Catherine Murrays litter the registers. Most of these individuals were imprisoned for drunk and disorderly behavior and vagrancy, suggesting a life on the streets.

29. "Punishment Ledger, 1839–1841," Philadelphia Prisons System Papers.

30. "Female Department," *JPDP*, January 1864.

31. "County Prison," *JPDP*, January 1865. In January 1877, the number of female inmates had tripled since June 1876, illustrating the increasing trend of female convicts. See "County Prison," *JPDP*, January 1877.

32. "Philadelphia County Prison," *JPDP*, January 1866; "County Prison," *JPDP*, January 1869.

33. "Philadelphia County Prison," *JPDP*, January 1866.

34. Teeters, *They Were in Prison*, 296.

35. "County Prison Agent," *JPDP*, January 1872.

36. In a given year, Agent Mullen helped thousands of potential inmates secure their freedom. In 1872, for example, he assisted 2,279 individuals and saved the prison almost $13,000 in housing costs. His work was needed to help manage the prison population and to aid helpless individuals avoid unnecessary imprisonment. He also acted as an advocate for the mentally ill, attempting to get them treatment at a hospital rather than being imprisoned. For specific examples of his work see numerous articles in the *JPDP* from January 1872, January 1873, January 1875, and January 1876.

37. Untitled letter by William Mullen, *JPDP*, January 1876; "Wm. J. Mullen's Report," *JPDP*, January 1878.

38. "Female Penitentiaries," *JPDP*, October 1848, 190.

Chapter 6

1. Thomas Larcombe, "Volume A: Admissions (20–1124), 1830–1839," Series I, State Penitentiary for the Eastern District Papers.

2. This chapter is focused mostly on Philadelphia and the work of reformers with the female prisoners of the city. Records on the reform program for the Western State Penitentiary in Pittsburgh do not seem to have survived. Furthermore, records for county prisons across the state are spotty at best and, when available, rarely discuss rehabilitation efforts.

3. Caldwell, *New Views on Penitentiary Discipline and Moral Education and Reform*, 2–3, 35; Smith, *Defence of the System of Solitary Confinement*, 23–24. Emphasis in original.

4. Roscoe, *Observations on Penal Jurisprudence*, 21, 100, 105. Emphasis in original.

5. Vaux, *Letter on the Penitentiary System of Pennsylvania*, 10; Lieber, *Popular Essay on Subjects of Penal Law*, 63, 64.

6. De Tocqueville and de Beaumont, *On the Penitentiary System*, 22.

7. Abzug, *Cosmos Crumbling*, 4; Griffin, *Ferment of Reform*, 49; Mintz, *Moralists and Modernizers*, xviii.

8. Walters, *American Reformers*, ix–x, 3–9; Mintz, *Moralists and Modernizers*, xv–xviii; Ginzberg, *Women in Antebellum Reform*, 3–5.

9. While some reform movements, like abolition or women's rights, could be seen as less socially controlling, movements like the push for colonization, some branches of the temperance movement, or even dietary- or health-related reforms can be viewed as restrictive to some degree. See Haynes, *Riotous Flesh*; Lasser and Robertson, *Antebellum Women*; Abzug, *Cosmos Crumbing*; Walters, *American Reformers*; and Ginzberg, *Women in Antebellum Reform*, for examples of this wide spectrum of attitudes toward antebellum reform.

10. Lewis, "Female Criminal and the Prisons of New York," 219; Shugg, *Monument to Good Intentions*, 19.

11. Graber, *Furnace of Affliction*, 147; Rafter, "Prisons for Women," 139–41.

12. Rafter, "Prisons for Women," 141. For more on female prison reformers, see Freedman, *Their Sisters' Keepers*; and for more general discussions on women in reform work, see Dorsey, *Reforming Men and Women*; Ginzberg, *Women in Antebellum Reform*; and Ginzberg, *Women and the Work of Benevolence*.

13. Manion, *Liberty's Prisoners*, 188–89.

14. Skotnicki, *Religion and the Development of the American Penal System*, 30.

15. Dix, *Remarks on Prison and Prison Discipline in the United States*, 60.

16. Skonicki, *Religion and the Development of the American Penal System*, 6, 39, 51.

17. Ibid., 83; Graber, *Furnace of Affliction*, 4–5, 28, 48, 156.

18. Vaux, *Brief Sketch of the Origin and History of the State Penitentiary*, 43, 49.

19. Skotnicki, *Religion and the Development of the American Penal Institution*, 59, 60; Vaux, *Brief Sketch of the Origin and History of the State Penitentiary*, 77.

20. Charles Demmé, "Eastern State Penitentiary," *Register of Pennsylvania*, February 12, 1831.

21. Charles Coxe, *Register of Pennsylvania*, February 5, 1831. This article consists of a letter written by the Prison Society's president.

22. *Annual Report of the Acting Committee of the Philadelphia Society for Alleviating the Miseries of Public Prisons*, 27.

23. Larcombe, "Volume A." Elizabeth Lemon, a twenty-year-old African American servant from Pennsylvania at the time of her incarceration in 1838, was a typical Eastern female inmate. "Descriptive Registers," ESP; Thomas Larcombe, "Volume B: Admissions (1125–1677), 1839–1843," Series I, State Penitentiary for the Eastern District Papers. Mary Jenkins, an African American servant from Wilmington, Delaware, was twenty-three at the time of her incarceration in 1839. "Descriptive Registers," ESP; Larcombe, "Volume B". Henry was a seventeen-year-old, "bright mulatto" woman from Easton, Pennsylvania. "Descriptive Registers," ESP; Larcombe, "Volume B." Wilson, a nurse, originally from Ireland, was thirty-five at the time of her incarceration and faced a ten-year sentence. "Descriptive Registers," ESP. See chapter 2 and 4 for more on Marian Wilson.

24. Larcombe, "Volume A"; Thomas Larcombe, "Volume D: Admissions (1941–2600), 1845–1850," Series I, State Penitentiary for the Eastern District Papers. Mary Ann Rogers, from New Jersey, was twenty-five at the time of her admission in 1845. "Descriptive Registers," ESP.

25. Larcombe, "Volume A." Eliza Smith, from Amsterdam, was a peddler incarcerated in 1835 at the age of twenty-nine. "Descriptive Registers," ESP; Larcombe, "Volume B." Lyas was a thirty-five-year-old mulatto servant from Baltimore when sentenced to two years for larceny. "Descriptive Registers," ESP.

26. Larcombe also met with male inmates. In looking at his entries with male inmates, we see similar editorial comments to what he made in his entries on women. For example, Alexander How, serving a seven-year sentence for horse stealing, was described as "desperately determined to evil," and Larcombe saw this as a reason that his character was going to be irretrievable. Other entries include comments that

vary in terms of Larcombe's satisfaction of reformation. Phrases such as "not entirely sane," "have some hope that he is reformed," and "no hope" are scattered throughout the entries. See Larcombe, "Volume A." In a perusal of the annual reports from the Inspectors to Eastern State Penitentiary, the moral instructor's comments never mentioned female inmates specifically. When an inmate's progress was mentioned, it was always a male prisoner. This omission seems to illustrate again the institution's overall focus on the welfare of male inmates at the expense of female ones.

27. *Report of the Board of Inspectors of the Western Penitentiary of Pennsylvania for the Year 1844*, 14. Nath. Callender reported as the moral instructor in 1842 and 1843. By the 1844 report, A. W. Black is in the position.

28. *Report of the Board of Inspectors of the Western Penitentiary of Pennsylvania for the Year 1845*, 14; *Report of the Board of Inspectors of the Western Penitentiary of Pennsylvania for the Year 1846*, 22.

29. *Report of the Board of Inspectors of the Western Penitentiary of Pennsylvania for the Year 1858*, 27.

30. "Female Penitentiaries," *JPDP*, October 1848, 190.

31. Ibid., 191; An Inspector, "In and Out of the County Prison," *JPDP*, April 1857. Emphasis in original.

32. Freedman, *Their Sisters' Keepers*, 21; Ginzberg, *Women in Antebellum Reform*, 45; Ginzberg *Women and the Work of Benevolence*, 21–22.

33. Ginzberg, *Women in Antebellum Reform*, ix. Emphasis in original.

34. Freedman, *Their Sisters' Keepers*, 18.

35. The Philadelphia Society for Alleviating the Miseries of Public Prisons was organized in 1787 (it was later renamed the Pennsylvania Prison Society). One of the PSAMPP's important functions was to provide regular visits to the penitentiaries and county prisons with its official visitors. By the late 1850s, there were twenty official visitors to the penitentiary, and another twenty who were in charge of visiting Moyamensing, the county prison. The committees of official visitors were "composed of citizens of respectable standing" who "desire to promote the moral and religious

improvement of the prisoners," many of whom give hours each week to meet with inmates. The penitentiary only allowed official visitors or individuals who had secured written permission from the Board of Inspectors to visit the penitentiary. See *Sketch of the Principal Transactions of the Philadelphia Society*; "The Eastern Penitentiary: Its Library, Visitors, etc.," *JPDP*, January 1858; *Acts of the General Assembly Relating to the Eastern State Penitentiary*, 16.

36. Dix, *Address by a Recent Female Visiter*, 3, 5–8, 10. Emphases in original.

37. Dix, *Letter to Convicts in the Western State Penitentiary*, 4–7, 11. Emphasis in original.

38. "Female Convicts and the Efforts of Females for Their Relief and Reformation," *JPDP*, April 1845, 111.

39. Ibid., 111–12.

40. Ibid. The Society for Alleviating the Miseries of Public Prisons provided these materials and seemingly supported the Female Prison Association financially. There is a link between the two groups, probably in an auxiliary capacity. The Female Prison Association does appear in the minutes of the Prison Society, particularly in the 1850s when the Female Prison Association sought to establish the Howard Institution for discharged female inmates.

41. "Roberts Vaux to Mary Waln Wistar," n.d., Series I, Box 5, Folder 13, Vaux Family Papers.

42. Meranze, *Laboratories of Virtue*, 272–73.

43. "Female Convicts and the Efforts of Females for Their Relief and Reformation," 112.

44. Halttunen, *Murder Most Foul*, 142.

45. "Female Convicts and the Efforts of Females for Their Relief and Reformation," 113–14.

46. Ibid.; "Eastern Penitentiary: Its Library, Visitors, etc.," 114. Emphasis in original.

47. For testimony, see McElwee, *Concise History of the Eastern Penitentiary*; and for an analysis of the investigation, see Meranze, *Laboratories of Virtue*.

48. Mary Anna Longstreth to Rebecca Collins, November 21, 1842, Rebecca Collins Papers. Rosanna Lacount and Maria Jones were both African American women, age twenty-one, who were convicted and sentenced to three years for larceny. Because their admission

and discharge records were for the same date and they have sequential inmate numbers, it is probable that they committed the crime together. "Descriptive Registers," ESP.

49. Mary Anna Longstreth to Rebecca Collins, January 22, 1843, Rebecca Collins Papers.

50. Ibid. Charles Dickens detailed his visit to Eastern State Penitentiary and provided a negative perspective on the penitentiary system in *American Notes for General Circulation*.

51. "Eastern Penitentiary," *JPDP*, January 1866; "Eastern Penitentiary," *JPDP*, January 1868.

52. "Female Convicts and the Efforts of Females for Their Relief and Reformation," 115.

53. Ibid., 116.

54. Ibid., 117.

55. "Fifth Annual Report of John J. Lytle," *JPDP*, January 1891; "Twelfth Annual Report of John J. Lytle, General Secretary," *JPDP*, January 1902.

56. Dorsey, *Reforming Men and Women*, 9.

57. Ginzberg, *Women and the Work of Benevolence*, 9, 69.

58. Ibid., 1, 13, 15; Cutter, *Domestic Devils, Battlefield Angels*, 101–3; Freedman, *Their Sisters' Keepers*, 1984.

59. "Female Convicts and the Efforts of Females for Their Relief and Reformation," 117. Although it appears that multiple tracts were published, I have only found the one retelling Julia Wilt's story.

60. *An Account of Julia Moore*.

61. "Descriptive Registers," ESP; *PPL*, May 14 and 27, 1839; "Miscellaneous Descriptive Books," ESP.

62. *An Account of Julia Moore*, 3–4.

63. Ibid., 5, 6, 8.

64. Ibid., 11, 14–15.

65. Ibid., 18. See the discussion of letter writing at the end of chapter 4.

66. Ibid., 18–19.

67. Vaux, *Brief Sketch of the Origin and History of the State Penitentiary*, 36, 50.

68. Mary Anna Longstreth to Rebecca Collins, May 28, 1843, Rebecca Collins Papers.

69. "Larcombe, "Volume A." The *Seventeenth Annual Report of the Inspectors of the Eastern State Penitentiary of Pennsylvania* noted that Julia, inmate 1109, entered with syphilitic

disease and eventually died of syphilis and erysipelas.

70. Adshead, *Prisons and Prisoners*, 116.

71. "The Religious Instruction," *JPDP*, January 1868.

72. Freedman, *Their Sisters' Keepers*, 33.

73. "Notices: No. 1, Philadelphia County Prison," *JPDP*, July 1849.

74. Regular visits did "much good by kind and wholesome instruction" as these women "endeavor to improve" the female inmates, who looked forward to these visits with "much impatience, and any interruption of the regular course [was] specially lamented." By the 1870s, women visitors from various religious traditions and reform groups visited the county prison each day, bringing advice, encouragement and tools for education. See "County Prison," *JPDP*, January 1869; as well as articles in the same journal from January 1867, January 1871, January 1874, and January 1878. These reformers became a source of advice for other cities on how to treat female inmates. Members visited Pittsburgh as well and reported on their observations. In 1869, one observer noted that in the western city "care should be taken to have female prisoners visited by persons of their own sex." As late as 1890, however, the Allegheny County Jail in Pittsburgh, still failed to meet approval from female reformers. Mrs. J. K. Barney, National Superintendent for the Women's Christian Temperance Union, reported to the Pennsylvania Prison Society that at the county jail, she "was glad to find a pleasant-faced matron in charge of the women, but could see little opportunity for reformatory influence." See A Member of the Philadelphia Society for Alleviating the Miseries of Public Prisons, "Letter to the Pittsburgh Prison Reform Society," *JPDP*, January 1869; "From Mrs. J. K. Barney," *JPDP*, January 1890.

75. "Female Convicts and the Efforts of Females for Their Relief and Reformation," 115–17.

76. "Report of the Philadelphia Society," *JPDP*, January 1880; "Visitors," *JPDP*, January 1867.

77. "Female Convicts and the Efforts of Females for Their Relief and Reformation," 117; "Acting Committee Minutes: Volume 7,"

October 12, 1852, Pennsylvania Prison Society Papers. Emphasis in original.

78. "Acting Committee Minutes: Volume 3," February 26, 1853, Pennsylvania Prison Society Papers; Holloway, *History of the Howard Institution*, 1. Holloway served as president of the Howard Institution in the early twentieth century.

79. Holloway, *History of the Howard Institution*, 1. The Howard Institution was named after the British prison reformer John Howard of the eighteenth century.

80. Information regarding the locations and occupations of the members of the Howard Institution came from the Institution's *Annual Reports of the Board of Inspectors* and McElroy's *Philadelphia City Directory* for the years 1858–60. See also Scheffler, "Wise as Serpents and Harmless as Doves."

81. *Annual Report of the Board of Managers of the Howard Institution*, 3–4; *Second Annual Report of the Board of Managers of the Howard Institution*, 3.

82. *Third Annual Report of the Board of Managers of the Howard Institution*, 6. See also "Minutes of the Pennsylvania Prison Society," January 12, 1857, Pennsylvania Prison Society Papers.

83. *Fourth Annual Report of the Board of Managers of the Howard Institution*, 3–4. Emphasis in original. See also *An Appeal to the Citizens of Philadelphia*.

84. *An Appeal to the Citizens of Philadelphia*.

85. *Fourth Annual Report of the Board of Managers of the Howard Institution*, 4–5; *An Appeal to the Citizens of Philadelphia*.

86. *Third Annual Report of the Board of Managers of the Howard Institution*, 10; *Fourth Annual Report of the Board of Managers of the Howard Institution*, 9.

87. Holloway, *History of the Howard Institution*, 3; *Fifteenth Annual Report of the Board of Managers of the Howard Institution*, 3–4. Throughout the later decades of the nineteenth century, the Institution received charges not only from prison, but from prison agent William Mullen, who sent young women there for reformation as an alternative to incarceration. See "Extracts from Mr. Mullen's Report," *JPDP*, January 1875; *Twenty-First Annual Report from the Board of Managers of the Howard Institution*,

5–6. By the end of the century, the Institution was focusing more attention on alcoholic women and less on female prisoners. For the Institution's work at the end of the century, see *Sixteenth Annual Report of the Board of Managers for the Howard Institution*, 6; *Twenty-Second Annual Report of the Board of Managers of the Howard Institution*, 5; *Twenty-Seventh Annual Report of the Board of Managers of the Howard Institution*, 6; *Twenty-Eighth Annual Report of the Board of Managers of the Howard Institution*, 7; and Holloway, *History of the Howard Institution*, 6.

Conclusion

1. As quoted in the *Eastern State Penitentiary Historic Structures Report*, 207. See also "Descriptive Registers," ESP.

2. At the Philadelphia County prison at Moyamensing, women who committed self-harm were often punished for their action (see chapter 5 of this book). What might be read as signs of mental illness or emotional stress to modern readers, appeared to have been seen by prison officials at the county and state levels as threats to prison discipline and were treated as such. See detailed descriptions of punishments used in at Eastern State in McElwee, *Concise History of the Eastern Penitentiary*.

3. Cassidy, *Warden Cassidy on Prisons and Convicts*, 24, 26, 31.

4. Ibid., 95–96.

5. Lewis, "Female Criminal and the Prisons of New York," 222–29.

6. Ibid., 229–32. Women prisoners in Illinois suffered similarly to those in New York and Pennsylvania. They were housed within the male penitentiary system until 1896 in Illinois when a separate facility was built. See Dodge, "One Female Prisoner Is of More Trouble Than Twenty Males," 918; and Dodge, "The Most Degraded of Their Sex, If Not of Humanity," 223–26.

7. Barnes, *Evolution of Penology in Pennsylvania*, 401.

8. Ibid., 402. Reformatories sprang up across the United States during the late nineteenth and early twentieth centuries. In addition to New York, institutions in Massachusetts, New Jersey, Maine, Connecticut, Ohio, Indiana, Iowa, Kansas, Minnesota, Nebraska, Wisconsin, Illinois, Arkansas, North Carolina, Virginia, and California opened for female inmates. See Rafter, "Prisons for Women," 148.

9. De Tocqueville and de Beaumont, *On the Penitentiary System*, xvii–xviii.

Archival Sources

Allegheny County Court of Quarter Sessions Dockets. Allegheny County Courthouse. Pittsburgh.

Bedford County Court of Quarter Sessions Dockets. Bedford County Courthouse. Bedford, Pa.

Cumberland County Court of Quarter Sessions Dockets. Cumberland County Archives. Carlisle, Pa.

Historical Society of Pennsylvania. Philadelphia.
Pennsylvania Abolition Society Papers. Collection 0490.

Pennsylvania Prison Society Papers. Record Group 1946.

Thompson Family Papers, 1607–1934. Manuscript Group 654.

Vaux Family Papers. Manuscript Group 684.

Huntingdon County Court of Quarter Sessions Dockets. Huntingdon County Courthouse. Huntingdon, Pa.

Indiana County Court of Quarter Sessions Dockets. Indiana County Clerk of Courts Office. Indiana, Pa.

John McClintock Papers. Manuscript, Archives, and Rare Book Library. Emory University. Atlanta.

Lancaster County Court of Quarter Sessions Dockets. Lancaster County Historical Society. Lancaster, Pa.

Lebanon County Historical Society. Lebanon, Pa.

Mifflin County Court of Quarter Sessions Dockets. Mifflin County Courthouse. Lewistown, Pa.

Pennsylvania State Archives. Harrisburg.
Court of Quarter Sessions Dockets
Adams County
Berks County
Chester County

Dauphin County
Erie County
Luzerne County
Record Group 15. Bureau of Corrections.
Eastern State Penitentiary Papers
Western State Penitentiary Papers

Philadelphia City Archives. Philadelphia.
Philadelphia County Court of Quarter Sessions Dockets

Philadelphia Prisons System Papers. Record Group 38.

Rebecca Collins Papers. Collection 1196. Quaker Collection. Haverford College. Haverford, Pa.

State Penitentiary for the Eastern District Papers. American Philosophical Society. Philadelphia.

United States Federal Census, Pennsylvania. Various counties.

Washington County Court of Quarter Sessions Dockets. Washington County Courthouse. Washington, Pa.

Westmoreland County Court of Quarter Sessions Dockets. Westmoreland County Courthouse. Greensburg, Pa.

York County Court of Quarter Sessions Dockets. York County Archives. York, Pa.

Periodicals

American Woman
Carlisle American Volunteer
Carlisle Herald and Expositor
Danville Intelligencer
Huntingdon Globe
Journal of Prison Discipline and Philanthropy
Lancaster Examiner and Herald
Lancaster Intelligencer
National Era
New York Times
Pennsylvania Freeman
Pennsylvania Inquirer and National Gazette

Philadelphia Inquirer and Daily Courier
Philadelphia Public Ledger
Pittsburgh Daily Dispatch
Pittsburgh Daily Gazette and Advertiser
Pittsburgh Daily Morning Post
Pittsburgh Gazette
Register of Pennsylvania
Saturday Visiter
Sullivan County Democrat
Williamsport Grit

Pamphlets and Official Reports

Adshead, Joseph. *Prisons and Prisoners.*
    London: Longman, Brown, Green,
    and Longman, 1845.
An Account of Julia Moore, A Penitent Female,
    Who Died in the Eastern Penitentiary
    of Philadelphia, in the Year 1843. 2nd
    ed. Philadelphia: Joseph and William
    Kite, 1844.
"An Act Concerning Divorces and Alimony."
    Statutes at Large of Pennsylvania 1187
    (1785): 94–99, http://www.chesco
    .org/DocumentCenter/View/5829
    /Divorce-Records.
Acts of the General Assembly Relating to the
    Eastern State Penitentiary and to the New
    Prisons of the City and County of Phila-
    delphia. Philadelphia: J. W. Allen, 1831.
Annual Report of the Acting Committee of the
    Philadelphia Society for Alleviating the
    Miseries of Public Prisons. Philadelphia:
    Published by the Order of the Society,
    1833.
Annual Reports of the Board of Inspectors of
    the Howard Institution. Philadelphia,
    1856–59, 1870–71, 1876–77, 1882–83.
    [Various publishers over the years.]
Annual Reports of the Inspectors of the Eastern
    State Penitentiary of Pennsylvania. Phil-
    adelphia, 1829–58. [Various publishers
    over the years.]
An Appeal to the Citizens of Philadelphia, for
    Means to Purchase a Lot and Suitable
    Building for the Howard Institution for
    Discharged Female Prisoners. Philadel-
    phia: Henry B. Ashmead, 1858.
Belisle, Orvilla S. *The Arch-Bishop; or, Roman-*
    ism in the United States. Philadelphia:
    Wm. White Smith, 1855.

Brown, David Paul. *The Forensic Speeches of*
    David Paul Brown. Philadelphia: King
    and Baird, 1873.
Caldwell, Charles. *New Views on Penitentiary*
    Discipline and Moral Education and
    Reform. Philadelphia: William Brown,
    1829.
Casey, Joseph. *Pennsylvania State Reports.* Vol.
    29, *Comprising Cases Adjudged in the*
    Supreme Court of Pennsylvania. Phila-
    delphia: Kay and Brother, 1858.
Cassidy, Michael J. *Warden Cassidy on Prisons*
    and Convicts. Philadelphia: Patterson
    and White, 1897.
Combe, Andrew. *Observations on Mental*
    Derangement: Being an Application of
    the Principles of Phrenology to the Eluci-
    dation of the Causes, Symptoms, Nature,
    and Treatment of Insanity. Boston:
    Marsh, Capen, and Lyon, 1834.
Confessions of Henry Fife and Charlotte Jones,
    Under Sentence of Death for the Murder
    of Geo. Wilson and Elizabeth M'Mas-
    ters: Together with a History of the
    Case and Statement of Monroe Stewart.
    Pittsburgh: Hunt and Miner, 1857.
Crooks, George R. *The Life and Letters of the*
    Rev. John M'Clintock, D.D., LL.D., Late
    President of Drew Theological Seminary.
    New York: Nelson and Phillips, 1876.
De Tocqueville, Alexis, and Gustave de
    Beaumont. *On the Penitentiary System*
    in the United States and Its Applica-
    tion in France. Translated by Francis
    Lieber. Philadelphia: Carey, Lea, and
    Blanchard, 1833.
Dimick, Rev. Augustus. *Private History and*
    Confession of Pamela Lee, Who Was
    Convicted at Pittsburgh, Pa., December
    19th, 1851, for the Wilful Murder of Her
    Husband and Sentenced to Be Hanged
    on the 30th Day of January, A.D. 1852.
    Pittsburgh: Lucas and Grant, 1852.
Dix, Dorothea Lynde. *An Address by a Recent*
    Female Visiter to the Prisoners in the
    Eastern Penitentiary of Pennsylvania.
    Philadelphia: Joseph and William Kite,
    1844.
———. *Letter to Convicts in the Western State*
    Penitentiary of Pennsylvania, in Allegh-
    eny City. N.p., 1848.

———. *Memorial Soliciting a State Hospital for the Insane: Submitted to the Legislature of Pennsylvania, February 3, 1845.* Harrisburg, Pa.: J. M. G. Lescure, 1845.

———. *Remarks on Prisons and Prison Discipline in the United States.* 2nd ed. Philadelphia: Joseph Kite, 1845.

The Factory Riots in Allegheny City: Judge Patton's Charge. Allegheny, Pa., 1849.

First Annual Report of the Board of Inspectors of the Philadelphia County Prison. Harrisburg, Pa.: J. M. G. Lescure, 1848.

Foulke, William Parker. *Remarks on the Penal System of Pennsylvania: Particularly with Reference to County Prisons.* Philadelphia: Printed for the Philadelphia Society for Alleviating the Miseries of Public Prisons; 1855.

A Full and Accurate Report of the Trial for Riot Before the Mayor's Court of Philadelphia, on the 13th of October, 1831, Arising out of a Protestant Procession on the 12th of July, and in Which the Contending Parties Were Protestants and Roman Catholics. Philadelphia: Henry Darley, 1831.

A Full and Complete Account of the Late Awful Riots in Philadelphia. Philadelphia: J. B. Perry, 1844.

Haviland, John. *A Description of Haviland's Design for the New Penitentiary, Now Erecting near Philadelphia.* Philadelphia: Robert Desilver, 1824.

Jarvis, Edward. *On the Comparative Liability of Males and Females to Insanity, and Their Comparative Curability and Mortality When Insane.* Utica: New York State Insane Asylum, 1850.

Lieber, Francis. *A Popular Essay on Subjects of Penal Law, and on Uninterrupted Solitary Confinement at Labor, as Contradistinguished to Solitary Confinement at Night and Joint Labor by Day, in A Letter to John Bacon, Esquire.* Philadelphia: Order of the Society, 1838.

The Life and Confessions of Martha Grinder, the Poisoner; Embracing a Complete History of the Crimes Committed by Her up to the Time of Her Execution. Pittsburgh: John P. Hunt, 1866.

Lovell, Laura. *Report of a Delegate to the Anti-Slavery Convention of American Women.* Boston: J. Knapp, 1838.

McCleane, Mr. *Report of the Committee to Visit the Western State Penitentiary.* Harrisburg, Pa.: Henry Welsh, 1834.

McElroy's Philadelphia City Directory. Philadelphia: Edw. C. and John Biddle, 1858–60.

McElwee, Thomas B. *A Concise History of the Eastern Penitentiary of Pennsylvania, Together with a Detailed Statement of the Proceedings of the Committee, Appointed by the Legislature, December 6th, 1834, for the Purpose of Examining into the Economy and Management of That Institution, Embracing the Testimony Taken on That Occasion, and Legislative Proceedings Connected Therewith.* Philadelphia: Neall and Massey, 1835.

The Olive Branch; or, An Earnest Appeal in Behalf of Religion, The Supremacy of Law, and Social Order: With Documents, Relating to the Late Disturbances in Philadelphia. Philadelphia: M. Fithian, 1844.

Parker, William. "The Freedman's Story, in Two Parts." *Atlantic Monthly*, February 1866.

Peirce, Charles. *The Portsmouth Miscellany.* Portsmouth, N.H.: Hill and Pierce, 1804.

Pennsylvania Secretary of the Commonwealth. *Pennsylvania Archives.* 1852–1935. [Various cities of publication and publishers over the years.]

Report of the Commissioners on the Penal Code, with Accompanying Documents. Harrisburg, Pa.: S. C. Stambaugh, 1828.

Report of the Secretary of the Commonwealth, Relative to the County Prisons of the State. Harrisburg, Pa.: E. Guyer, 1839.

Report of the Select Committee Relative to the Management of the Eastern Penitentiary, Mr. Curtis, Chairman. Harrisburg, Pa. 1838.

Reports of the Board of Inspectors of the Western Penitentiary of Pennsylvania. Pittsburgh, 1844–46, 1848, 1858. [Various publishers over the years.]

Roscoe, William. *Observations on Penal Jurisprudence and the Reformation of Criminals.* London: T. Cadell, W. Davies, and J. and A. Arch, 1819.

Rush, Benjamin. *An Enquiry into the Effects of Public Punishments.* Philadelphia: James, 1787.

Sketch of the Principal Transactions of the Philadelphia Society for Alleviating the Miseries of Public Prisons, from its Origin to the Present Time. Philadelphia: Merrihew and Thompson, 1859.

Smith, George W. *A Defence of the System of Solitary Confinement of Prisoners Adopted by the State of Pennsylvania: With Remarks on the Origin, Progress, and Extension of this Species of Prison Discipline.* Philadelphia: E. G. Dorsey, 1833.

Spurzheim, J. G. *Observations on the Deranged Manifestations of the Mind; or, Insanity.* Boston: Marsh, Capen, and Lyon, 1836.

"Supplement to the Act, Entitled 'An Act Concerning Divorces and Alimony.'" *Statutes at Large of Pennsylvania.* 2495 (1804): 834–35, http://www.chesco .org/DocumentCenter/View/5829 /Divorce-Records.

The Trial and Conviction of Mary Myers and John Parker for the Murder of John Myers (the Husband of Mary Myers), Late of Rockland Township, Venango County, Penna, by Administering Arsenic. Franklin, Pa: E. S. Durban, 1847. Courtesy of the Venango County Historical Society.

The Trial of Lucretia Chapman: Otherwise Called Lucretia Espos y Mina, Who Was Jointly Indicted with Lino Amalia Espos y Mina, for the Murder of William Chapman . . . in the Court of Oyer and Terminer, Held at Doylestown, for Bucks County, December Term, 1831, Continued to February Term, 1832. Philadelphia: G. W. Mentz and Son, 1882.

Tyson, Job R. *Essay on the Penal Law of Pennsylvania.* Philadelphia: Law Academy, Mifflin and Parry, 1827.

Vaux, Richard. *Brief Sketch of the Origin and History of the State Penitentiary for the Eastern District of Pennsylvania, at Philadelphia.* Philadelphia: McLaughlin Brothers, 1872.

Vaux, Roberts. *Letter on the Penitentiary System of Pennsylvania: Addressed to William Roscoe, Esquire, of Toxteth Park, Near Liverpool.* Philadelphia: Jesper Harding, 1827.

Secondary Sources

Abelson, Elaine S. *When Ladies Go A-Thieving: Middle-Class Shoplifters in the Victorian Department Store.* New York: Oxford University Press, 1989.

Abzug, Robert. *Cosmos Crumbling: American Reform and the Religious Imagination.* New York: Oxford University Press, 1994.

Allgor, Catherine. *Parlor Politics in Which the Ladies of Washington Help Build a City and a Government.* Charlottesville: University of Virginia Press, 2000.

Bacon, Margaret Hope. *The Quiet Rebels: The Story of the Quakers in America.* New York: Basic Books, 1969.

Baker, Paula. "The Domestication of Politics: Women and American Political Society, 1780–1920." *American Historical Review* 89, no. 3 (1984): 620–47.

Barnes, Harry Elmer. *The Evolution of Penology in Pennsylvania: A Study in American Social History.* Indianapolis: Bobbs-Merrill, 1927.

Baron, Ava, ed. *Work Engendered: Toward a New History of American Labor.* Ithaca: Cornell University Press, 1991.

Beyer-Purvis, Amanda. "The Philadelphia Bible Riots of 1844: Contest over the Rights of Citizens." *Pennsylvania History: A Journal of Mid-Atlantic Studies* 83, no. 3 (2016): 366–93.

Boromé, Joseph A. "The Vigilant Committee of Philadelphia." *Pennsylvania Magazine of History and Biography* 92, no. 3 (1968): 320–51.

Branson, Susan. *Dangerous to Know: Women, Crime, and Notoriety in the Early Republic.* Philadelphia: University of Pennsylvania Press, 2008.

———. *These Fiery Frenchified Dames: Women and Political Culture in Early National*

Philadelphia. Philadelphia: University of Pennsylvania Press, 2001.

Bridenbaugh, Carl. *Cities in Revolt: Urban Life in America, 1743–1776*. New York: Knopf, 1955.

Brower, D. H. B. *Danville, Montour County, Pennsylvania: A Collection of Historical and Biographical Sketches*. Harrisburg, Pa.: Lane S. Hart, 1881.

Brown, Ira V. "'Am I Not a Woman and a Sister': The Anti-Slavery Convention of American Women, 1837–1839." *Pennsylvania History* 50, no. 1 (1983): 1–19.

———. "Racism and Sexism: The Case of Pennsylvania Hall." *Phylon* 37, no. 2 (1976): 126–36.

Clark, Dennis. *The Irish in Philadelphia: Ten Generations of Urban Experience*. Philadelphia: Temple University Press, 1973.

Clinton, Catherine. *The Other Civil War: American Women in the Nineteenth Century*. Rev. ed. New York: Hill and Wang, 1999.

Colvin, Mark. *Penitentiaries, Reformatories, and Chain Gangs: Social Theory and the History of Punishment in Nineteenth-Century America*. New York: St. Martin's Press, 1997.

Corrigan, John. *Business of the Heart: Religion and Emotion in the Nineteenth Century*. Berkeley: University of California Press, 2002.

Cott, Nancy F. *The Bonds of Womanhood: "Woman's Sphere" in New England, 1780–1835*. New Haven: Yale University Press, 1977.

Cutter, Barbara. *Domestic Devils, Battlefield Angels: The Radicalism of American Womanhood, 1830–1865*. DeKalb: Northern Illinois University Press, 2003.

Daniels, Christine, and Michael V. Kennedy, eds. *Over the Threshold: Intimate Violence in Early America*. New York: Routledge, 1999.

Davis, Allen Freeman, and Mark H. Haller, eds. *The Peoples of Philadelphia: A History of Ethnic Groups and Lower-Class Life, 1790–1940*. Philadelphia: Temple University Press, 1973.

De Grave, Kathleen. *Swindler, Spy, Rebel: The Confidence Woman in Nineteenth-Century America*. Columbia: University of Missouri Press, 1995.

Dickens, Charles. *American Notes for General Circulation*. New York: Penguin, 2000.

Dodge, L. Mara. "'The Most Degraded of Their Sex, If Not of Humanity': Female Prisoners at the Illinois State Penitentiary at Joliet, 1859–1900." *Journal of Illinois History* 2, no. 3 (1999): 205–26.

———. "'One Female Prisoner Is of More Trouble Than Twenty Males': Women Convicts in Illinois Prisons, 1835–1896." *Journal of Social History* 32, no. 4 (1999): 907–30.

———. *Whores and Thieves of the Worst Kind: A Study of Women, Crime, and Prisons, 1835–2000*. DeKalb: Northern Illinois University Press, 2002.

Doll, Eugene E. "Trial and Error at Allegheny: The Western State Penitentiary, 1818–1838." *Pennsylvania Magazine of History and Biography* 81, no. 1 (1957): 3–27.

Dorsey, Bruce. "Freedom of Religion: Bibles, Public Schools, and Philadelphia's Bloody Riots of 1844." *Pennsylvania Legacies* 8, no. 1 (2008): 12–17.

———. *Reforming Men and Women: Gender in the Antebellum City*. Ithaca: Cornell University Press, 2002.

Dublin, Thomas. *Transforming Women's Work: New England Lives in the Industrial Revolution*. Ithaca.: Cornell University Press, 1994.

———. *Women at Work*. New York: Columbia University Press, 1979.

Du Bois, W. E. B. *The Philadelphia Negro: A Social Study*. Philadelphia: Published for the University, 1899.

Dumm, Thomas. *Democracy and Punishment: Disciplinary Origins of the United States*. Madison: University of Wisconsin Press, 1987.

Dunbar, Erica Armstrong. *A Fragile Freedom: African American Women and Emancipation in the Antebellum City*. New Haven: Yale University Press, 2008.

Eastern State Penitentiary Historic Structures Report, Volume I. Philadelphia: Philadelphia Historic Commission, 1994.

http://www.easternstate.org/sites/easternstate/files/inline-files/history-vol1.pdf.

Eggert, Gerald G. "The Impact of the Fugitive Slave Law on Harrisburg: A Case Study." *Pennsylvania Magazine of History and Biography* 109, no. 4 (1985): 537–69.

———. "'Two Steps Forward, a Step-and-a-Half Back': Harrisburg's African American Community in the Nineteenth Century." *Pennsylvania History* 58, no. 1 (1991): 1–36.

Enstad, Nan. *Ladies of Labor, Girls of Adventure: Working Women, Popular Culture, and Labor Politics at the Turn of the Twentieth Century.* New York: Columbia University Press, 1999.

Epstein, Barbara Leslie. *The Politics of Domesticity: Women, Evangelism, and Temperance in Nineteenth-Century America.* Middletown: Wesleyan University Press, 1981.

Feldberg, Michael. "The Crowd in Philadelphia History: A Comparative Perspective." *Labor History* 15, no. 3 (1974): 323–36.

———. *The Philadelphia Riots of 1844: A Study of Ethnic Conflict.* Westport, Conn.: Greenwood Press, 1975.

———. *The Turbulent Era: Riot and Disorder in Jacksonian America.* New York: Oxford University Press, 1980.

Foner, Philip S. *History of Black Americans: From the Emergence of the Cotton Kingdom to the Eve of the Compromise of 1850.* Westport, Conn.: Greenwood Press, 1983.

Foucault, Michel. *Discipline and Punish: The Birth of the Prison.* Translated by Alan Sheridan. New York: Vintage Books, 1995.

Fox-Genovese, Elizabeth. *Within the Plantation Household: Black and White Women of the Old South.* Chapel Hill: University of North Carolina Press, 1988.

Freedman, Estelle B. *Their Sisters' Keepers: Women's Prison Reform in America, 1830–1900.* Ann Arbor: University of Michigan Press, 1981.

"Fugitive Slave Act of 1793." *US History*, n.d. http://www.ushistory.org/presidentshouse/history/slaveact1793.php.

Geffen, Elizabeth M. "Violence in Philadelphia in the 1840s and 1850s." *Pennsylvania History* 36, no. 4 (1969): 380–410.

Genovese, Eugene. *Roll, Jordan, Roll: The World the Slaves Made.* New York: Vintage Books, 1974.

Ginzberg, Lori D. *Untidy Origins: A Story of Woman's Rights in Antebellum New York.* Chapel Hill: University of North Carolina Press, 2005.

———. *Women and the Work of Benevolence: Morality, Politics, and Class in the Nineteenth-Century United States.* New Haven: Yale University Press, 1990.

———. *Women in Antebellum Reform.* Wheeling, Ill.: Harlan Davidson, 2000.

Graber, Jennifer. *The Furnace of Affliction: Prisons and Religion in Antebellum America.* Chapel Hill: University of North Carolina Press, 2011.

Graham, Hugh Davis, and Ted Robert Gurr, eds. *Violence in America: Historical and Comparative Perspectives.* Beverly Hills, Calif.: Sage Publications, 1979.

Griffin, C. S. *The Ferment of Reform, 1830–1860.* New York: Thomas Y. Crowell, 1967.

Griffler, Keith P. *Front Line of Freedom: African Americans and the Forging of the Underground Railroad in the Ohio Valley.* Lexington: University Press of Kentucky, 2004.

Grimsted, David. *American Mobbing, 1828–1861: Toward Civil War.* New York: Oxford University Press, 1998.

———. "Rioting in its Jacksonian Setting." *American Historical Review* 77, no. 2 (1972): 361–97.

Gross, Kali. *Colored Amazons: Crime, Violence, and Black Women in the City of Brotherly Love, 1880–1910.* Durham: Duke University Press, 2006.

———. *Hannah Mary Tabbs and the Disembodied Torso: A Tale of Race, Sex, and Violence in America.* Oxford: Oxford University Press, 2016.

Halttunen, Karen. *Murder Most Foul: The Killer and the American Gothic Imagination.*

Cambridge: Harvard University Press, 1998.

Harris, Barbara J. *Beyond Her Sphere: Women and the Professions in American History.* Westport, Conn.: Greenwood Press, 1978.

Harrold, Stanley. *Border War: Fighting over Slavery Before the Civil War.* Chapel Hill: University of North Carolina Press, 2010.

Hayden, Erica Rhodes, and Theresa R. Jach, eds. *Incarcerated Women: A History of Struggle, Oppression, and Resistance in American Prisons.* Lanham, Md.: Lexington Books, 2017.

Haynes, April R. *Riotous Flesh: Women, Physiology, and the Solitary Vice in Nineteenth-Century America.* Chicago: University of Chicago Press, 2015.

Hensel, W. U. *The Christiana Riot and the Treason Trials of 1851: An Historical Sketch.* Lancaster, Pa.: New Era Printing Company, 1911.

Hewitt, Nancy A. *Women's Activism and Social Change: Rochester, New York, 1822–1872.* Ithaca: Cornell University Press, 1984.

Hindus, Michael. *Prison and Plantation: Crime, Justice, and Authority in Massachusetts and South Carolina, 1767–1878.* Chapel Hill: University of North Carolina Press, 1980.

Hirsch, Adam Jay. *The Rise of the Penitentiary: Prisons and Punishment in Early America.* New Haven: Yale University Press, 1992.

Hobsbawm, E. J. *Primitive Rebels: Studies in Archaic Forms of Social Movement in the 19th and 20th Centuries.* Manchester: Manchester University Press, 1959.

Hoeber, Francis W. "Drama in the Courtroom, Theater in the Streets: Philadelphia's Irish Riot of 1831." *Pennsylvania Magazine of History and Biography* 125, no. 3 (2001): 191–232.

Hoffert, Sylvia D. *Jane Grey Swisshelm: An Unconventional Life, 1815–1884.* Chapel Hill: University of North Carolina Press, 2004.

———. *When Hens Crow: The Woman's Rights Movement in Antebellum America.*

Bloomington: Indiana University Press, 1995.

Holloway, Emma B. M. *A History of the Howard Institution.* Philadelphia: n.p., 1945.

Horton, James Oliver. "Freedom's Yoke: Gender Conventions among Antebellum Free Blacks." *Feminist Studies* 12, no. 1 (1986): 51–76.

Horton, James Oliver, and Lois E. Horton. *In Hope of Liberty: Culture, Community, and Protest Among Northern Free Blacks, 1700–1860.* New York: Oxford University Press, 1997.

Houts, Mary D. "Black Harrisburg's Resistance to Slavery." *Pennsylvania Heritage* 10, no. 1 (1977): 9–13.

Hull, N. E. H. *Female Felons: Women and Serious Crime in Colonial Massachusetts.* Urbana: University of Illinois Press, 1987.

Ignatieff, Michael. *A Just Measure of Pain: The Penitentiary in the Industrial Revolution, 1750–1850.* London: Macmillan, 1978.

Janofsky, Jennifer. "'There Is No Hope for the Likes of Me': Eastern State Penitentiary, 1829–1856." Ph.D. diss., Temple University, 2004.

Jeffrey, Julie Roy. *The Great Silent Army of Abolitionism: Ordinary Women in the Antislavery Movement.* Chapel Hill: University of North Carolina Press, 1998.

Johnson, David R. *Policing the Urban Underworld: The Impact of Crime on the Development of the American Police, 1800–1887.* Philadelphia: Temple University Press, 1979.

Kahan, Paul. *Eastern State Penitentiary: A History.* Charleston, S.C.: History Press, 2008.

Kann, Mark E. *Punishment, Prisons, and Patriarchy: Liberty and Power in the Early American Republic.* New York: New York University Press, 2005.

Kashatus, William C. "Punishment, Penitence, and Reform: Eastern State Penitentiary and the Controversy over Solitary Confinement." *Pennsylvania Heritage* 25, no. 1 (1999): 30–39.

Katz, Jonathan. *Resistance at Christiana: The Fugitive Slave Rebellion, Christiana,*

Pennsylvania, September 11, 1851. New York: Thomas Y. Crowell, 1974.

Kerber, Linda K. "Separate Spheres, Female Worlds, Woman's Place: The Rhetoric of Women's History." *Journal of American History* 75, no. 1 (1988): 9–39.

———. *Women of the Republic: Intellect and Ideology in Revolutionary America.* Chapel Hill: University of North Carolina Press, 1980.

King, Wilma. "'Mad' Enough to Kill: Enslaved Women, Murder, and Southern Courts." *Journal of African American History* 92, no. 1 (2007): 37–56.

Kleinberg, S. J. *Women in the United States, 1830–1945.* London: Macmillan, 1999.

Klepp, Susan E. *Revolutionary Conceptions: Women, Fertility, and Family Limitation in America, 1760–1820.* Chapel Hill: University of North Carolina Press, 2009.

Knobel, Dale T. *Paddy and the Republic: Ethnicity and Nationality in Antebellum America.* Middletown: Wesleyan University Press, 1986.

Landers, Jane. *Black Society in Spanish Florida.* Urbana: University of Illinois Press, 1999.

Lane, Roger. *Murder in America: A History.* Columbus: Ohio State University Press, 1997.

———. "Urban Police and Crime in Nineteenth-Century America." *Crime and Justice* 15 (1992): 1–50.

Lannie, Vincent P., and Bernard C. Diethorn. "For the Honor and Glory of God: The Philadelphia Bible Riots of 1840." *History of Education Quarterly* 8, no. 1 (1968): 44–106.

Lapsanksy, Emma. "'Since They Got Those Separate Churches': Afro-Americans and Racism in Jacksonian Philadelphia." *American Quarterly* 32, no. 1 (1980): 54–78.

Lasser, Carol, and Stacey Robertson. *Antebellum Women: Private, Public, Partisan.* Lanham, Md.: Rowman and Littlefield, 2010.

Lee, John Hancock. *The Origin and Progress of the American Party in Politics: Embracing a Complete History of the*

Philadelphia Riots in May and July, 1844. Freeport, N.Y.: Books for Libraries Press, 1970.

Lewis, W. David. "The Female Criminal and the Prisons of New York, 1825–1845." *New York History* 42 (July 1961): 215–38.

Liebman, Robert, and Michael Polen. "Perspectives on Policing in Nineteenth-Century America." *Social Science History* 2, no. 3 (1978): 346–60.

Linaberger, James. "The Rolling Mill Riots of 1850." *Western Pennsylvania Historical Magazine* 47, no. 1 (1964): 1–18.

Lombroso, Cesare, and Guglielmo Ferrero. *Criminal Woman, the Prostitute, and the Normal Woman.* Translated by Nicole Hahn Rafter and Mary Gibson. Durham: Duke University Press, 2004.

Lyons, Clare A. *Sex Among the Rabble: An Intimate History of Gender and Power in the Age of Revolution, Philadelphia, 1730–1830.* Chapel Hill: University of North Carolina Press, 2006.

Maier, Pauline. "Uprisings and Civil Authority in Eighteenth-Century America." *William and Mary Quarterly* 27, no. 1 (1970): 3–35.

Manion, Jennifer. *Liberty's Prisoners: Carceral Culture in Early America.* Philadelphia: University of Pennsylvania Press, 2015.

Marietta, Jack D., and G. S. Rowe. *Troubled Experiment: Crime and Justice in Pennsylvania, 1682–1800.* Philadelphia: University of Pennsylvania Press, 2006.

Martin, Scott C. *Devil of the Domestic Sphere: Temperance, Gender, and Middle-Class Ideology, 1800–1860.* DeKalb: Northern Illinois University Press, 2008.

Masur, Louis P. *Rites of Execution: Capital Punishment and the Transformation of American Culture, 1776–1865.* New York: Oxford University Press, 1989.

Matthews, Glenna. *The Rise of Public Woman: Woman's Power and Woman's Place in the United States, 1630–1970.* New York: Oxford University Press, 1992.

McQuown, M. L. *History of Capital Crimes, Confessions, and Death Penalties in Clearfield County from 1816 to July 1, 1914.* Clearfield, Pa: Raftsman's Journal

Print, 1914. Courtesy of the Clearfield County Historical Society.

Meinig, D. W. *The Shaping of America: A Geographical Perspective on 500 Years of History: Volume 1, Atlantic America, 1492–1800*. New Haven: Yale University Press, 1986.

Meranze, Michael. *Laboratories of Virtue: Punishment, Revolution, and Authority in Philadelphia, 1760–1835*. Chapel Hill: University of North Carolina Press, 1996.

Miller, E. Willard, ed. *A Geography of Pennsylvania*. University Park: Pennsylvania State University Press, 1995.

Mintz, Steven. *Moralists and Modernizers: America's Pre–Civil War Reformers*. Baltimore: Johns Hopkins University Press, 1995.

Monkkonen, Eric. "History of Urban Police." *Crime and Justice* 15 (1992): 547–80.

Nash, Jonathan. "An Incarcerated Republic: Prisoners, Reformers, and the Penitentiary in the United States, 1790–1860." Ph.D. diss., State University of New York at Albany, 2011.

Newman, Simon P. *Embodied History: The Lives of the Poor in Early Philadelphia*. Philadelphia: University of Pennsylvania Press, 2003.

———. *Parades and the Politics of the Street: Festive Culture in the Early American Republic*. Philadelphia: University of Pennsylvania Press, 1997.

Norton, Mary Beth. *Liberty's Daughters: The Revolutionary Experience of American Women, 1750–1800*. Glenview, Ill.: Little, Brown, 1980.

Oblinger, Carl. "New Freedoms, Old Miseries: The Emergence and Disruption of Black Communities in Southeastern Pennsylvania, 1780–1860." Ph.D. diss., Lehigh University, 1988.

Painter, Nell Irvin. *Sojourner Truth: A Life, a Symbol*. New York: W. W. Norton, 1996.

Papke, David Ray. *Framing the Criminal: Crime, Cultural Work, and the Loss of Critical Perspective, 1830–1900*. Hamden, Conn.: Archon Books, 1987.

Parke, John E. *Recollections of Seventy Years and Historical Gleanings of Allegheny, Pennsylvania*. Boston: Rand, Avery, 1886.

Parsons, Elaine Frantz. *Manhood Lost: Fallen Drunkards and Redeeming Women in the Nineteenth-Century United States*. Baltimore: Johns Hopkins University Press, 2003.

Patrick, Leslie. "Ann Hinson: A Little-Known Woman in the Country's Premier Prison, Eastern State Penitentiary, 1831." *Pennsylvania History* 67, no. 3 (2000): 376–96.

Pease, Jane H., and William H. Pease. *They Who Would Be Free: Blacks' Search for Freedom, 1830–1861*. New York: Atheneum, 1974.

Pestritto, Ronald J. *Founding the Criminal Law: Punishment and Political Thought in the Origins of America*. DeKalb: Northern Illinois University Press, 2000.

Preyer, Kathryn. "Penal Measures in the American Colonies: An Overview." *American Journal of Legal History* 26, no. 4 (1982): 326–53.

Prince, Carl E. "The Great 'Riot Year': Jacksonian Democracy and Patterns of Violence in 1834." *Journal of the Early Republic* 5, no. 1 (1985): 1–19.

Rafter, Nicole Hahn. *Partial Justice: Women in State Prisons, 1800–1935*. Boston: Northeastern University Press, 1985.

———. "Prisons for Women, 1790–1980." *Crime and Justice* 5 (1983): 129–81.

Richards, Leonard L. *"Gentlemen of Property and Standing": Anti-Abolition Mobs in Jacksonian America*. New York: Oxford University Press, 1970.

Rothman, David. *The Discovery of the Asylum: Social Order and Disorder in the New Republic*. Boston: Little, Brown, 1971.

Rowe, G. S. "Infanticide, Its Judicial Resolution, and Criminal Code Revision in Early Pennsylvania." *Proceedings of the American Philosophical Society*. 135, no. 2 (1991): 200–232.

———. "Women's Crime and Criminal Administration in Pennsylvania, 1763–1790." *Pennsylvania Magazine of History and Biography* 109, no. 3 (1985): 335–68.

Rudé, George. *The Crowd in History: A Study of Popular Disturbances in France and*

England, 1730–1848. New York: John Wiley & Sons, 1964.

Runcie, John. "'Hunting the Nigs' in Philadelphia: The Race Riot of August 1834." *Pennsylvania History* 39, no. 2 (1972): 187–218.

Rung, Albert M. *Rung's Chronicles of Pennsylvania.* Vol. 1. Huntingdon, Pa.: Huntingdon County Historical Society, 1977.

———. *Rung's Chronicles of Pennsylvania.* Vol. 2. Huntingdon, Pa.: Huntingdon County Historical Society, 1984.

Ryan, Mary. *Womanhood in America: From Colonial Times to the Present.* New York: New Viewpoints, 1975.

Saxton, Martha. *Being Good: Women's Moral Values in Early America.* New York: Hill and Wang, 2003.

Scheffler, Judith. "'Wise as Serpents and Harmless as Doves': The Contributions of the Female Prison Association of Friends in Philadelphia, 1823–1870." *Pennsylvania History: Journal of Mid-Atlantic Studies* 81, no. 3 (2014): 300–341.

Segrave, Kerry. *Women and Capital Punishment in America, 1840–1899: Death Sentences and Executions in the United States and Canada.* Jefferson, N.C.: McFarland, 2008.

Shipman, Marlin. *"The Penalty Is Death": U.S. Newspaper Coverage of Women's Executions.* Columbia: University of Missouri Press, 2002.

Shugg, Wallace. *A Monument to Good Intentions: The Story of the Maryland Penitentiary, 1804–1995.* Baltimore: Maryland Historical Society, 2000.

Skotnicki, Andrew. *Religion and the Development of the American Penal System.* Lanham: University Press of America, 2000.

Slaughter, Thomas P. *Bloody Dawn: The Christiana Riot and Racial Violence in the Antebellum North.* New York: Oxford University Press, 1991.

Slotten, Martha C. "The McClintock Slave Riot of 1847." *Cumberland County History* 17, no. 1 (2000): http://gardnerlibrary.org/journal-issue/2000-summer-volume-17-issue-1.

Smith, Caleb. *The Prison and the American Imagination.* New Haven: Yale University Press, 2009.

Smith, David G. *On the Edge of Freedom: The Fugitive Slave Issue in South Central Pennsylvania, 1820–1870.* New York: Fordham University Press, 2013.

Smith, Kimberly K. *The Dominion of Voice: Riot, Reason, and Romance in Antebellum Politics.* Lawrence: University Press of Kansas, 1999.

Smith, Merril D. *Breaking the Bonds: Marital Discord in Pennsylvania, 1730–1830.* New York: New York University Press, 1991.

———. *Women's Roles in Eighteenth-Century America.* Santa Barbara, Calif.: Greenwood, 2010.

Smith-Rosenberg, Carroll. *Disorderly Conduct: Visions of Gender in Victorian America.* New York: Oxford University Press, 1985.

Smith-Rosenberg, Carroll, and Charles Rosenberg. "The Female Animal: Medical and Biological Views of Woman and Her Role in Nineteenth-Century America." *Journal of American History* 60, no. 2 (1973): 332–56.

"A Tale of Passion and Poison." In *Remembering the Past: A Photo History of the Danville Area,* 203–4. Danville, Pa.: Danville News, 1992.

Tarter, Michele Lise, and Richard Bell, eds. *Buried Lives: Incarcerated in Early America.* Athens: University of Georgia Press, 2012.

Tate, Gayle T. *Unknown Tongues: Black Women's Political Activism in the Antebellum Era, 1830–1860.* East Lansing: Michigan State University Press, 2003.

Taylor, Nikki M. *Driven Toward Madness: The Fugitive Slave Margaret Garner and Tragedy on the Ohio.* Athens: Ohio University Press, 2016.

Teeters, Negley K. *The Cradle of the Penitentiary: The Walnut Street Jail at Philadelphia, 1773–1835.* Philadelphia: Sponsored by the Prison Society, 1955.

———. *They Were in Prison: A History of the Pennsylvania Prison Society, 1787–1937, Formerly the Philadelphia Society for*

Alleviating the Misery of Public Prisons. Philadelphia: John C. Winston, 1937.

Teeters, Negley K., and John Shearer. *The Prison at Philadelphia, Cherry Hill: The Separate System of Penal Discipline, 1829–1913.* New York: Published for Temple University Publications by New York University Press, 1957.

Theriot, Nancy M. *Mothers and Daughters in Nineteenth-Century America: The Biosocial Construction of Femininity.* Lexington: University Press of Kentucky, 1996.

Thibaut, Jacqueline. "'To Pave the Way to Penitence': Prisoners and Discipline at the Eastern State Penitentiary, 1829–1835." *Pennsylvania Magazine of History and Biography* 106, no. 2 (April 1982): 187–222.

Thompson, E. P. *Customs in Common.* New York: New Press, 1991.

———. *The Making of the English Working Class.* New York: Vintage Books, 1966.

Tomek, Beverly C. *Pennsylvania Hall: A "Legal Lynching" in the Shadow of the Liberty Bell.* New York: Oxford University Press, 2013.

Tonkovich, Nicole. *Domesticity with a Difference: The Nonfiction of Catherine Beecher, Sarah J. Hale, Fanny Fern, and Margaret Fuller.* Jackson: University Press of Mississippi, 1997.

Varon, Elizabeth R. *We Mean to Be Counted: White Women and Politics in Antebellum Virginia.* Chapel Hill: University of North Carolina Press, 1998.

Wainwright, Nicholas B., ed. *A Philadelphia Perspective: The Diary of Sidney George Fisher Covering the Years 1834–1871.* Philadelphia: Historical Society of Pennsylvania, 1967.

Waldstreicher, David. *In the Midst of Perpetual Fetes: The Making of American Nationalism, 1776–1820.* Chapel Hill: University of North Carolina Press, 1999.

Walters, Ronald. *American Reformers, 1815–1860.* New York: Hill and Wang, 1978.

Welch, Michael. *Punishment in America: Social Control and the Ironies of Imprisonment.* Thousand Oaks, Calif.: Sage Publications, 1999.

Welter, Barbara. "The Cult of True Womanhood, 1820–1860." Pt. 1. *American Quarterly* 18, no. 2 (1966): 151–74.

Wheeler, Kenneth H. "Infanticide in Nineteenth-Century Ohio." *Journal of Social History* 31, no. 2 (1997): 407–18.

Wilson, Erasmus, ed. *Standard History of Pittsburg, Pennsylvania.* Chicago: H. R. Cornell, 1898.

Wolfe, Linda. *The Murder of Dr. Chapman: The Legendary Trials of Lucretia Chapman and Her Lover.* New York: Harper Perennial, 2004.

Wood, Gordon S. *The Creation of the American Republic, 1776–1787.* Chapel Hill: University of North Carolina Press, 1998.

———. "A Note on Mobs in the American Revolution." *William and Mary Quarterly* 23, no. 4 (1966): 635–42.

———. *The Radicalism of the American Revolution.* New York: Vintage Books, 1991.

Yellin, Jean Fagan, and John C. Van Horne, eds. *The Abolitionist Sisterhood: Women's Political Culture in Antebellum America.* Ithaca: Cornell University Press, 1994.

Zagarri, Rosemarie. *Revolutionary Backlash: Women and Politics in the Early American Republic.* Philadelphia: University of Pennsylvania Press, 2007.

Websites

"Historical Census Browser." University of Virginia Library Geospatial and Statistical Data Center. http://fisher.lib.virginia.edu/collections/stats/histcensus/index.html. Site discontinued.

"Pennsylvania Geography." Diana, Goddess of the Hunt. http://dgmweb.net/Ancillary/Geog/PA/PA-Cos.html.

CPSIA information can be obtained
at www.ICGtesting.com
Printed in the USA
BVHW072041101120
593011BV00002B/128

9 780271 082271